"This is a beautifully written, deeply felt, and ultimately tragic love story about a deracinated Jewish writer wildly in love with European culture, who discovers, too late, that European culture does not love him back. What makes *The Impossible Exile* doubly tragic is the way that Zweig mistook his best self for Europe, just as Europe was mistaking its worst self for Zweig. The double suicide that resulted is, in Prochnik's expert hands, as fascinating as it is unsettling."
—Jonathan Rosen, author of *The Life of the Skies*

"A deeply moving study of one writer's struggle to adapt to a life outside the European culture whose values he helped create. In *The Impossible Exile*, George Prochnik has illuminated the facts of Stefan Zweig's life and work with his own family's experience of exile, creating a remarkably rich, multi-dimensional portrait of loss, longing, and despair."
—Sherill Tippins, critically acclaimed author of *February House* and *Inside the Dream Palace*

"*The Impossible Exile* is not only a riveting study of one of the major literary émigrés of the Nazi era, but also a profound meditation on the nature of fame, the intersection of politics and art, and the condition of exile itself. Tracing the final, tumultuous phase of Zweig's career from cosmopolitan Vienna to the small city in Brazil where he met his melancholy end, Prochnik brings a sympathetic but unsparing eye to his subject and in the process makes the best case I've read for the continued importance of this cultured, humane, yet fascinatingly complicated figure."
—James Lasdun, author of *Give Me Everything You Have*

"This elegant and very engaging book lays out with great sensibility Zweig's descent into intellectual paralysis and self-destruction. It is at once an excellent intellectual and personal account which also serves as a convincing portrait of modern Europe's darkest days."
—Patrice Higonnet, Goelet Professor of French History at Harvard University and author of *The Four Centuries' History of a French Protestant Village in Southern Europe*

"Though he escaped the madness of Hitler's Europe, Stefan Zweig was a war casualty nonetheless, succumbing to the exile's humiliating erasure as he tried to find his way in North and South America. In this learned and luminous volume, George Prochnik uses the last, tragic phase of Zweig's career as a metaphor for the condition of exile itself. Part literary biography, part cultural history, part meditation on war, art, and death, *The Impossible Exile* gives us the pulse and fever of Zweig's desperate and fascinating days."
—David Laskin, author of *The Family: Three Journeys into the Heart of the Twentieth Century*

"It would have been enough to rescue Stefan Zweig from his undue obscurity and to bring him virtually to life for a new generation of readers. George Prochnik has accomplished this and much more: viewing the popular literary titan of pre-Anschluss Vienna from the revealing perspective of his desperate final wanderings through France and England, New York and Brazil, he renders Zweig as the flawed but fascinating hero of his own tragedy as well as an exemplary character in the century's agonies. With vast scholarship and a light touch, an incisive eye for the telling anecdote and a poignant reflection of his family's immigrant legacy, Prochnik illuminates every place and time he glances at, including the present day, and offers surprising angles on the big questions: the American character, Jewish identity, the Viennese cultural heritage, the pressure of political engagement in trying times, the crucial and enduring experience of exile."
—Richard Brody, of *The New Yorker*

"'I am not able to identify myself with the me of my passport,' wrote this man of letters, yearning after a dozen favorite cafés in his native Vienna, in Rome and Paris and Berlin. Zweig's descent from European stardom into a private hell of enforced exile as a Jew and obscurity as a 'guest' in England, America, and Brazil lingers in the mind. Pitch perfect, Prochnik tells the somber story, culminating in the events of February 1942 and in the publication in that year of *The World of Yesterday*, Zweig's late and bitter masterpiece. This author's research is far-ranging, his occasional meditations on his own family's history, to the point. Though it is a dirge he composes, he writes with the élan that distinguished Zweig's own work. Absorbing."
—Flora Fraser, author of *Pauline Bonaparte: Venus of Empire*

THE IMPOSSIBLE EXILE

ALSO BY GEORGE PROCHNIK

In Pursuit of Silence: Listening for Meaning in a World of Noise

*Putnam Camp: Sigmund Freud, James Jackson Putnam,
and the Purpose of American Psychology*

THE
IMPOSSIBLE
EXILE

STEFAN ZWEIG AT THE END OF THE WORLD

George Prochnik

GRANTA

Granta Publications, 12 Addison Avenue, London W11 4QR

Published in Great Britain by Granta Books, 2014
First published in the US in 2014 by Other Press, New York

A CIP catalogue record for this book is available from the British Library.

1 3 5 7 9 10 8 6 4 2

ISBN 978 1 78378 114 0
eISBN 978 1 78378 115 7

Text Designer: Jennifer Daddio / Bookmark Design & Media, Inc.
This book was set in 13.5 Centaur by Alpha Design & Composition of Pittsfield, NH.

Offset by Avon DataSet Limited, Bidford on Avon, Warwickshire

Printed and bound by CPI Group (UK) Ltd, Croydon, CR0 4YY

www.grantabooks.com

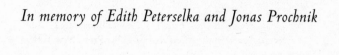

In memory of Edith Peterselka and Jonas Prochnik

"Always the same default in mankind,
a thorough lack of imagination!"

–SZ DIARY, FALL 1939

INTRODUCTION

Late on a November morning in 1941, Stefan Zweig, one of the world's foremost literary celebrities—a wealthy humanist who'd considered himself friends with the likes of Sigmund Freud, Albert Einstein, Thomas Mann, Herman Hesse, and Arturo Toscanini, a Viennese cosmopolitan just shy of his sixtieth birthday who wrote with violet ink and rarely traveled without his tails, awoke on a narrow black iron bed beside the iron bed of his wife, Lotte, drew his teeth from a glass, and pulled on his rumpled slacks and shirt. Pack animals clopped by on the stones below. Birds screeched in the canopy of trees while insects crept over his skin.

Lighting the day's first cigar, he walked out the door of their moldy little bungalow, descended the steep stairs overgrown with hydrangeas, and crossed the road to the Café Elegante. There, in the company of dark-skinned mule drivers, he enjoyed a delicious

coffee for half a penny and practiced his Portuguese with the sympathetic proprietor. It was difficult; his Spanish interfered continuously. Then he remounted the steps and seated himself for a few hours of work on the covered veranda that functioned as his living room, gazing off now and again over the emerald fans of palm fronds toward the splendid panorama of the Serro do Mar mountains. Lotte, who was twenty-seven years his junior and had once been his secretary, worked nearby, correcting a draft of the manuscript of a short story he was writing about chess—the royal game. Inside, the maid struggled with their smoky wood-burning stove.

After a rather primitive lunch—chicken, rice, and beans were staples—Stefan and Lotte played through a contest from a book of master chess games. Following the match, they took a long walk away from the main streets of Petrópolis, the town in the hills above Rio where they'd come to rest, onto an old path that led into a picturesque jungle rife with wildflowers and little streams. And then back to the bungalow for more work. Correspondence. Note-taking from a dusty Montaigne he'd found in the cellar. ("Then as today the world torn apart, a battlefield, war raised to the apotheosis of bestiality," he wrote: "in such times the problems of life for man merge into a single problem: How can I remain free?") Then sleep. And so it went. Day after day. Week after week.

But on this day, the sheer implausibility of his situation overcame him. In a letter to Lotte's family, he burst out in astonishment: "I would not have believed that in my sixtieth year I would sit in a little Brazilian village, served by a barefoot black girl and miles and miles away from all that was formerly my life, books, concerts, friends, conversation." All the property he'd left behind in Austria, his stake in the family textile business in Czechoslovakia, the remnant of his belongings he'd managed to bring away to England, where he'd based himself after first going into exile in 1934, he regarded as lost. The spectacular array of manuscripts and musical scores he'd gathered over a lifetime of passionate collecting was scattered all over the world. To his sister-in-law in London he repeated "my urgent wish, that you may use all clothes, underwear, linen, overcoats and also whatever we have there . . . You do me only a favour and you will see that I feel much better with this idea. I have then less regret of what I shall never see more."

Yet here was the extraordinary thing: despite their removal from everything that had composed his existence hitherto, Stefan asserted, "we feel extremely happy here." The landscape was exquisite. The people were lovely. Life was cheap and flavorful. He and Lotte were gathering the strength necessary to face the dark times—"alas, we will want much strength," he wrote. Their happiness was marred only by thoughts of the unspeakable suffering engulfing their former home. The news of everyday life in the Nazi-occupied territories was more depressing even than reports of the military situation. Stefan feared that millions would starve while Brazil continued to bask in peace and prosperity. The country's sense of immunity from Europe's fit of self-destruction had sparked a new nationalism among Brazil's powerful, who fantasized about the influential role they would play in shaping the outcome of the war. But the kindness of the Brazilian people remained. "I wish we could send you some chocolate or coffee and sugar, which is ridiculously cheap here," he wrote, "but we have not yet found any possibility."

The image of Stefan Zweig marooned on his lush perch in Petrópolis, where, he wrote, Europe with all its troubles was as far from the thoughts of locals as China's struggles used to seem from Europeans like himself—is as improbable as it is haunting. How had one of the most lionized writers in the world, a man who prided himself on serving as a connector between the intellectual and artistic luminaries of Europe even more than on his literary output, ended up living what he described as a monk's life at 34 Rua Gonçalves Dias? Yet this very distance—what he characterized to his publisher as the "complete isolation" of his Brazilian refuge—had also freed him, he wrote, to finish his memoir, *The*

World of Yesterday, and "completely revise" all the material he'd composed before. The countryside around him in Petrópolis "seems to be translated from the Austrian into a tropical language," he told one fellow exile. As Vienna sank further into shadows, the city's imaginary character as an artistic utopia glowed ever brighter for Zweig. In this sense he resembled his old friend Joseph Roth, of whom it was once noted, "His Austrian patriotism grew apace as Austria shrank smaller and smaller, reaching its climax when his homeland ceased to exist."

While donkeys carrying loads of bananas passed beneath him, and his maid sang gently in the kitchen next door, Zweig revisited the most vibrant scenes of his past. None was more precious to him, because of the testimony it offered to the aesthetic fervor of his native milieu, than the moment when Viennese society assembled for the last time at the old Burgtheater in 1888, before this grand building was torn down. Hardly had the curtain fallen on the final performance, Zweig wrote, when the entire audience, consumed with sorrow, leapt to the stage to pry away "a relic of the boards upon which the beloved artists had trod." For decades afterward in ornate bourgeois homes all around the Ringstrasse these splinters from the Burgtheater could be seen "preserved in costly caskets, as fragments of the Holy Cross are kept in churches." It was, Zweig concluded, nothing less than "a fanaticism for art," one in which all classes of Vienna participated. Moreover, this consuming obsession enabled the artists themselves to reach new heights of creative achievement, since not just appreciation but overestimation fed the drive. "Art always reaches its peak where it becomes the life interest of a people," he declared. And when he looked up from the page, his eyes filled with dark green and golden palms, with swooping hills buried in verdure, with giant empty skies. Where had every-one in his life gone? he marveled. No one was more worldly than Zweig. He thought he'd heard everything. Yet he'd never heard anything like the quiet of his new home.

There are lives we turn to because their genius—creative or malign—provokes an itch to snatch the secret. And then there are characters who seize our interest because they serve as potent lenses, refracting momentous times.

Stefan Zweig—affluent Austrian citizen, restless wandering Jew, stupendously prolific author, tireless advocate for pan-European humanism, relentless networker, impeccable host, domestic hysteric, noble pacifist, cheap populist, squeamish sensualist, dog lover, cat hater, book collector, alligator shoe wearer, dandy, depressive, café enthusiast, sympathizer with lonely hearts, casual womanizer, man ogler, suspected flasher, convicted fabulist, fawner over the power-ful, champion of the powerless, abject coward before the ravages of old age, unblinking stoic before the mysteries of the grave—Stefan Zweig falls into the category of those who incarnate the enchant-ments and corruptions of their environment.

To this day, Zweig's work is abundantly available in new edi-tions across much of Europe. In France, his novellas are regularly reissued and almost invariably sprint up the best-seller lists all over again. Zweig's books fill shop windows and airport carousels. He's popular in Italy and Spain, and has his admirers in Germany and Austria. But in the English-speaking world, and the United States in particular, until just a few years ago Stefan Zweig had all but vanished. During the years I was growing up and studying

literature, I never encountered a single work by Zweig. When I asked friends about him, I found almost no one who'd even heard his name. As I started to grasp just how widely he'd been read even in North America up through the early 1940s, the totality of his disappearance perplexed and intrigued me. What made Stefan Zweig fall quite so far out of sight?

For all that his story reveals about the cultural life of pre-war Europe, the insights his exile offers into what became of that culture when it was translated into the idiom of the New World are equally provocative. Zweig's life illuminates abiding questions of the artist's responsibility in times of crisis: the debt owed one's fellow sufferers relative to the debt owed one's muse; the role of politics in the arts; and the place of art in education. His tale also raises questions of how we come to belong anywhere—of responsibility to family and ethnic roots relative to ideals of cosmopolitanism. The number of lives Zweig touched through his writing, and the haven he made of the terrace of his home above Salzburg, where scores of Europe's humanists and artists came to sit and talk in the leafy shade, made Zweig both a catalyst and a cross-channel for currents of thought vital to his age. *"And meet the time as it seeks us,"* reads the epigraph to his memoir. The line from Shakespeare opens itself to different interpretations throughout Zweig's story, as he falls in and out of step with the present.

Zweig himself saw even his own plunge from glory to darkness as symptomatic of a larger phenomenon. "Never . . . has any generation experienced such a moral retrogression from such a spiritual height as our generation has," he asserts at the opening of *The World of Yesterday.* Yet the fact that his fate was shared didn't cushion the impact of the fall. He never ceased to be amazed by his own ejection from the Olympus of European artistic celebrity into a miserable, nomadic existence over the course of a handful of years. "I have been detached, as rarely anyone has in the past, from all roots and from the very earth which nurtures them," he proclaims in an apostrophe that seems to suffer, at moments, from delusions of non-grandeur.

———

He crafted this preface in the summer of 1941, shortly before leaving the United States for Brazil, while he was living in Ossining, New York, where the first draft of his autobiography was written. If his home in Petrópolis was wild and remote, his domicile in this Hudson River town a mile uphill from Sing Sing prison felt abased and forlorn. "There is nothing whatsoever to be done or seen in Ossining," Lotte wrote her family back in England. Sing Sing was its only claim to fame and, she noted, "One rather tries to forget this fact." Stefan's friend Jules Romains, the president of European PEN, questioned Zweig's choice of this "*banlieue sinistre*," as he called it, for a residence and worried that the place would further blacken his spirits.

One July afternoon Suse Winternitz, Zweig's stepdaughter from his first marriage, took a series of photographs of Stefan in a rattan chair on the lawn of this house at 7 Ramapo Road. He is dressed, as always, with meticulous care: soft, light trousers, a white shirt, and a bow tie dancing with tiny polka dots. Though he's fifty-nine years old, his neat, clipped mustache and hair, swept finely back from his high brow, remain dark, of a piece with his opaque black eyes. Only the crinkles radiating from the corners and bunching in convoluted folds below expose his age. He leans forward, right leg crossed over the left, perhaps to an interlocutor. In one photograph shot that day, the tension animating his pose suggests that he's just heard something that arrests his attention. In another, the current has gone slack and he looks like the saddest man in the world. In both images, there's a stunned quality to his gaze. People often remarked on Zweig's bird-like social manner. In these pictures, the bird might just have cracked into a sheet of glass mistaken for sky.

"My todays and each of my yesterdays, my rises and falls, are so diverse that I sometimes feel as if I had lived not one, but several existences," he observed in his autobiography. He'd been forced to skulk away "like a criminal" from the "super-national metropolis" in which he'd grown up one of fortune's blessed, absorbing Vienna's cultural riches, and welcomed into the coffeehouse conversation. The extremity with which Zweig *felt* the drama he was living through in his American exile was palpable to everyone he met. When Klaus Mann bumped into Zweig on Fifth Avenue one sunny day in June 1941, the figure Mann had long admired as a "tireless promoter of striving talents" looked bizarre—unkempt and entranced. Zweig was so rapt in some dark train of thought that he was oblivious to Mann's approach. Only when directly addressed did Zweig jolt "like a sleepwalker who hears his name," abruptly changing into the polished cosmopolitan of old. Still, Mann could not rid himself of the memory of that first wild look—a stare Carl Zuckmayer, the refugee playwright, encountered a few weeks later when, over dinner, Zweig asked him what the purpose was of continuing to live as a shadow. "We are just ghosts—or memories," Zweig concluded.

Above all, Zweig understood that exile wasn't a static condition but a process. "You are just starting a life of exile," he remarked to André Maurois in 1940. "You will see how, little by little, the world refuses itself to the exiled." By then, Zweig had already been ricocheting around Europe long enough that he would thumbnail his status to another friend: "Formerly writer, now expert in visas." The consular stamps, with their dates and seals, their signatures and hand-scrawled numbers, their strictly notated conditions of entry and limitations of validity, which were added to Zweig's British passport between March 1940 and the end of his sojourn in Ossining at the close of August 1941, cover nineteen pages with graphic inscription so dense and arcane that his traveling papers take on the character of a spell-encrusted talisman from *The Arabian Nights.*

What makes the good exile? Is there a calculable equation of inner fortitude, openness of mind, and external support networks that determines a refugee's odds of survival? Why did Thomas Mann, Carl Zuckmayer, and Zweig's friend the conductor Bruno Walter flourish in the United States, while Zweig, Bertolt Brecht, and the dramatist Ernst Toller recoiled from almost every aspect of their New World experience? Goebbels laughed at the entire pack of émigré authors, calling them "cadavers on leave." And this mockery of course speaks to the great fear of the exile, which Zweig was haunted by: the notion that uprooting translates into death by disconnection. It was an apprehension unmitigated by the size of the European community that was then being reconstituted on New World shores.

The wartime emigration of artists and intellectuals was so vast that historians have turned back to the flight of Greek scholars after the fall of Byzantium for a point of comparison. Zweig's life in the Americas gives a lens onto the hotels across the New World in which the fragmented mind of Europe was suspended in the 1940s—a chain of rooms, hundreds of way stations in an impossible flight from nowhere to nowhere. All the lobbies and coffeehouses where the exiles gathered in their loose pants and bulky coats to murmur among themselves without the pretense to translation—the benches in slightly off-center neighborhoods to which they retreated, where the legacy of earlier refugees, a shop, a name, a fragment of architecture, evoked home—before returning to the overwhelmed ministries of limbo, seeking papers and work, and working papers.

Bruno Walter attributed the secret of a happy exile to remembering the distinction between "here" and "over there." Zweig, the quintessential exile manqué, offers a formula for toxic migration—what might be called Lot's wife syndrome. Understanding to a fault the difference between his former home and his current environs, he could not stop looking back over his shoulder. Composing his memoir at 7 Ramapo Road, from what he called "the abyss of despair in which today, half-blinded, we grope about with distorted and broken souls," Zweig wrote of staring up "again and again to those old star-patterns" of his lost continent.

In our own era of perpetual dislocation and upended cultural values, Zweig's experience of watching the world deny itself to him bit by bit—his loss of home, language, cultural reference points, friends, books, sense of vocation, hope—seems not just moving but oracular. It suggests a line from Thomas Mann's brother, Heinrich: "The vanquished are the first to learn what history holds in store."

One June day, I made a trip up the Hudson to see the home where Zweig was based in that critical interlude of his American exile during which he sometimes wrote more than seventy pages of his autobiography in a single week. I wanted to see what was left; whether his presence had been marked; what he might have looked out on from his windows. I wanted to try to imagine what it would have been to take the train north from the monumental edifice of Grand Central Station at a time when the sea of dark fedoras on the businessmen was increasingly sprinkled with khaki wedges and round white navy "dixie cups" as the nation girded for war.

How many times did Zweig ride these rails, passing abruptly from the gray and silver quiver of city scrapers to the folds of green and sheaves of stone bordering the river beyond Manhattan? Segues are softer in Vienna, where loose gardens spin nature through the city and the Wienerwald with its historic vineyards presses romantic landscapes close on three sides. With all Zweig's obsessive writing about the supreme value of individual freedom, how must it have affected him to arrive at his station just after passing the walls of Sing Sing, the watchtowers ringed by searchlights?

I climbed up a long slope from the depot, past stark churches and scarred strip malls, cutting across a baseball diamond onto Ramapo Road itself, a stub of a cross-street in a small development built shortly before Zweig's move there, though his own home is older than those around it. The very house he was living in while writing *The World of Yesterday* had been uprooted, having been dragged uphill on chains from its original site in an orchard or butcher yard some distance below. The steep lot on which the house sits was scattered with new plantings, low shrubs, a scarlet Japanese maple. Only one thick, old oak between the front door and driveway looked as if it might have survived from that summer of 1941, its roots buckled up through the uneven ground like a heap of snakes.

Paint was molting from the white wooden columns that supported the little arch above the main entrance of the house, but there was no longer any walkway leading to the front door, which had been boarded over. I walked around the side of the house and peered through a dusty window, past a wilting spider plant and a faded rainbow of plastic pansies in white baskets underneath a green and yellow faux Tiffany lamp into a dark room. Next to the side door was a gold sign reading "Beware of Occupants." A decal affixed to the glass of the screen door itself announced, in florid gothic script, "Beyond this point . . . Dragons."

I knocked on the door and waited, and waited, and was about to walk away again when the inner door unhitched and swung back to reveal a heavyset woman with a tiny, round, pale head; enormous plastic glasses; spare, curly auburn hair that went bone-white at the roots; and a baggy T-shirt printed with one word in red: "DEVILS."

She looked at me skeptically and did not move to unlock the screen. I gave her my name and asked whether she knew that a famous European writer named Stefan Zweig had once lived in her house. She broke into my spiel. "Yes, I do know! Ten years ago some woman who was writing a book came around here telling me the same thing. She wanted me to let her inside. I told her, *I don't know where this man sat when he was writing his books.* I don't know whether he sat upstairs or downstairs or in the porch or in the basement. How can anyone know? I don't know what window he stared out of when he looked up from the page. I have no idea what he could see from where he was working. I don't know what he ate. I don't know what he wore. Wherever he sat, his chair's not here. His desk is gone. I don't have any of his pens. I don't have his typewriter. Even the lawn out front isn't the same, because of a false claim about the property line in which I was supposed to pay for cutting down trees that did *not belong to me*. I wrote the city a letter, I said, 'You go right ahead and try to hold me responsible when I have copies of the original deeds right here that prove . . .'"

She went on for some time. I nodded, and nodded, my gaze drifting to a line of tall, bountiful old trees beyond her back fence that might have been shadowing the grass when the photograph of Zweig in the rattan chair was snapped.

In a touching essay written just before he departed England, Zweig speculates that the calm demonstrated by the English in the face of world war has less to do with their cultivation of manners or the British educational system than with the national passion for gardening. Deeper than all else, he writes, is "the constant union with nature that transmits unseen a measure of its composure to each individual in a perpetual union, one on one." Poor Zweig, pondering the mystery of English cool as his own feverish spirit withered away.

Abruptly, my host veered back from her legal woes to say that after the last unfortunate Zweig seeker had left, she herself had gone to the library and looked up the writer this interloper had been researching.

Ah, I thought, so I had been too quick to view this encounter as further proof of Zweig's erasure from the American scene. "What did you find?" I asked.

"Well—when Mr. Stefan Zweig was living in Europe, who do you think happened to be living just down the street from him?"

I shook my head.

"A certain housepainter by the name of Adolf Hitler. Boy, do I wish Mr. Zweig had knocked him off his ladder!"

———

My father escaped Hitler's Vienna in 1938 after my grandfather, a successful doctor, was tipped off by an ex-patient who was a high-ranking Nazi: he and his family were on a Gestapo list to be rounded up the next morning. The family went into hiding with Gentile friends and managed to get out of the country on a train for Switzerland a few days later. To this day, my father—as zealous a gadget hound as ever lived—can't stop chuckling with a slightly dazed expression at the fact that only the absence of computers saved his family from arrest at the border. Had their names been added to the roster consulted by the Nazis who stripsearched the passengers for money and valuables, they would never have been let out of Austria.

The family traveled first to Zurich, whence my father and his brother were packed off to a Catholic orphanage in the Alpine foothills, since my grandparents had no means of providing for them. My father's memories of this time center on being forced out of bed in the middle of the night to clamber down a treacherously steep path from the orphanage into the nearest village on missions to procure liquor for the alcoholic head nun. After one bad spill, he and his brother contrived somehow to run away and get back to my grandparents in the city. By this time, their Swiss visas were about to expire and the Swiss authorities were preparing to send the family punctually back to Austria when my grandfather managed to make contact with an American whom he'd chanced to treat after this individual fell ill on a tourist junket. The man had not forgotten my grandfather and agreed to provide the precious affidavit vouching for the family's solvency, necessary to acquire the visas that would enable them to gain admission to the United States. Without the gracious intervention of this unknown Texan, the family would have gone to the camps. Other mishaps followed. Money was stolen; a set of identity papers and tickets went missing. But somehow they traveled from Zurich to Genoa, and in Genoa, through machinations involving friends of an Italian branch of the family who'd hidden money for them, they booked passage to New York on the SS *Rex*.

Like the stories of other refugees from this war—indeed from any engulfing conflict—it's a tale riddled with moments of "if it weren't for," "barely," and "just before." But too often, because it makes a neater ending, these recollections end with the émigrés' arrival in the harbor of refuge—the default land of promise. In my own family's case, the story more or less closed this way: "Yet with all the narrow escapes, lo and behold they managed, by God, to make it to the United States. And though times were hard at first, living in a grim New York tenement building, eventually they made their way to Boston, where your grandfather was able to resume his medical practice and get both his sons into Boston Latin School and Harvard. The End."

It took a long time for me to understand how much was irrecoverably lost over the course of the family's harrowing flight. If only a third of European Jewry survived Hitler, only a tiny fraction of those who did escape made it out with their former identities and sense of humanity intact. Zweig's life on the run draws me in in part for the way it presents, as in a *tableau vivant*, archetypal stages of refugee experience shared by others fleeing a state turned murderous. His story is particularly revealing for what it says about the predicaments of exile that aren't resolved when freedom is regained.

It's true that after a few years living on welfare, my already elderly grandfather was able to learn enough English to pass his medical boards and be recertified in the United States, but his American practice never grew large enough for my grandparents to do more than muddle by. And far sadder than their loss of material well-being, though partly rooted in this hardship, was what became of their relationship.

My grandmother had a cousin, known to us as Aunt Alice, who also escaped Vienna and became a successful, rather terrifying psychiatrist in Manhattan. Where other people had manners, Aunt Alice had stories. She swore she'd been employed for years by one of Mussolini's offspring to help concoct a resettlement plan for Europe's Jews, perhaps in Uganda. She said she'd been palling around in Cuba with Hemingway and his gang during the revolution. Hemingway was hungry to bed her, she said—refusing to disclose whether or not she complied. He drove her to the airport as Batista's regime was collapsing, forcing her into the last plane off the island. Her proudest claim was that she'd managed by pure force of will to badger the guards at Buchenwald into releasing her husband after he was interred there. She divorced him soon after—and then remarried him years later. I glimpsed him once, a slightly shabby figure with a heavy chin, cringing in the lobby of the Beaumont Theater, where Alice had taken me to a matinee production of *The Merchant of Venice*. She passed him without a word, but then—in a magnificently enigmatic gesture—reached her hand backward to squeeze him as we swept by. Only years later, with a dangerous twinkle in her eye, did she reveal the identity of the man we'd snubbed; by then they were separated again.

Aunt Alice knew my grandparents well during the years in which they lived in Vienna, in a large apartment near the Belvedere Gardens. She often rode with them in their dark Opel Olympia to one cultural spectacle or another. She shared meals in their home and visited them in the Alpine chateau they rented for summer holidays. Whenever Aunt Alice spoke of my father, a fond, mildly condescending smile would flicker over her lips. "Poor Martin," she would say. "He was so *neglected* as a young boy." Then she would sigh. "People think it has such a terrible effect on children when parents fight. Believe me, this is nothing compared to how *stunting* it is when they get along too well. Your grandparents loved each other so much when he was a child that Martin was *abandoned*."

Certainly my father had the opportunity to evaluate both sides of the coin of parental interaction. For in America, the more than twenty-year-old hermetic bond between my grandfather and grandmother splintered. They fought often and dreadfully. The toll of these battles was brought home to me one day in adolescence when my father, staring glumly at something stupid on TV, abruptly said, "You know people always complain about 'Oh it's so awful, families watch television now around the dinner table and they don't talk together.' Well, it wasn't such great shakes sitting around *my* dinner table talking, let me tell you. God, did my parents have awful fights!" His hand went to his brow. "I wish to hell we'd had a television set!"

The subjects of these battles were various, and unsurprising. There were perennial money woes. At some point, there may have been an affair. But the real subject of their marital strife was the sudden, radical disequilibrium in their social worlds brought about by life in a new country. We usually think of the exile's plight in terms of a transfigured relationship to the outside world, whereby everyday routines become defamiliarized—charged with difficulty. The estrangement from domestic ties formed in one's native land

can be equally harsh, however. Sometimes, as in my grandparents'
case, there was a reversal of power. My grandmother's flair as a
classical pianist, and her appetite for the social whirl, had greater
charisma in Vienna than did my grandfather's clinical practice.
She went from being the doctor's effervescent beloved, with a wide,
voluble circle of friends and a full book of engagements, to being
isolated in an alien home with two young children: doubly exiled just shy of her fortieth birthday. Meanwhile, my grandfather,
though ten years older, by virtue of the desperate need to work had
to learn English rapidly and was forced out into the world, where
he managed to reconstruct some semblance of an active social life.
(Often the switch in power went the other direction; the classic
Austro-German *Hausfrau* was overburdened with domestic chores.
"It is only here that many European women see a different way of
living and therefore so many are in the typical 'U.S.A. rapture,'"
observed one refugee.)

Sometimes, rather than an inversion of the previous dynamic,
there was an intensification of it, which could prove just as disorienting. This, I believe, was the case with Stefan and Lotte.
Cast away to a tiny mountain town within the vast unknown
of Brazil, they found the world beyond their marriage less and
less accessible. Letters Lotte wrote to her brother, Manfred, and
sister-in-law, Hanna, who lived in England, revert again and
again to the helplessness she feels at being unable to lift Zweig's
despair. Just before the Zweigs left New York for the last time,
Lotte remarked to a friend, in words that darkly echo Ruth's
in the Bible, that there was no longer anything she could do for
Stefan except compel him to drag her along with him wherever
he should choose to go.

With so much left behind, it's easy to assume that the experience of exile consists only of relinquishing a former identity. And yet these stories are not exclusively ones of loss, for the exiles, as they move through their new world, scatter around them the aura of past lives, like powder from beating wings—in this case, the splendor and toxins, the black iridescence, of pre-Anschluss Vienna. A photograph taken of my grandmother in the 1920s counterpoints the image of Zweig's despondency in Ossining in 1941. She reached adulthood when Zweig was at the height of his fame, and Austria was enjoying its last efflorescence of culture. The shot reveals her in a dark flapper dress with a great ovular gold brooch at the waist and a cloche hat set at a rakish angle on her head. Her hands are at her hips, fingers aimed down; her left leg is crossed over the right, heel up with cocky panache. A long loop of pearls dangles down her white blouse. She grins out at the world with an expression of vivacious certitude. And when I see her fearless, incandescent smile, I'm reminded of the way that, when she came into the suburban northern Virginia world where I grew up, everything about her seemed disproportionate—the big, wet smooch she gave me and my siblings, the freedom of her laugh, the symphonies playing in her apartment—her giant amber eyes and lips and bosom as she bobbed in the popsicle-blue swimming pool, her generosity with candy and blithe dismissals of those she deemed inferior. She appeared in Fairfax a kind of Jewish Gulliver. And I took from her bearing a challenge to look outward at the greater world. The passion for cultural enlightenment she radiated, shared by so many from her former milieu, kindled my own imagination.

Max Brod felt a version of this excitement when he stepped into Zweig's bachelor flat in Vienna as a young man fresh from

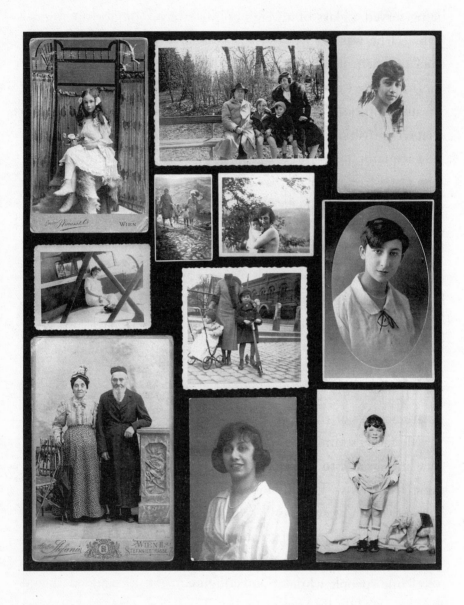

tiny Prague and saw countless books in foreign languages while being served a glass of Zweig's gold-confettied liquor that made him feel he was enjoying "the height of racy urban sophistication." Other people noted the fascination Zweig's ambience continued to exert after he'd gone into exile. Visitors to the "beautiful rooms" he'd rented on Hallam Street in London described transfixing evenings there during which, as one Viennese acquaintance wrote, "for hours on end, writers read aloud to each other from their works in progress, and listened respectfully while others read." Such scenes epitomized for some refugees the "in-between life" of the early years of exile, during which intellectuals and artists lurched "between pretentions to nobility and a *vie de bohème*"—between displaced compatriots and eccentric locals. In this period Zweig himself used to wander the streets of London, seeking out the memorial plaques of earlier exiles— Marx, Lenin, and Sun Yat-sen among them—in order to still feel part of a familiar community of elite global citizens; trying to convince himself that the bowl of lights around Piccadilly Circus was the center of the world.

My father's family was not of Zweig's social rank. Mutti's parents immigrated to Vienna from Czechoslovakia. Opah's parents came from L'viv. They'd both been *Ostjuden* (Eastern Jews) not long ago. But Zweig himself scoffed at the class pretentions that dictated behavior in his parents' world, mocking the way that as children he and his brother were always being told that so-and-so were "fine" people while others were not. "Every friend's pedigree was examined back to the earliest generation, to see whether or not he came from a 'good' family, and all his relatives, as well as his wealth, were checked," he recalls. And yet, he coolly points out, only fifty years or at most a century earlier, all these Jewish families came from the same ghetto.

As he grew older, Zweig grew more tolerant of the game, however, as he came to believe that it was less about the fight for pure status than a symptom of the greater Jewish striving to rise up to "a higher plane of culture in the intellectual world"—one that in fact applied to Jews of every socioeconomic category. A "good" family, he came to realize, was ultimately defined as one free of the constricted outlook impressed upon them by the narrow, humiliating life of the ghetto—a family free to adopt "a different culture and even possibly a universal culture." In this sense, my grandparents, who'd traveled so far beyond the horizons of their own parents' humble village worlds, were exemplary. The holiday confidence emanating from the image of my grandmother was hard-won. How incredible it seems that the expression could have been erased from her features in the blink of a few years. It was, Zweig noted, merely another in the "eternal paradoxes of Jewish destiny" that the "flight into the intellectual" had become as disastrous for the Jews as their former confinement to material concerns. Who could have foreseen the Nazi prohibition on Jews taking part in the so-called "intellectual professions," such as medicine and law? Zweig wondered. And how could this deep investment in the life of the mind have proven to be just as enraging to the masses as the Jews' former preoccupation with business had been?

When I began reading Zweig's work and researching his life, I found that his story brought my grandparents closer, and this has made me reluctant to leave the study, even after many years. If the chance to end their exile is gone, perhaps in charting the wanderings of this intricate character I can at least show something of what the long process of exile consisted in—trace its prelude in Europe and its evolving character in the New World, where garish novelties and gilded memories alike disoriented the refugees. But, truth be told, I also liked to linger among these Viennese phantoms just for the mystery of their fate, even after I came to understand how much darkness the city always cradled amid its scintillation.

The explosion of creativity in early-twentieth-century Vienna is often depicted as a kind of beautiful dream. A rose fire glowed at the last hour of European civilization before some primal savagery reared up and extinguished that renaissance. Yet there were murky overlaps, as well, between the realm of the flowering spirit and the clenching fist. Rather than a binary opposition between good and evil there, Zweig's story reveals ways that the two sides were fatally interlocked. The artists and intellectuals in Vienna were grappling with many of the same problems and aspirations that fueled the violent passions of their archenemies. Just as Hitler's agenda was dominated by pan-Europeanism in the Napoleonic sense—to be achieved through conquest and maintained through the hegemonic rule of one nationalist culture—Zweig's program was inspired by the dream of pan-Europeanism on a humanist model, to be achieved through peaceful, transnational understanding and ruled over by an elite assembly of scholars and artists. People on both sides of the cataclysmic debates over Europe's destiny were educated in the same stultifying school system, shaped by the same sinister admixture of sexual repression and jingoistic militarism. They'd passed through the same faith-obliterating war, and lived with the lingering socioeconomic devastation of that conflict.

The inspiringly cultured Viennese shared more of their nemeses'
concerns about the future of Europe and the need for a profound
spiritual rejuvenation than we have yet reckoned with.

Zweig himself had recognized—and even, momentarily,
endorsed—the allure of National Socialism. After the September
1930 elections in Germany, when support for the National Socialists shot up from under a million votes two years before to over
six million, he blamed the stuffiness of the country's old-fashioned
democrats themselves for the Nazi victory, calling the results "a
perhaps unwise but fundamentally sound and approvable revolt
of youth against the slowness and irresolution of 'high politics.'"
Klaus Mann, twenty-five years Zweig's junior, had to remind him
that "not everything youth does and thinks, is a priori good and
pregnant with future. If German youth now turns radical should
we not ask, above all, for the sake of which cause it rebels?"

While Zweig and his Fascist adversaries drew antithetical conclusions about what the European crisis meant and how to address
it, they had, as we say, a lot of history together—and sometimes
even the same ideas about advancing human civilization. For this
reason, by the time Zweig went into exile he'd begun to question
the entire notion of progress and productivity in a European sense.
With all the technological and social achievements introduced between the world wars, Zweig wrote in his autobiography, "there is
not a single nation in our small world of the West that has not lost
immeasurably much of its *joie de vivre* and its carefree existence."
How could one even imagine anymore an Austria such as that they
had known in their youth, "so lax and loose in its joviality, so pi-
ously confiding in its Imperial master and in the God who made

life so comfortable for them?" But it was precisely to overthrow this lazily conventional, clownish, and hierarchical world of security that the revolutionary artistic movements to which he and his peers so fervently subscribed had been launched.

A riddle lies at the heart of Zweig's story about the place where the path forks, and the urge to create separates from the urge to annihilate. If the crossroads could be mapped on the physical city of Vienna I'd locate it at Schillerplatz, the little park before Vienna's Academy of Fine Arts, where Hitler's application to study painting was rejected and a venerable collection of European art remains open to the public. In the center of this park stands a statue to the poet Schiller, the "Apostle of Freedom," of whom Gershom Scholem, the scholar of Jewish mysticism, once noted, "The intellectual encounter with Friedrich Schiller was for many Jews more real than their encounter with empirical Germans." Zweig chose a citation from Schiller about how "the secret workings of the forces of desire" become "conspicuous and stupendous when passion is strongly aroused" as the epigraph for his study of Sigmund Freud. And it was from Schiller's poetry that Zweig absorbed the lesson which underlay his moral philosophy that freedom could be realized only in dreams, just as deep beauty blossomed only in song.

At the base of the Schiller statue is a bronze medallion engraved with a large face contorted in wide-eyed horror. It's an allegorical mask of tragedy. But if you stare carefully into the wild swirls of hair surrounding this countenance, you'll find they hide a laughing satyr: the allegorical face of comedy. Tragedy and comedy are inextricably enmeshed in this icon, which renders the true Viennese dilemma. Comedy, far smaller, and obscured by tragedy's long hair, has its eyes partly shut. Tragedy looks completely mad. The story of Zweig's impossible exile—of Zweig himself *as* an impossible exile—resonates with that profoundly troubling, paradoxical image. If we can look harder at the conundrum, what might we see?

Chapter One

ODYSSEUS TO OEDIPUS

After dark on the 4th of June, 1941, a sizable crowd of European refugees from all social classes descended on the Wyndham Hotel in Midtown Manhattan for an unheard-of event: Stefan Zweig was throwing a cocktail party. It was the first large gathering he'd hosted since leaving his home and first wife, Friderike, in Salzburg seven years earlier. Even in Austria, he couldn't have hosted a party like this, since at the Wyndham he was throwing open the doors to émigrés—asking just about every refugee he knew. Klaus Mann made his way from the house in Brooklyn Heights he shared with W. H. Auden and Gypsy Rose Lee, among others, for the occasion. Hermann Broch, whose dicey health did not curtail his appetite for seeing friends, might have ridden the train up from Princeton. The German novelist Hermann Kesten and Jules Romains, the president of PEN

International, were almost certainly present. Friderike Zweig, with whom Stefan's life was still embroiled, was definitely invited.

The sight of the arrival at the hotel of all these men and women—many of whom were now utterly destitute and most of whom had suffered more severe calamity than Zweig before reaching America—may have raised a few eyebrows around Park Avenue east of the Wyndham. As an émigré sociologist wrote not long after this event: "One refugee is a novelty, ten refugees are boring, and a hundred refugees are a menace."

After returning to Manhattan in late January from a lecture tour of South America, Zweig had done his best to avoid the huge crowd of his acquaintances who'd ended up in the city. Throughout the winter, he'd preserved what he considered a hermitic existence. He confined his social energies mostly to Alfred, his older brother, who'd run the family textile concern in Europe and who managed to transfer sufficient funds before Hitler's ascendancy to ensconce himself on the Upper East Side; to Ben Huebsch, his stalwart editor at Viking Press; to Lotte's beloved twelve-year-old niece, Eva, who'd been evacuated to the United States to escape the Blitz, and for whom the Zweigs were serving as guardians; and to Friderike. But by springtime the barriers he'd tried to erect against the larger émigré community had begun to crumble and his nerves were on edge.

No subject crops up more frequently in his New York letters than his feeling of being smothered by the needs of his fellow refugees. "It exhausts me to have to see five or six people every day," he complained. "The telephone rang from early till late at night . . . I now am acquainted with from 200 to 300 people in New York; all of them would be hurt if I didn't get to see them." Worse still, Zweig fretted, he hadn't acquired Thomas Mann's shrewd capacity of being economical with his time. "He gets rid of each visitor in-side of an hour. All of my people stay at least three hours."

It wasn't, then, only his neighbors who might have felt uncer-tain about the gathering. Many of the guests themselves, knowing of Zweig's newfound reclusiveness, must have wondered what they were doing there. Did Zweig have some ringing announcement to make? Was he finally going to speak out about the plight of Europe's Jews and call for military action, as his fellow refugees had been waiting for him to do? Guest after guest wandered through the small hotel lobby and shot up the elevator to knock at Zweig's door. They pressed into the crowd thronging his surprisingly modest two-room suite. They caught a view out the windows of what Zweig once called Manhattan's "billion artificial stars," arrayed in skyscrapers that resembled "stone pulp with spiky tips." They chatted. They drank schnapps. They ate snacks. They peeked around and waited for more.

Less intimate friends might have been disappointed to see so little evidence of Zweig's purported great wealth in the hotel rooms he kept in New York. Those who knew him better would have been aware that he'd already divested himself of all but a tiny portfolio from his collection of hundreds of valuable original manuscripts, along with virtually the whole of his ten-thousand-book library. But what he kept with him on his travels was telling. Most of his remaining treasures were musical scores, including several pieces by Mozart, Beethoven's *Kurz ist der Schmerz* (Brief is the pain), a work by Handel, and one by Schubert. He collected almost nothing but music by the mid-1930s, and when he told one correspondent in 1937 that the true foundation of his being lay in art, it was music that occupied his thinking as the medium best able to overcome humanity's divisive sorrows, forging a solidarity of the spirit.

Such faith harkened back to a deep-rooted Viennese conviction that the city's special grace lay in its capacity to blend sensual traditions of the people with elevated aesthetic yearnings. Vienna, the town's devoted dreamers believed, had found a way of traceably kneading spirit into matter—and uniting the different sectors of society. In an essay he wrote about Zweig, Klaus Mann described how in Zweig's Vienna "the Baron and the *fiaker* driver understood each other; they had the same vocabulary and mostly the same ideas." On their first meeting in 1930, Zweig told the working-class poet Walter Bauer of his belief that the life of the spirit was rooted in the inarticulate masses—they constituted the depths from which enlightenment would ultimately arise. The same faith explains why Zweig had long treasured above all those manuscripts in his collection that were the most worked over, smudged, and bespattered, displaying their author's efforts to wrest the sublime from the corporeal at its stormiest pitch. The divine ink jar had toppled over Vienna. Angels' fingerprints stained the air; nowhere more so than inside the spacious opera house, where, Zweig recalled in his memoir, his awe "treading on that stage exceeded that of Virgil when he mounted into the holy circles of Paradise."

Some of Zweig's friends were convinced that love of music could have been his salvation, if only he'd indulged it more actively. Madame Gisella Selden-Goth, a musicologist with whom Zweig carried on a lively correspondence throughout the years of his exile, declared that if in Petrópolis Zweig had been able to have a "chamber music ensemble playing in his home, or the opportunity to listen now and then to an orchestra led by one of his master-conductor friends," he would have been able to bear his agonized vision of humanity's future and his personal fate. The image of a therapeutic chamber-music ensemble jammed inside Zweig's little mountain bungalow on the edge of a dense Brazilian forest in 1942 is as preposterous as it is poignant. Zweig certainly strained to "keep the world of music pure and free from this cacophony of politics," as he wrote another friend. It's one reason he chose to continue collaborating with Richard Strauss, even after Strauss had been appointed president of the Reichsmusikkammer by Goebbels.

However, the effort to preserve an impossible division between the arts and the events making headlines also doomed him to contortions and pathos. Watching the Salzburg Festival for the last time in 1935, already self-exiled from Austria, he yet described the town that had proven so porous to National Socialism with generosity and love, celebrating its success at resolving "melodiously in stone and through atmosphere that which is usually crudely opposed in reality." The secret to this resolution of dissonances, Zweig wrote, had been taught to Salzburg by music. And on "those rare days when one sees a union of sky and landscape," while the most eminent artists of the time performed "the most sublime works, such as *Fidelio, The Magic Flute* or *Orpheus and Eurydice*, at the heart of a shattered world, in these shattered times, one feels sometimes borne towards the solemn spheres, one experiences that state of grace uniquely produced when nature and art, art and nature exchange a kiss."

The sound of German overflowed Zweig's hotel rooms— perhaps loudly enough to provoke a degree of consternation, or at least distaste among other residents of the Wyndham. Newspapers were filled with signs of America's impending entry into

the war—predictions that more than a million new defense workers would be hired in the coming months; President Roosevelt's
backing of a bill to allow seizure of any private property deemed
important to the war effort; calls for "gasless Sundays" to preserve
petroleum for the coming battle. Two days before Zweig's cocktail
party, one New Jersey congressman returned from a tour of the
region to announce that spies infested the forts all around New
York and "could wreck the entire defense of the New York area."

The city was on edge about the allegiance of its quarter-million-
strong German population. Zweig had only just missed being in
New York two years earlier when twenty-two thousand members
of the German-American Bund, the predominant American Nazi
organization, held a rally on George Washington Day in Madison
Square Garden: the *Times* reported a sea of "anti-Jewish, pro-Nazi
banners, the uniformed Bund members and the Bund emblems and
flags." Flushing Meadows had recently been the sight of militia ma-
neuvers aimed at preparing Nazi sympathizers for the hour when
blood would flow throughout the streets of the United States. Bund
plots to hang a handful of big bankers to destabilize the government
had been exposed. Vigilant citizens pricked up their ears when they
heard the German language, on the lookout for possible saboteurs.
The *Aufbau*, a leading German-language newspaper of the refugees,
printed large-type warnings for its readers who hoped to American-
ize: "Do not speak German on streets and public places! If you do
not know enough English yet, speak with a low voice!"

Discretion was the watchword now. And Zweig, having been in
England two years earlier when it declared war on the Reich, was
well aware of how one's status could snap overnight from "refugee"
to "enemy alien."

But for this one evening, it seems, Zweig could suspend his angst. He floated among the guests with sympathetic warmth. Lotte deftly assisted. Friderike gloated over the fact that her former husband, who'd *requested* her to keep using his last name, had no qualms about appearing in public by her side. She'd been married to him, after all, for nearly two decades, while his frail, withdrawn ex-secretary had become his wife just two years ago. Zweig was able to reassume the role of consummate host for which he'd been well-known in Austria. There, he would dart from one group to another, "with a light and easy step in which there is something of the dancer, of the Mercury," wrote Charles Baudouin, the Swiss-French psychoanalyst. Baudouin was enchanted by the way Zweig deployed "his whole talent as an intermediary." Zweig's manner was almost feline, "if this word could evoke only a picture of a certain native elegance of movement without any implication of cruelty or cunning." Beneath the creature of intelligence, Baudouin wrote, "there is a being of instinct and flair, a taste for the hunt converted and turned toward the seeking out of human contacts."

A remarkable scrap of film survives of Stefan Zweig at a garden party in Salzburg in the summer of 1933—six months after Hitler became chancellor of Germany—half a year before he fled into permanent exile. At five feet, eight and a half inches, he's taller than most of the other guests. His head is large. His hair is dark, short, and slicked back. His brow gleams. His eyes are small, black, and bright. His nose is aquiline. He's not wearing a jacket, and his striped tie looks chic and bold. His fingers lightly pinch a cigar. Zweig's appearance in the movie lasts only a few seconds, but his ceaseless animation, embracing smile, and limber grace are riveting. He pivots this way and that; bends into people and back; starts to catch one person's eye, laughs, then swings

his gaze in another direction; stretches his hand out toward one man, then abruptly switches the gesture and brings his hand in again to scratch the back of his head; takes a woman's hand, folds supplely from the waist to kiss it, then straightens once more, twisting his head to chuckle toward the camera before rotating back into the scene. His hands, eyes, and ears appear attentive in all directions simultaneously. Zweig looks the very definition of the social animal, as though, through all his senses, he's taking the impression of those around him the way heated clay absorbs the imprint of whatever it touches.

More than one person who knew Zweig spoke of his "genius for friendship." Klaus Mann wrote of how not just Zweig's house in Salzburg but "every hotel room he occupied, whether for a few days or weeks, became a center of literary activities." But the gift went beyond his charisma in groups to encompass a genuine joy in bringing pleasure to others. Romain Rolland declared that for Zweig, friendship was a kind of religion. And in this vein Carl Zuckmayer recounted a story of how, when he was a young man of very limited means, he and his wife moved to a small village near Salzburg. Zweig learned that the budding playwright was living close by and immediately invited him to visit him at his home. He drew Zuckmayer deftly into his "circle of notables," an artistic elite that would otherwise have been inaccessible to him. Then he visited Zuckmayer in the old house he'd purchased. The house had an unusable stove, and when Zweig turned up, Zuckmayer and his wife were lamenting the fact that they would have to replace it with a modern version. Zweig beamed when the couple recounted their troubles. He asked for the dimensions of their living room, then vanished. The next day a truck rumbled up to Zuckmayer's home bearing an old Salzburg tiled stove, forest green and exquisitely ornamented.

"It fitted the corner where it was to go with perfection," Zuckmayer marveled. He asked Zweig where he'd found it. "It was just lying around with a lot of junk in a storeroom of my house," Zweig said dismissively. But Zuckmayer guessed that Zweig had in fact bounded all over Salzburg for hours to track down a stove that would ideally match the house.

There were countless more serious acts of generosity as well. Thomas Mann asserted that few if any really knew the extent of Zweig's largesse. He described one scene witnessed by a friend of his at a dinner to which Zweig had invited a ragged-looking older man. At a certain point, Zweig surreptitiously slid a hundred marks across the tablecloth.

"This belongs to you," Zweig murmured.

"No—why?" the man responded.

"I tell you that it is for you," Zweig quietly countered.

"Dear Mr. Zweig, I confess, it is only too welcome," the man answered.

"Exactly—precisely," Zweig said.

How many times must similar scenes have repeated themselves over the years? Mann asked himself.

The guests at the Wyndham that evening in 1941 certainly saw flashes of Zweig's fabled grace and generosity. He was in his element—enveloped in others and enveloping them with his attentions—himself a kind of master conductor making the disparate assembly of émigrés harmonize. And the party was a success. Nearly everyone remained not just for a cocktail but deep into the night, as Lotte later reported. Yet there was no special denouement. People left no wiser than they'd come as to why they'd been invited. A letter to Manfred and Hanna reveals that Zweig had simply decided to hold "a great spring cleaning," to which he invited "all those people I had to see to one cocktail." He was no longer interested in surrounding himself with people to be nurtured, it seems, but to sponge away a sea of obligations in one swipe—leaving himself free in a perfect void.

It was this same spring that Carl Zuckmayer came down to Manhattan from the farm he'd leased in Vermont to have dinner with Zweig. The old friends relaxed over a meal in a small French restaurant. For a time, Zuckmayer wrote, Zweig was "as usual, lively, interested, full of sympathetic understanding for other people's affairs and doings and plans."

Zuckmayer had plenty to share. And he was always, Elias Canetti recalled, a zesty raconteur, "dramatic, bubbling with enthusiasm"—his repartee made all the more riveting by his massive head, a model of which became a trophy in the collection of Viennese busts sculpted by Anna Mahler, Gustav Mahler's illustrious daughter. That summer Zuckmayer was full of the renewing experience of his communion with nature in the American wilderness. He'd abandoned what he called his "serfdom" in Hollywood not long before, declaring, "Never have I been so wrapped in the mists of depression as in this land of eternal spring, in whose irrigated gardens, with their chlorinated swimming pools and dream castles perched on the slopes of canyons, short-lived pleasure is at home, while in the depths sprawls a dreary, murderous wasteland."

New York City, meanwhile, was financially impossible for him, and at the age of almost fifty he felt that, "surrounded by a foreign language and an unfamiliar mentality," there was no hope for the sort of abrupt reversal in fortune he'd believed in as a young man in Berlin. He considered his work preparing the farm, to which he and his wife would move that fall, his "salvation." Zuckmayer surely regaled Zweig, as he did most everyone, about the exhilaration he felt going to bed each night after nailing up new walls in the old house, repairing pipes, and clearing rocks from the earth—too exhausted to think about the news. He listened to the howls of a lynx from a nearby granite cliff and swam in a pristine pond fashioned by the owner of the property some fifty years before. "Backwoods," as his Vermont rental was called, struck Zuckmayer as the last chance for him and his wife "to forge a life for ourselves by free, self-chosen work." Like a number of other exiles—filmmakers in particular—he had discovered the wellspring of an inspiring American mythology in the landscape.

But I suspect that Zuckmayer's rhapsody to the outdoors life would only have made Zweig feel anew his own dissociation from nature—and, even more than the existential parameters of that condition, his physical inability to pursue the kind of Thoreau-like course Zuckmayer prescribed as the only real escape route left to the American exile. For Zweig turned their conversation to age and lost time, asking Zuckmayer whether he remembered how they celebrated his fiftieth birthday. Wishing to avoid the official rigmarole customary for a figure of his prominence, Zweig had persuaded Zuckmayer to sneak off with him from Salzburg to a fusty Jewish restaurant in Munich, where the discreet waiters pretended not to recognize their famous guest and the pair shared a meal of blue carp, braised goose, and brandy.

"It was ten years ago!" Zweig marveled. "Sixty," he said, anticipating his next birthday. "I think that's enough."

Zuckmayer laughed and said that people like them ought to live to the age of ninety or a hundred in order to see life get back to normal again. Since their first acquaintance, Zuckmayer had been struck by Zweig's fear of aging, which he had never seen exhibited so intensely by anyone, "not even a woman." He assumed this was just another outbreak of that chronic anxiety. But now he realized the degree to which this long-standing tic had become part of a more engulfing blackness.

Zweig's eyes became "incredibly mournful," Zuckmayer wrote, and he remarked that this return to normalcy would never happen. "Not for us. The world we loved has gone beyond recall," Zweig wrote. "What we have to say will not be understood—not in any language. We shall be homeless in all countries. We have no present and no future."

When did Zweig's sense of being in exile really begin? One striking feature of that fleeting image of him on film is how youthful he appears. Zweig was fifty-one in 1933, and for all his dimpled conviviality before the camera, his mental state had already plummeted. Shortly before that year's Salzburg Festival, he informed a friend of his resolve to close his house on the Kapuzinerberg for the winter, if not longer. "Much, alas, has changed here, not least inwardly," he wrote; "my joy in developing my home, my collection . . . is completely dead, I am thinking of making my life simpler and thus more mobile, to leave my homeland (though the pressure for this certainly did not come from within)."

His excitement about the upcoming festival, at which both his idol Richard Strauss and his friend Bruno Walter were to conduct, was tainted by Hitler's imposition of the "Thousand-Mark Tariff." In an effort to disrupt the pre-Anschluss Austrian government by sabotaging the festival, which had been dominated by German artists and audiences, the Nazis imposed an enormous tax on crossing the border that prevented many fans and musicians from attending.

More savage intrusions followed. If Zweig chanced to be strolling down the hill on which his house was located for the festival opening, he might have seen two black formations of German planes suddenly flying into view across the nearby Alpine border. The planes kept coming and coming, thundering overhead, then all at once unleashed huge quantities of propaganda leaflets down over Salzburg's medieval streets. The brochures urged Austrians to commit treason against the government and remove all their money from the banks. "Brothers, Clench Your Fists!" screamed the headline on one. To terrify the populace, the Nazis also simulated bomb attacks by setting off firecrackers tied to telephone poles. How could Zweig not have been mortified? Almost every night along the border Nazis were hurling bricks at Austrian guards in the hope of provoking an incident that would give Hitler an excuse for invading. Some nights, Zweig swore he could hear the rumble of German tanks.

Zweig's façade of affable charm at the festival, notwithstanding such provocations, reflected his training in Vienna, where ambiguities of character became a point of pride. He was fond of quoting Nietzsche's dictum that "every genius wears a mask," and had always been seen as something of a protean figure by friends and detractors alike. Klaus Mann saw his hybrid nature as typically Austrian. "Only Vienna produced that peculiar style of behavior," Mann wrote. "French suavity with a touch of German pensiveness and a faint tinge of Oriental eccentricity." In the *Bestarium Literaricum*, a satirical volume published in 1920, Zweig was caricatured as "the Steffzweig . . . an artificial product created on the occasion of a Vienna poets' congress from the feathers, skin, hair, etc. of every possible European animal."

But after Hitler's assumption of power, Zweig's multiplicity of personae began to blur as he confessed to increasing uncertainty about where his integral self abided. He'd lost his ability to concentrate, he complained to friends. "I need counterweights like music, people, and it is Rome or London that attracts me most, only not to drift into some corner of émigrés," he wrote the German author Erich Ebermayer. One must go out in the world to seek "a substitute for what one has lost at home (for the German language is my home indissolubly)." By the summer of 1933 Zweig had begun to toy with the idea of exile from Austria. The book burnings and the banning of his work in Germany had begun to push him toward this condition. He himself took the next step by decamping that autumn for his first protracted stay in London, testing the waters of emigration, in a city where politics felt far away.

But eight years deeper into exile he was no closer to finding a palliative for all he'd lost. At times in New York he seemed to be trying out different possible roles for himself like so many costumes. Perhaps he would resume his role as a transnational ambassador of humanism? The party at the hotel wasn't Zweig's first large social event of the season, after all. In May he'd taken part in two important fund-raisers on behalf of his fellow refugees. At the same time, he was constantly writing friends about his monkish existence in the New World, in which he saw no one and—unthinkable renunciation!—no longer even attended concerts or the theater. Perhaps he would go to LA and become an American-style superstar? Hollywood itself kept making overtures to Zweig. At the end of 1933, a group of producers had made him what he called "a financially quite fantastic" offer to fly to California for ten weeks to work with them, and he was told by friends that the studio would triple that sum to secure his presence. The next spring, Ben Huebsch had a meeting with three top executives of Warner Brothers ("cultured persons, who know who you are") and reported to Zweig that they were "confident that, if you were to come over here ostensibly to lecture, as the result of your presence, what with interviews and the usual publicity for a distinguished foreigner, you would receive first-rate offers from the various motion picture firms." To one young German author who met him in the mid-1930s Zweig appeared a film buff's stereotype of the famous writer: "worldly, elegant, well-cared for, with a gentle melancholy in his dark gaze . . . a castle in Salzburg and a lady-like secretary."

The possibilities unfolding around him suggest an eerie revival of a game Zweig played on his first trip to New York three decades earlier. On that occasion, after a few days meandering the city as a solitary flaneur, at a time when Manhattan had fewer galleries, libraries, and museums, Zweig decided to "play" emigrant. He pretended to be one of the new Americans drifting around New York, with only seven dollars in his pocket, and no connections or friends. He visited different employment bureaus and studied the job notice boards. In two days, he found five positions for himself. Three decades later, notwithstanding his connections, friends, and money, he discovered he'd actually become one of the lost émigré horde, someone who—for all the different paths theoretically open to him—had no real vocation.

Again and again, Zweig's life reversed the order of Marx's famous comment about history repeating itself, the first time as tragedy, the second time as farce. In Zweig's case it was always farce first and tragedy the second time around.

Millions of copies of Zweig's books were circulating across Europe and the Americas in the 1920s, when he was in his prime, up through the first half of the 1930s. Though he also wrote plays, poems, and innumerable essays for the newspapers, he was best-known for his biographies and novellas. The former, such as his portrait of Marie Antoinette, were fast-moving studies of hapless individuals ravaged by the spinning gears of world-historical events. The short fictions—smooth, distilled letters of passion, almost always of passion catastrophically thwarted—were dramatized, publicly read, and, like the biographies, adapted for the movies.

Just a few years after his fame began to take off, Zweig had attained the kind of success he deemed most valuable: the creation of "a community, a dependable group of people which looked forward to each new book, which bought each new book, which trusted one and whose trust one dared not disappoint," he wrote in his autobiography. Even his briefest novellas sold at a clip usually reserved for best-selling novels. When he published a small collection of historical miniatures—studies of key turning points ranging from the discovery of El Dorado and the creation of the transatlantic telegraph to the composition of "La Marseillaise"—it sold 250,000 copies in a flash. Zweig's storytelling style held to premodernist conventions, but he anticipated the shift in readers' tastes away from nineteenth-century triple-deckers to sleek volumes that were tightly focused, easy to carry, and digestible in a few sittings. He was recognized by sleeping-car conductors and given special treatment by customs officers. Effervescent young women fluttered about him at his innumerable public appearances. Every delivery of mail brought "piles of letters, invitations, requests, inquiries."

Zweig describes his success in his autobiography as "a guest who settled himself most benevolently, a guest whom I had never expected." Reading of his works' reception calls to mind another analogy: as an author, Zweig had the Midas touch. Unlike the mythic king, Zweig didn't lust after this gift whereby everything from his pen turned to gold. He just had it. With their penchant for revealing erotic secrets and muting exterior reality, Zweig's stories conveyed a sense of intimacy to mass audiences. Readers curled around them like cats before fires.

Zweig himself attributed his popularity to "a personal flaw": radical impatience. In words that sound startlingly contemporary, Zweig expressed irritation at any work that didn't maintain a breathless clip from beginning to end. Ninety percent of what he read, Zweig reported, struck him as padded, arid, high-flown—just not thrilling enough. More surprising still, though Zweig indulged a typically Viennese disdain for America's mass-market coarsening of literature, he once floated a scheme that might have made even some U.S. publishers uncomfortable: a series of great works by Homer through Balzac and Dostoevsky to Mann's *Magic Mountain* with any hint of excess verbiage slashed out. Thus, he would give the classics a new lease on life, he boasted. Zweig venerated the traditional canon, but that didn't mean he felt obliged to treat masterpieces with kid gloves. The typical Austro-German disdain for America was premised on claims to a better understanding of the past and a less materialistic approach to the present. But it sometimes just betrayed angst that the New World had scooped the Old when it came to scrambling high and low culture.

Zweig himself was later dismissive of his first collection of poems, published when he was only nineteen. He'd been "composing verses full of passion to women before I knew what it was to be erotically aroused," he confessed, tossing off poems with "a polished ease of versified expression" that he abandoned once he learned to know "things of true value." Yet even this precious, jejune work was reviewed everywhere that mattered and almost universally celebrated as the work of a tremendously promising young man. When he turned to drama, his second play was published in book form and immediately sold twenty thousand copies—unheard of for a printed script. When he decided to write about a truly unpleasant character, Napoleon's police chief, Joseph Fouché, his publisher wanted to print ten thousand copies for the first run. Zweig advised him to cut that number in half. Lacking any love interest, focused on a nasty manipulator, this book was never going to sell, he warned. Yet in a single year in Germany alone, the biography sold fifty thousand copies. Zweig was dizzyingly popular in Russia, and when he was invited by the Communist government to represent Austria at the celebration of Tolstoy's centenary, four thousand people attended his talk. By the end of that trip, he signed off a letter to Friderike, "Your seven thousand times photographed, filmed and much radioed, *Stefan*." His later success in South America rocketed him to new heights of renown. To Zweig's own surprise, whatever he wrote, wherever he appeared, another windfall greeted his arrival: the showering jingle of falling coins; the clickety swish of chips sliding to his place at the table. As he joked to Romain Rolland not long after departing Austria, he was one of ten authors writing in German who could actually afford to be exiled.

Though he professed to have no interest in the personal side of celebrity because of the restrictions it brought to his freedom, Zweig had lived with its consequences and perks since the 1920s. Now, with the advent of Hitler, success, his surprise guest, had begun making motions to leave. To New York City's conductors, waiters, and porters Zweig was invisible. To women, he was an aging unknown with fear in his eyes and a thick accent on his mustache-smudged lips. U.S. government authorities did not defer to his name, let alone to the sight of his face. Who exactly *was* he now?

The fall into anonymity was, of course, common to many refugees who'd been celebrated in their homelands—an experience that could have its liberating aspect as well. Martin Gumpert, the exiled German physician, writer, occasional lover of Erika

Mann, and expert adviser on the progress of syphilis to her father, Thomas Mann, for his work on *Doctor Faustus*, wrote of the opportunity exile provided for self-reinvention. It would be "ungrateful to deny the tremendous stimulus brought on by emigration," he wrote in a chronicle of his own refugee experience. "Many of us over there were what many of you are over here—dead men who walked, lives lived in a vacuum, adding machines, robots for whom there was virtually no salvation from the dreary inferno of life . . . We all plainly suffered from a neurosis of civilization that consigned adult men to premature old age at the very prime of their life. When one is ruthlessly put out into the street at such a stage, the elements of youth are revitalized; one has to . . . find one's way in a modern life in which heretofore one had played but the role of pensioner."

Zweig himself once struck a similar note, remarking to Rolland that he felt thankful to "Mr. Hitler" for having infused him with a new élan, freeing him from the perils of becoming a settled bourgeois. But this was in 1934, during what, in retrospect, might be called the honeymoon phase of his exile. After seven years of wandering, the release from everything he'd once been no longer felt so enlivening.

Nonetheless, he shared Gumpert's intimation of the opportunity exile presented for resurrecting stagnant creative powers. Indeed, it awed Zweig to realize, as he told a *New York Times* reporter, that despite his own shattered concentration, "vast realms of experience" were being opened up by the conflict from which artists would one day be able to draw inspiration. For, he continued, "on each ship, in each travel bureau, in each consulate, one may hear from quite unimportant, anonymous people the stories of adventures and pilgrimages which are no less dangerous and thrilling than those of Odysseus."

References to the epic dimension of their displacement crop up repeatedly among the exiles. One refugee author made an observation akin to Zweig's, but with a twist: "I often think that we have the same adventures to undergo as Odysseus, only the gods are not in the story." Hannah Arendt, who also arrived in New York that spring of 1941, gave a yet darker spin to the analogy. Considering the Jewish flight from Europe, she wrote of "the desperate confusion of these Ulysses-wanderers who, unlike their great prototype, don't know who they are."

An Odysseus bereft of his sense of identity is worse off than one deprived of his gods. This is Odysseus as Oedipus. It's a conflation that gets at the heart of the experience of many European Jews who'd imagined themselves to be integrated members of their homelands before Hitler's rise.

"Who can make plans! Who can say 'I will' 'I intend,'" Zweig wrote in anguish to Lotte's family one gloomy afternoon from the Wyndham. Hour after hour, he paced the floor of their little suite, squeezing alternate wrists with his delicate, slender hands in a nervous gesture that had become habitual, lurching from disgust at the glitter of Manhattan to confusion about what to do next, trying to figure out where he might yet flee and find peace—how he could manage to actually reach a true place of refuge, if one even existed. All the while, their claustrophobic rooms piled higher and higher with pages of his manuscripts. "Poor Lotte does not know where to correct five different copies, the bed, the floor, all is always overflooded with typerighted pages," he confessed. Lotte herself wrote at one point of struggling not to become utterly lost in the mountains of paper that were amassing. The two of them were being literally buried in his writing—mummified in his scribbled sheets.

By that spring, moreover, Zweig was acutely conscious of the fact that other refugees were proving to be better at exile than he was—more energetic and nimble. Thinking of those who'd resettled in California, Zweig noted that whereas most of the émigrés had "established themselves in little houses and started a new life," he and Lotte remained unsure "how long we shall stay and how to decide—will it be possible to go to Brazil? Will there still be ships and planes? . . . So we wait and waiting is not very appropriate for concentrated work."

Zweig felt paralyzed by the most corrosive type of suspension—that form of waiting in which one feels one's fate pinned at every joint to world events and the decisions of authorities beyond one's powers of petition. The sense of dependency on massive, faceless entities for the freedom even to toddle forward or back a few steps was infantilizing, and may help explain the note of narcisstic self-pity that crept into his letters around this time. Bertolt Brecht—who rivaled Zweig at flunking his U.S. exile—left an account of the American naturalization process that adroitly caricatures this regressive quality: "First the consul makes us walk around the block four times on all fours. Then we are asked to produce a medical certificate to establish that we are free of calluses. After that we are compelled to swear, while staring at the whites of the consul's eyes, that we do not hold an opinion. But then he sees through us and asks us to prove that we have never once held an opinion in our entire life."

The philosopher Günther Anders—who was married to

Hannah Arendt for a time and also immigrated to New York—recounted in his diary how, after going into exile, "the expression 'old boy' suddenly sounded meaningful . . . Because we occupied the *chambres garnies* of a temporary existence, because we regarded our weekday as a mere intermezzo, because we arranged our life as only an antecedent to the day after tomorrow . . . we engaged in a totally *invalid life*, in a condition that, on the basis of its similarity to the lifestyle of adolescents, could be labeled, 'puberty.'"

To Zweig this "day after tomorrow" seemed a lifetime away, for he saw the whole world reverting to an earlier phase of development in consequence of war. Describing the conditions in which he was writing his autobiography—the absence of his books, notes, and letters and the information stored in friends' memories—he observed: "We all live apart from each other, just as we did hundreds of years ago before the invention of steamships and railways, air travel and the postal system." As for himself, "everything was torn apart, broken to pieces, and I knew that I would have to begin again—yet again!—after the war was over."

The day after hosting the cocktail party at the Wyndham, he wrote the German writer Paul Zech, who'd immigrated to Argentina, that their generation would die like Israel's children, aimlessly wandering the desert without ever seeing the Promised Land. "We are placed wrongly in every sense," he lamented. "Today one should be either 20 or 80—have life all in front of you or already behind you. Only one thing is left for us and that is work. Even in this time when it has no impact, it still remains a distracting force." His struggle in the Americas was not to determine how far he could reascend the ranks of fame, but with fundamental questions of why he should continue to walk the earth. For at every

turn Zweig was confronted with reminders that his prior identity
had been propped up by the scaffolding of an entire world.

A nd yet, nonetheless, one day that season Zweig walked out the
door of the Wyndham on his way to a doctor who was giving
him a course of unusual treatments. He'd already pressured Lotte
into embarking on a lengthy regimen of antibody cocktails aimed
at curing her asthma, though her symptoms in the wake of these
shots often worsened. For all his criticism of American faddish-
ness, Zweig couldn't let go of the possibility that when it came to
redeeming the body, there might be something in all this novelty.

When Zweig reached the door of his mysterious doctor, I suspect vanity made him cast a furtive glance back to make sure he
would enter unseen—though he might have heard that none other
than Sigmund Freud was once operated on by the Viennese physi-
ologist Eugen Steinach, a pioneering figure in such treatments. Exactly what happened there we can't know, but at some point Zweig
bared his skin to take the next round in a series of special hormone
injections. For that spring of despair Zweig had also begun an in-
novative regimen intended to reverse the effects of age. In his final
letter to Romains, he revealed that the last phase of his life had
been so charged with disquiet that he couldn't stop asking himself
where he might find the fountain of youth. New York had suggested the possibility of a pharmaceutical solution.

Not only did the city make the refugees question who they
were, but New York itself seemed to harbor multiple identities.
"Manhattan is America's alphabet," declared the German-Czech
exile Hans Natonek. Every block "contains a sample of the eventual

America." Claude Lévi-Strauss, walking New York's streets for the first time in 1941, described the city as a place where anything seemed possible. Its urban, social, and cultural fabrics were riddled with holes, he wrote. "All you had to do was pick one and slip through if, like Alice, you wanted to get to the other side of the looking glass and find worlds so enchanting they seemed unreal." What made for these charms, he wrote, was the way the city was at once "charged with the stale odors of Central Europe"—the residue of a world that was already finished—*and* injected with the new American dynamism by which Europe was about to be invaded.

Part of Zweig still dreamed that in New York he might find the formula to recover his lost youth. It's a painful, *Blue Angel* image—an elderly man's fumbling gambit to trick time. Yet it is one that also shows Zweig hadn't quite abandoned all hope that summer, if only he could rekindle his depleted energies. Zweig had fantasized before about absorbing some of America's vibrancy. "A barbarian music sounding in a wild tempo, a triumphal song for humanity, emanates from American cities," he wrote after visiting Manhattan earlier in his exile. Despite the exhaustion it induced, "you keep rushing to see more—more people, more streets; unconsciously you adapt to the rhythm." These American metropolises, he lyricized, radiate "the wonderful rhythm of life itself which seems strongest here in New York, for here is the utmost outpost of the Old World."

Chapter Two

THE BEGGARS
AND THE
BRIDGE

S tefan Zweig made his first trip to New York in 1911, when he was just thirty, fresh and high-spirited, brimming over with enthusiasm to discover the country of Walt Whitman, whose verse celebrated "the coming brotherhood of the whole world." Whitman's role as the polestar for alienated Europeans in the first decades of the twentieth century cannot be overstated. For Klaus Mann, the "youthful impulse to reorganize the world," the essentially religious "revolutionary élan of every new generation," was guided by four archangels: Plato, Nietzsche, Novalis, and Whitman. But it was Whitman, in his own words "a Kosmos, of mighty Manhattan the son," who'd linked the urge to love humanity expansively and erotically with the highest principles of democracy. Thus he'd embodied the most universal features of the American promise. Mann and his compatriots looked for signs of Whitman's "athletic democracy" in the "land of open spaces and towering cities . . . the land of Lincoln and Sacco and Vanzetti, the land of the stunning mixtures and contradictions." One of Carl Zuckmayer's first acts on going into exile was to make a pilgrimage to the house in which Whitman was born and wave his hat high "in tribute to the great 'camerado.'" Zweig's friend the novelist Franz Werfel proclaimed his love for Whitman as the genius who revealed that there was no topic too commonplace for the poet to write about.

Above all, Whitman embodied the dream of open-minded, fraternal optimism that was already evaporating in Europe by the time of Zweig's inaugural American visit. No sooner did he arrive in New York than he flung himself at his hotel receptionist and asked directions to Whitman's grave. The man stared at him in confusion. Zweig couldn't make himself understood! Whitman! Walt Whitman! The man who made of the whole universe one divine homeland! But it was no use. The poor fellow, an Italian immigrant, had never even heard the name.

Along with the notion of rhapsodic democracy, in which all humanity would be embraced body and soul, Whitman also inspired Zweig with the "wild, cataractic" force of his lines, and it was in this realm that he found echoes of his actual New York experience. Zweig's first impression of the city was of an overwhelming rhythmic magnitude, and gazing down from Brooklyn Bridge at the harbor, or wandering "the stone canyons of the avenues, was discovery and excitement enough."

The trip had been undertaken on the advice of the Jewish industrialist and über-diplomat Walter Rathenau, a Berliner ten years Zweig's senior. Rathenau came to fascinate Zweig as much for what Zweig called the "blinding brilliance" of his intellect as for the fact that, with his "deep unrest and uncertainty," he seemed more than anyone Zweig had ever met to personify the tragedy of the Jew. In words that anticipate those that would later be applied to Zweig himself, Zweig speculated that Rathenau's "ceaseless activity was nothing but an opiate to cover up an inner nervousness and to deaden the loneliness that surrounded his inner life." During a conversation in 1907, Rathenau remarked that Zweig would never understand England until he'd seen that island's colonial holdings, and never grasp the meaning of the Continent until he'd stepped outside it. "Why not travel to India and America?" Rathenau asked. Eager to become a true world citizen, Zweig leapt at the suggestion and set off almost immediately for India. Once there, his self-consciousness about being kowtowed to as a privileged European discomfited him almost as much as did the sight of the country's caste system and wretched poverty.

His visit to the Americas a few years later—which took in Panama, Canada, Cuba, and Puerto Rico along with the United States over several months—was far more enlivening, but the seeds of an abiding disdain for New York culture were already planted. At a trip to the opera, he chuckled over the audience's dislike of darkness, observing that once they'd bought their libretti for fifty cents, they were determined to read them. Suddenly "little flashes of light appear accompanied by a soft click, as the provident switch on the electric torches they have brought along with them. To the right and to the left one can see the little quivering cones of light dancing on the open pages of the libretti. Sacred festival drama in the land of the practical!" Once the curtain went down, Zweig noted, everyone in the audience fought to show that he could applaud more vigorously than his neighbor—and then went on to engage in a second battle over the ice cream in the foyer. This latter was understandable, Zweig said, as ice cream "is really the best thing to be had in America."

The next time he landed in the city, in 1935, Zweig was fifty-four years old and near the height of his fame. He was also defensive, depressive, and wracked by fears that his every move as a public figure was being scrutinized and found wanting. Nazi sympathizers in Salzburg, having already commended the burning of his books in Germany, had recently begun accusing Zweig of inciting the world against Austria. The Jewish émigré press, meanwhile, was lambasting Zweig for continuing to work with Richard Strauss, even after Strauss had been officially named the chief musical ambassador for Hitler's regime. He was also being accused of cowardice for his continued unwillingness to demand international action to save Germany's Jews—and of "epicurean-ism" for preaching to the exiles to remain politically neutral, "just as Christianity averts its gaze from the world," as one prominent refugee charged.

This barely scratches the surface of Zweig's woes. He'd finally been forced to leave his beloved Insel Verlag press in Germany—the publishing house with which he'd built his whole career—because of its ham-fisted accommodation of Hitler's regime. And Herbert Reichner, the Viennese editor whom Zweig was grooming as his new publisher, provoked his friend Joseph Roth to a torrent of scorn. "A little analphabetical cacker, a Weltbühne yid, can't be your literary representative!" Roth exploded. "Don't put yourself in the hands of someone who THROUGH YOU can suddenly acquire prosperity and influence, and who at the same time will go on shamelessly bad-mouthing you in his shitty intimate circle of 'Jewish-aware' and 'Progressive' illiterates.'" Zweig's marriage to his first wife, Friderike, was collapsing. His affair with Lotte was only just beginning and might never go further—she was almost thirty years younger, after all. His recent decision to go into preemptive exile in London, where Lotte was living—partly to escape the mad pressures of Austria, and partly to flee his claustrophobic home life in Salzburg—had been widely reported in the press. Activist émigrés were no doubt appalled when Zweig, asked about his move by the press in London, gave feebly anodyne responses about what a nice, quiet place England was to work in—in addition to boasting great libraries and an awfully good music scene—making no mention of the fact that he was fleeing the encroachment of National Socialism, the ascendancy of homegrown Austrian Fascism, and the ever-more-virulent anti-Semitism throughout Central Europe.

But none of this mess had much impact on Zweig's golden literary reputation. He'd just published his study of Erasmus of Rotterdam, "a thinly veiled self-portrait," as he described it, which depicted the agon between that worldly humanist—Erasmus as Zweig—and the fanatical man-of-action Martin Luther as an allegory for Europe's contemporary struggles. The book met with broad critical acclaim, and despite all the Nazi restrictions on publishing works by Jews, Zweig's *Erasmus* was deemed safe for publication even inside Germany, where purchases roughly kept pace with the healthy sales of the work elsewhere across Europe and the United States. Only a few months earlier he'd told a Viennese journalist that he was convinced Europe and America were drawing culturally nearer, and was keenly anticipating his impending trip to the United States. Now, in January 1935—the start of a new year—many people expected Zweig to take advantage of the attention garnered by his New York visit to finally make a bold public statement about Nazi atrocities.

Ben Huebsch called a press conference in the offices of Viking Press on 48th Street to appease the reporters clamoring for Zweig's opinions. The pressmen duly showed up. Zweig was ushered into the room and seated at a desk surrounded by a semicircle of interviewers. Flashbulbs began popping. Zweig murmured some trivial observations on the changes he'd noticed in America since his last

trip twenty-six years earlier. Before he got far, questions started to be fired at him from all directions. What was happening in Europe? What did he have to say about Hitler? What ought the world to do about Hitlerism?

Zweig gazed out at the gathered reporters with his typical "languid composure," as one interviewer described his look at this time.

"It is three years since I have been in Germany," he responded.

"But you have followed events—you have spoken with people who have come out of Germany?"

Zweig objected. "But people visiting Germany for a fortnight or so can't know what's really going on," he said. "How can they judge the state of mind of the Germans? How do they know what new alliance will develop the next day to alter the entire situation?"

His interviewers were unconvinced.

"I have been in America a fortnight and after this brief visit I couldn't say whether the people are satisfied with President Roosevelt," Zweig persisted. For Germany, "prophecies are impossible. Every prophecy already uttered has been disproved. Every single one has been wrong.

"I will make no prophecy. I would never speak against Germany," Zweig announced. "I would never speak against any country."

Some of those present, seeking excuses for Zweig's reticence, concluded that "it was the historian and biographer talking, the artist who sought to write only after he had gained the proper perspective of time," as one journalist wrote. But the reporters were confounded when Zweig then abruptly switched tack and began expressing fears about the behavior of Jewish settlers in Palestine. "Palestine is displaying a tendency to become a dangerous nationalist movement," he remarked.

"Weren't you yourself associated with Doctor Herzl and other pioneer Zionists?" a reporter asked.

"I was never a real Zionist," Zweig countered. "I hate all kinds of nationalism. I wouldn't want the Jews to become nationalists."

One of the journalists at the conference, Joseph Brainin, kept trying to draw Zweig out of his shell. Brainin, who would go on to become a defender of Julius and Ethel Rosenberg, asked about the responsibility of the artist today, drilling Zweig to elicit a quotable condemnation of Hitler's persecution of the Jews.

Zweig wouldn't give in. "The artist who believes in justice can never fascinate the masses nor give them slogans to rally around," he declared. "The intellectual should remain close to his books. No intellectual has ever, in the history of the world, been properly equipped for the needs of popular leadership."

But *why* exactly couldn't the intellectual succeed in politics? the reporters wanted to know.

By this point, Zweig had become visibly engaged by the discussion. He leaned forward on the desk toward the crescent of interviewers, once in a while lapsing from English into a German phrase and looking to Huebsch for translation.

"The true intellectual cannot be 'a good party man,'" he asserted. "To be intellectual is to be too just, to understand the opponent and thus weaken the conviction of your own righteousness."

Brainin kept pushing Zweig to speak directly to the current world situation, and finally he edged closer to the present.

Not a single one of the present world dictators, Zweig pointed out, had the slightest academic or intellectual background. "The masses at the moment distrust the intellectual. They seek leadership from within themselves—from the masses. It is so with

Mussolini, Hitler, Stalin, the late Dollfuss and now, in France, with Laval."

The reporters duly quoted his words but could not have been expected to understand how significant a tenet this was for Zweig. It wasn't until six years later, writing his memoir, that he spelled out the implication of these remarks. Then he went so far as to declare that the outside world never understood the true reason why Germany had so catastrophically underestimated the person and the rising power of Hitler. Not only was Germany a class-conscious society, Zweig argued, but the country had "always borne the burden of a blind over-estimation and deification of 'education.'" Reverence for *Bildung*, that magically potent idea of holistic, rigorously intellectual character development, predicated on fluency in the canon of Western knowledge, had made it impossible for educated Germans to take Hitler seriously, Zweig wrote. It was simply inconceivable that this "beer-hall agitator" who had not even finished high school, let alone college, "should even make a pass toward a position once held by a Bismarck, a Baron von Stein, a Prince Bülow." In consequence, Zweig said, even after 1933 the vast majority still believed Hitler was only a kind of stopgap, and that the Nazis would prove a transient phenomenon.

What Zweig did not make explicit in his memoir was that he'd made this mistake himself. No one placed a greater trust in the redemptive power of cultural education than did Zweig, who expressed his faith, even after Hitler's appointment as chancellor, that the Third Reich would prove only a brief hiccup en route to the unification of Europe—the coming "world Switzerland," as he labeled it. It took years for Zweig to really absorb the notion that the masses' indifference to intellectual and cultural achievements

might be a lasting condition. The fact that his own books continued to prove so wildly popular with mass audiences throughout
the German-speaking world (as well as in the dictatorships of Italy,
the Soviet Union, and France) must have contributed to his belief
that the German *Volk* would soon wake up. The best response to
Hitler's popularity was not to demonize his supporters, Zweig believed, but to communicate to them the value of the rich German
cultural legacy that was being jeopardized by Nazi policies.

It's easy in hindsight to mock Zweig's faith that intellectual
enlightenment might still rouse German moral consciousness as
late as 1935. But given the mostly disastrous consequences of our
own efforts to violently intervene against brutal leaders and glob-
ally threatening organizations, I'm not sure we should be so quick
to judge Zweig. Had he been able to muster wider international
support for his appeal to the Germans' own better impulses, his
approach might have yielded better results than what actually ensued. Perhaps the guilt for the failure of Zweig's agenda does not
lie with him alone.

Be that as it may, the intense valuation of *Bildung* that lay behind Zweig's comments in the Viking offices was lost on most of
his American interviewers. The point, as they saw it, was that no
matter how hard Brainin prodded, Zweig refused to come right out
and indict the National Socialist regime for its crimes against the
Jews. He was still lumping all the dictators together, rather than
recognizing Hitler's singularity. Escaping "trap after trap," one reporter wrote, Zweig always ultimately gave the same response: *"I
am not a politician—I am only a writer."*

What Zweig's auditors failed to hear in this self-characterization
—just as, early in the conference, they decided that his hesitancy

about passing judgment on Germany reflected the fact that he was speaking as an artist—was Zweig's own belief that it was precisely as an artist that he could help the people rise above the quagmire of politics altogether. Essentially, what Zweig sought to communicate was that when intellectuals deliver topical diatribes against state policies, the main beneficiary of these objections is just the public standing and narcissistic self-regard of the intellectuals themselves.

Again it's easy to charge Zweig with evading his public duty at a time of dire need. But it's important to recognize the distinction he was attempting to draw. Zweig wasn't suggesting that intellectuals should do *nothing*, but rather that they got nowhere by simply vilifying their adversaries. Truth be told, the track record of even the most righteous artists and intellectuals at effecting political change by denouncing evil governments is pretty lame—though it can certainly feel good to shout out with indignation. If you really want to demonstrate that you are not the scum your enemies portray you to be, Zweig suggested, make some lasting work that will stand as irrefutable evidence of your great humanity. Thus, in Zweig's own mind, his continued collaboration with the musical genius Richard Strauss was not flattering the Reich's power, but defeating Nazi doctrine by proving what Jews were capable of. However, Zweig's nuance was often missed, and his argument perplexed far more people than it won over in those turbulent times.

He wrote a friend in England that he'd been unable to issue the indictment the New York press hungered for because he could not lose sight of the way his words might influence the fate of Jews still inside Germany. "They are hostages," Zweig argued, "and anything we who are free say or do will be revenged on these defenceless people. We must do nothing now that involves a personal

polemical demonstration." His real feeling was that his strengths
as an artist lay in his capacity for embracing, à la Whitman, humanity's sublime variety, rather than in condemnation. "I can only
write positive things; I can't attack," he told the reporters in New
York. If this was to be read as a sign of weakness, he proclaimed
himself willing to "accept the stigma." While this was undeniably
self-serving—Zweig shunned conflict of every sort—it was also his
genuine, considered position. He wasn't trying to dodge questions;
he believed he *had* answered them, yet had failed to give the answers
his interrogators wanted.

Brainin was one of those who left Viking's offices completely
exasperated. Indeed, the experience rankled him so badly that a
few days later he cornered Zweig at his rooms in the Wyndham
to challenge him again. At first on this occasion as well, Zweig
kept up his façade of proud reserve—but something happened in
the course of their hour-long conversation that unnerved Brainin.
As Zweig chattered on, shifting and stumbling, Brainin started to
realize that Zweig's "incurable Europeanism" was not just a factor
of the Continent being, in some abstract sense, his spiritual homeland, but rather that Europe was "something physical integrated in
his own being, the very breath of his life." At this point, Brainin
glimpsed Zweig's "tortured soul." He grasped that when Europe
"began to split up into little cubicles," Zweig "suffered the pain of
physical dismemberment."

Eventually, Zweig began regaling Brainin with the grand project
he'd dreamed up in the wake of Hitler's appointment. He wanted
to found an international Jewish literary periodical that would enlist "the best minds of Europe, without regard to nationality." The
monthly journal would be published in English and German, but

would include outstanding contributions printed in their original languages, from Yiddish and Hebrew to French, Polish, Russian, and Spanish. Its goal, he told Brainin, would be "to cement, by its high ethical and literary standards, an aristocratic European brotherhood that eventually would be able to counteract the demagogic propaganda unleashed by those forces that were trying to bring about the moral destruction of Europe." The best response to Nazi racism would be a cornucopian showcase of positive Jewish achievement. If the world could only see how much extraordinary writing the Jews produced, the nations would never permit the Jews to be mistreated! Over and over Zweig repeated, "We must never permit ourselves to descend to the intellectual level of our opponents."

There were moments while he was pacing the floor when Zweig worked himself up into a fever of enthusiasm. He began reeling off the names of Jewish leaders who'd promised their support. Rabbi Stephen Wise was committed! Zweig had meetings with the elite in Manhattan. He himself would devote himself exclusively to this project! His body lost its rigidity. He seemed to shed years. Even so, Brainin was moved by the sense that he was seeing "the real face of Stefan Zweig," and that it was the face "of a disillusioned man who was trying frantically to hold on to the mirage of a Europe that no longer existed but which he still refused to mourn as dead."

Brainin remained skeptical about Zweig's aspirations. But he couldn't know how many similar quixotic projects had preceded this idea—how much time and energy Zweig had dedicated to the faith that people's instincts for tolerance could yet be awakened by learning positive truths about their supposed enemies. Among the most touching of these previous endeavors was a manifesto Zweig wanted to collaborate on with Albert Einstein after Hitler's victory that was to have enlisted all the well-known artists and writers who'd been expelled from Germany to defend the legitimacy of the Jewish people by way of their contributions to the arts, the sciences, and psychology. Reviewing his plans with Einstein in June 1933, Zweig described how the manifesto was not to be "full of moans and complaints, but thoroughly positive and responsible in approach, setting out our position for the world with the utmost calmness." Zweig envisioned the manifesto "as a classic and lasting piece of German prose, as a permanent cultural and historic document, composed jointly by the best, and signed by all." He wrote pages of notes for this project, which would have cited the creation of the Bible, "the holiest and most precious book of all time," as proof that Jews were not inferior. It seems at once poignant and slightly bizarre that the only individual Zweig chose to single out by name as representative of recent Jewish achievement was Paul Ehrlich, the scientist who discovered a cure for syphilis. Ehrlich's work alone, which had contributed so much "to the happiness of millions in Germany and the world, would have been enough for us to compensate for all the faults and offenses that the hatred of today accuses us of," Zweig wrote.

Though Einstein was intrigued, the manifesto didn't advance beyond Zweig's initial drafts. Egoistic quibbling among the Jews themselves undermined the project, Zweig informed Einstein. His efforts to reach out to their colleagues "already indicated that most asked first, in a petty way, who was to be represented and who not, and so I abandoned the plan."

The journal likewise never came to fruition. Ben Huebsch, whose faith in Zweig's literary powers and whose greater commitment to publishing refugee writers never blunted his business judgment, had tried to convince Zweig that, from an American perspective, the concept of a multilingual periodical was dead at the gate. But Zweig wanted to believe that American dollars might still salvage the endeavor. He floundered around New York trying to drum up support. Though he wasn't begging alms for his own pockets, Zweig found himself forced to adopt the persona of one of those exiles pleading for financial assistance who'd begun harrying his life back in England. And for all that he'd anticipated finding new cultural affinities between Europe and America, what Zweig actually observed was how difficult it was for émigrés to sustain themselves in Manhattan.

The city's skyscrapers were taller and more overpowering than they'd been twenty-four years earlier; those surrounding Central Park now reminded Zweig of a massive castle wall framing an inner courtyard. The castle keep resisted his assaults. This time around, New York seemed to confirm Zweig's sense that he could no longer make himself heard, that all his values had become obsolete. He left the city even sadder than he'd come, having secured neither funding for the periodical intended as his high-minded contribution to the European struggle, nor the personal vindication that might have come had he issued a stirring denunciation of Hitlerism.

By the mid 1930s, Zweig's sense of being attacked from right and left simultaneously made him feel all the more like Erasmus—and also as though he was approaching his personal limit. Thinking about the interview some years later, Joseph Brainin reflected that of all the Continental authors who'd been driven into exile, "Stefan Zweig was perhaps the most bruised and battered."

———

When Zweig made his third visit to New York, in December 1938, it was nine months after the Anschluss, which had plunged him into a vacuum, as he wrote one friend. And yet he was infected with a touch of euphoria. True, his homeland had ceased to exist and he'd just finalized his break from his first wife—and his last German-language publisher—but with so much loss, he also felt liberated. On his 1938 trip, Zweig suddenly became the classic guy in late middle age who says to hell with everything and goes off on a fling. Moreover, he was about to launch his most successful American lecture tour yet: 2,400 people would turn up for his speech at Carnegie Hall! Lotte accompanied him. She wrote her niece, Eva, a dazzled letter during their Atlantic crossing, listing the nearly two dozen cities in which Zweig was booked to speak. It was a beautiful passage, warm sun and smooth seas. Every afternoon there was a Punch and Judy show, followed by a motion picture. This time, Zweig wrote Huebsch, "I want to see a little of America and not only be seen." He added that he would like to keep a low profile in New York, remaining "an anonymous guest of Harlem and the Rainbow-cabaret" before being condemned to transform into "a dignified lecturer at universities." He expressed his hope that Huebsch would accompany him on these adventures. "I feel the duty to show to my publisher and friend a little of New York," he teased the staid father of two. Clearly, Lotte's presence helped reinvigorate Zweig's nighthawk propensities.

He might not have made it as far north as Harlem, but he did get to the newly reopened Cotton Club, which had recently moved from Harlem down to Broadway and 48th Street, not far from the Wyndham. The club's guests were almost exclusively limited to the wealthy white elite, while the performers were all black, with chorus girls selected to be as light-skinned as possible—"tall, tan and terrific," in the words of the Cab Calloway ode. Zweig noted to Lotte that the atmosphere of the place was not what it had been when it was still in Harlem—though the entertainment was presented by Negroes, the club was now trying to "Europeanize" the experience. *The New York Times* mocked this kind of nostalgia, noting that it was "easy to say that there will never be another colored show like some of those they used to do up at the—not the 'old' but the old, OLD Cotton Club." But the inauthenticity Zweig was attuned to, wherever it began, shows that he was in search of something other than theatrical exoticism.

The Zweigs also visited the sixty-fifth floor of Radio City Music Hall, where the Rainbow Room and Grill were located, which promised guests "the world's highest high life" and had gained a reputation as one of the few night resorts in the world that justly evoked a small-town movie fan's vision of the elegant life. When they'd opened the club a few years earlier, the Rockefellers had sought to set the social tone of the place by staffing it with "Social Registerites," even among the telephone girls.

The Zweigs shot up first to the observation deck, just as the sun was setting. A fierce wind split apart the clouds. Lotte found the panorama with all the illuminated skyscrapers, roads, and views of both rivers mesmerizing. She would go back time and again. The dream of a vantage point from which they could acquire some perspective on the chaos here teasingly materialized. But at last they descended to the lofty, domed Rainbow Room itself, with its mirrors and glossy metal work, where tables banked the emerald-green terraces set around a revolving dance floor, and prices were high enough that a single evening was said to demand a "heroic spending performance." Lotte seemed far more impressed with the views up above and the "fantastic special elevator" that soared and plunged so far, so fast.

The Zweigs stayed in Manhattan through New Year's Eve. The liveliest celebrations in a decade had been planned for sites all over New York. Festivities had been linked to the 1939 World's Fair, taking as their theme "Dawn of a New Day," the title of a Gershwin song. Zweig might not have been humming along with the refrain, but he and Lotte did their share of tripping the light fantastic, attending dinner parties and theatrical premieres of friends such as Thornton Wilder and George Bernard Shaw, seeing a good deal of Klaus Mann, going to concerts, shopping at Macy's, and visiting other nightclubs. The whole trip was a triumph—the most improbable of Zweig's American interludes, its success buoyed by the exorbitant MGM film of Zweig's best-selling biography of Marie Antoinette, which had been released shortly before the trip to become one of the blockbusters of the 1930s.

Just before setting sail back to London in January, Zweig gave an interview to the writer Thomas Quinn Curtiss, who was Klaus Mann's lover at the time, in which he stated that his American lecture series had been only a pretext. The real purpose of the visit, Zweig said, was "not to breathe the ominous air of Europe for some time," and to become more familiar with the United States. "It is intolerable for me to always think in European dimensions when it becomes smaller and more petty from year to year," Zweig declared. "I again sense here a stronger and more optimistic rhythm of life. Without European vanity, I must acknowledge that we are being definitively superseded . . . Only in this country has architecture endeavored to express the times symbolically in new forms, and for me the beauty of New York, the non-historic, absolutely modern beauty of today, has something intoxicating."

When Curtiss asked whether he was homesick, Zweig's voice took on a sad note. "Owing to the occupation," he said, Austrian culture had definitively ceased to be "a creative factor in the spiritual and intellectual life of Europe." With its rich mix of races, Austrian culture, Zweig said, had always formed a bridge "to humanity and international friendship—two ideas which are scorned in the Germany of today." Now the bridge was gone. What most struck Curtiss during their conversation was Zweig's amazing youthfulness. He looked "barely forty-five." His eyes had a "piercing clearness and lively movement," Curtiss wrote. His face was unlined; his hair was unchanged; his mustache was as black as ever.

"Our generation has gradually learned the great art of living without security," Zweig stated near the end of the interview; "we are prepared for anything." And besides, he concluded, "there is a mysterious pleasure in retaining one's reason and spiritual independence particularly in a period when confusion and madness are rampant."

Two years later, just before sailing to New York for the last time, Zweig was stung when an official filling out forms for some police identity papers wrote down in his description of Zweig: "Hair, grey." "No wonder," he remarked to Friderike. Not long before, a friend seeing Zweig for the first time in years was shocked to see that all the "aristocratic" elements of his countenance had vanished. In their place, the Jewish features had become more pronounced. In a weird, crowning touch, this old acquaintance wrote that Zweig's beautifully refined, long-fingered hands had sprouted a layer of hair.

Zweig's four experiences of New York suggest a cartoon arc of the "Four Ages of Man." Having passed from youth to middle age and then to midlife crisis, now, in the winter of 1941, Zweig had abruptly struck old age.

"You cannot imagine how I hate New York now with its luxury-shops, its 'glamour' and splendour—we Europeans remember our country and all the misery of the world too much," Zweig railed after arriving in Manhattan from a Brazilian lecture tour. Only days after disembarking, he made a beeline for the British Consulate to discuss going back to England, but was informed that flights were full for months, while German U-boats now made sea travel impossible. When an opportunity arose to decamp to New Haven for a couple of months, Zweig seized on the chance to escape. It wasn't only that he'd lost all taste for the opulence that seemed to advertise New York's indifference to Europe's woes, but also that he felt constantly besieged by the refugees crowded into the city, "the whole [of] Vienna, Berlin, Paris, Frankfurt and all possible towns." He didn't like New Haven, which he found to be "a little place, not nice, and one is lost in America without a car," but at least he wasn't bothered by the other exiles, and life was cheaper away from New York's daily expenses "and the Schnorrers."

That word again—"*Schnorrers*"—it had begun popping up all across his letters. Why did a man famous for the warmth of his generosity start tossing around the derogatory Yiddish term for spongers when referring to bereft refugees? How had recent events contrived to bring out Zweig's own resistance to the needs of others?

"*Panic plus the pain of departure,* that was the emotional situation of many travelers headed for America," recounted Hans Natonek, for whom Zweig loomed as "one of the great ones" of the age. "For weeks," Natonek recalled, "we had been swept along in the awful maelstrom of an entire continent being evacuated . . . as if we were in an overfilled lifeboat that couldn't get away from the sinking ship, or rather, from the sinking shore. Panic encourages more the use of your elbows than your altruism."

Natonek arrived in New York in 1940 with less than four dollars to his name and survived for days on supermarket apples. In his memoir, he recounted his initial visit to the National Refugee Service near Times Square. The office, he wrote, is "not as large as the destitution which created it, but it is growing larger daily." Filled with "reception desks, departments for all kinds of misery, pneumatic interoffice mail service, waiting rooms and inner waiting rooms, hurrying messenger boys, forms, forms, forms and questionnaires: 'Have you any money? Any income? Jewelry? Other valuables? Relatives in Europe? In America? What is your color? Who gave you your affidavit? Have you any technical experience? Any trade? Profession? Are you a farmer?' No—no—no—no—*no!* I am truly sorry, ladies and gentlemen, I seem to be made up of negations!"

The sense of being composed of negations became a commonplace among the exiles. Zweig had always been unstinting in his charity, dispensing money and gifts wherever he felt able to alleviate hardship, but the process had been in his control. I picture him through youth and middle age like a graceful swimmer advancing smoothly through the sea of others' needs, scooping from his coffers and distributing as he chooses. He fulfilled the precept of the opening couplet in Hugo von Hofmannsthal's *Der Rosenkavalier,*

"One must be light of heart and hand, / Holding and taking, holding and letting go." But it's as if suddenly, in the mid-1930s, this graceful swimmer struck choppy seas. And instead of tempering over time, the breakers just grew rougher and more harsh. All at once Zweig was living the second couplet of Hofmannsthal's verse: "Those who are not so, life punishes, / And God has no mercy upon them." At a certain point, Zweig found he could not stay afloat. Already by 1939, he'd begun writing friends that he hadn't the energy to keep up the pace of charity work demanded of him—"Helping on all sides, though unable to help myself."

There's abundant evidence of how much Zweig did in fact do on behalf of the unfortunates—deploying his myriad connections to find employment for the jobless, procuring visas to Portugal and the Americas for scores of individuals and families, making contributions from his own funds and helping to gather donations from others. A whole crop of letters among disparate refugees in London reveals the degree to which he'd become a one-man welfare office. *Go around to 49 Hallam Street*, these letters advise. *Ring at Number 17. You can get some money there.* But whatever Zweig did, he knew it could never be enough, and his tone gradually turned nasty. To one acquaintance he characterized the latest flood of refugees as mostly second-rate beggars who'd delayed their escape too long. In another letter he wrote that "people all want something, and like dogs not yet house-trained leave traces of their mess, their cares and worries, behind." To Rolland he declared himself "the victim of an avalanche of refugees . . . Yes, one gives advice and money, but one's brain and heart can no longer bear these painful stories. And how to help these writers who even in their own country were only small fry?"

Lion Feuchtwanger, a German novelist and acquaintance of Zweig's, recounted how typical it was for the good qualities of the refugees to reverse themselves under the pressure of exile. "Most of them became egocentric, lost their judgment and sense of measure," he wrote. "They were like fruit that had been ripped too soon from the tree, not ripe, but dry and bitter."

New York proved far more intrusive even than London. More than a million refugees from Central Europe were rumored to be in the United States. Another five hundred thousand were said to be scrambling to enter the country. Zweig's sense that the need he now confronted was bottomless left him feeling ravaged—praying for greater selfishness and recoiling emotionally from the petitioners. The incommensurability of any individual response with the misery generated by this mass forced migration was an unprecedented challenge to the older, more intimate notion of charity based on personal relationships that came naturally to Zweig. It anticipated the pattern of our own time, in which we see philanthropic organizations struggling to "put a human face" on crises of immeasurable scale, with the United Nations estimating current numbers of refugees at more than forty-five million, and where two or three stories are often singled out to emblematize unassimilable suffering—as publicity stand-ins for a cataclysm that overwhelms narrative.

In a kind of negative avatar of his former celebrity, while Zweig was a nonentity to the public on the street, all the Central European exiles knew exactly who he was, and the most wretched among them seized upon him as their ticket to salvation each time he stepped out the door. At times Zweig clearly felt physically trapped in his room at the Wyndham—picturing himself mobbed by hordes waving grubby documents if he dared show his face. He could not strike a balance between giving to others and the writing, reading, and conversation with friends that nurtured his inner life—between the labors of compassion and creation.

But was any such balance really possible then? Wouldn't the equilibrium he craved have required a culpably antiseptic disengagement from those pleading for charity?

For some, it was self-evident that when real crisis struck, one was "all in" or one was not really "in" the event at all. Then there were those who felt driven to hold something back—whether because of pure selfishness or, as in Zweig's case, a more ethically complex sense of obligation to some lifelong vocation. Regardless, Zweig was certainly among those who resisted absorption in the refugees' struggles—and this withholding was sniffed by those around him in their hour of need, even though he kept on giving cash, time, and sheer space of mind.

Increasingly, all Zweig thought about was finding some still point in the storm. In the same letter to Lotte's family in which he deplored New York's gilded excesses, he wrote of how vital it had become for him to discover some place where he could work quietly: "It becomes more and more necessary after so many months of travelling and unrest." For all Zweig's indignation at Manhattan's riches, in truth, he was most affected by a kind of profound motion sickness in the city. He'd experienced this back in 1935 on the Brooklyn Bridge, where, he wrote, people and vehicles rushed by at a relentless pace, creating a nonstop din, inciting a feeling of dizziness that made you grab the railing, but the moment you did so, "you get a strange sensation, you feel the steel vibrating under your hand . . . the whole bridge is shaking, sometimes more powerfully, sometimes more faintly, but in a never-ending rhythm, like the finest nerve in the human body . . . trembling in every molecule, while everyone on it sways in the massive surge of fluctuations." New York City has "a will to the elementary," he proclaimed. By 1941, the wild, shifting seas of the refugees' needs—exile experience as such—and the roiling melee of everyday life in New York struck him as kindred phenomena.

Carl Zuckmayer recalled his own introduction to New York exile in 1939 as a ceaseless drifting, "absorbing the vulgar noises and the popcorn smell of Times Square, the sudden hollow silences in side streets, the torrents of lights, the screeching of brakes, and the distant howling of ships' sirens . . . Everything, including the dangers of the city, gave us the feeling of having landed on a wild continent where you had to be unremittingly prepared for adventures and surprises." "The United States were too big for me," Zweig confessed at one point, in words that seem to echo Freud's quip that "America is a mistake—a gigantic mistake it's true, but still a mistake."

When we think about Hitler's exiles in New York it's easy to imagine this huge influx flooding over a stable environment and disrupting it, but the city itself was off-kilter and at times menacingly volatile. New York's crime rate had soared lately, felonies leaping 25 percent from June 1939 to June 1940. One in every fifty-three New Yorkers was arrested that year alone for infractions that did not include traffic violations or disobedience of city ordinances. And criminologists were not sanguine about the future. The United States and the world at large faced "swiftly changing conditions," reports noted, and "it has been the experience of the past that in such times as those which are approaching there comes an increase in crime."

Unemployment remained a problem throughout the country. My father's first memory of America in 1938 was of driving uptown in the car the refugee aid society provided to take his family from the docks to the Upper West Side apartment where they would lodge for the night. He stared out the car window, transfixed by repeated scenes of men clustered around burning oil drums, pressing their hands to the flames to keep warm. And this lingering economic hardship sometimes provoked the kinds of protests that remain familiar. "I think refugees should be stopped from coming here," wrote one citizen in a letter to the editor. "These refugees . . . will work for less, because they can live on less. Thus they will put a lot of Americans out of work . . . America for Americans . . . Down with immigration forever."

Still, after their European experiences, most refugees found New York's sociopolitical uncertainties less disorienting than its physical magnitude and changeability. "The piled-up, monolithic hulks of the buildings resemble enormous, jagged meteorites cast down by awful forces of original creation," Natonek wrote, echoing many émigrés who felt the city embodied a primordial dynamism. "New York was decidedly not the ultra-modern metropolis I had expected," Claude Lévi-Strauss declared, "but an immense horizontal and vertical disorder attributable to some spontaneous upheaval of the urban crust rather than to the deliberate plans of builders. Here, mineral strata, ancient or recent, were still intact in spots; while elsewhere peaks emerged from the surrounding magma like witnesses to different eras which followed one another at an accelerated rhythm." "Every day America's destroyed and re-created," Auden lyricized from his bohemian retreat in Brooklyn Heights.

Martin Gumpert shared Zweig's sense of depletion amid New York's incessant activity, likening the exhaustion that befell almost every newcomer to a "magic spell." When Bruno Walter first arrived in New York, the heat of his hotel room drove him out onto the street though it was still before dawn. On his initial promenade down Manhattan's avenues, he imagined "with a shudder of horror" that he was "walking at the bottom of immensely deep rocky canyons." As the sun rose, his eyes caught sight of an enormous billboard on top of a building displaying the words "U.S. Tires." In a daze he thought to himself, "Yes, it does—true enough—but why is this fact being advertised to me from the rooftops?"

New York's weather compounded the city's prostrating effect. Zuckmayer recounted how the "oven temperature that persisted day and night" melted the asphalt until the streets seemed mired in mud, like unpaved roads. The best metaphor Zweig could devise in his autobiography for what it was like to travel from England to Vienna in the mid-1930s was to compare it to suddenly stepping out of an air-conditioned room into a New York street in July. Even New York rain, Camus observed after his own first encounter with the city in the mid-1940s, was "a rain of exile. Abundant, viscous, and dense; it pours down tirelessly between the high cubes of cement into avenues plunged suddenly into the darkness of a well . . . I am out of my depth when I think of New York," he acknowledged. Camus wrote of wrestling with "the excessive luxury and bad taste" of New York, but also with "the subway that reminds you of Sing Sing prison" and "ads filled with clouds of smiles proclaiming from every wall that life is not tragic."

There were surprises having to do with the national psychology as well. The image of the United States that had been transmitted to Europeans through high literature and popular culture was of a land of fierce individualism, but Americans in the flesh seemed to have little sense of private space and less capacity for solitude.

The exiles marveled at the skyscrapers where blinds and curtains were never drawn, no matter what was going on behind the glass. Zuckmayer writes of looking with astonishment at the nighttime view through the open windows of rear apartments where "totally unclad people" were "slumped in rocking chairs, sitting at desks, or bustling about the kitchen, as if New York were one gigantic nudist colony." The refugee writer Erich Kahler noted, "What strikes me most in America is that these fantastically individualistic Americans are habitually the most collective people I have ever met." The refugees also had an eye for lyric fragments of the city to which locals had become inured. Natonek describes the Chrysler Building as "a gigantic silver unicorn nibbling at a leaf of cloud."

In Hitler's exiles, the United States received a veritable army of thousands of astute observers—real-life versions of Montesquieu's imaginary Persian visitor to France whose outsider perspective enabled him to incisively caricature the absurdities of contemporary Parisian society. But their virgin insights rarely got them anywhere. As Natonek stood beneath the Chrysler Building with his head flung back to survey the spire, a crowd gathered, craning their necks to discover what captivated him. However, he wrote, "there is nothing for them," and after a time, they all walked away, shaking their heads. Bertolt Brecht observed that the exile's real "laborious job" was "continued hoping." When this proved too much, the pileup of giant American wonders sometimes shut down the outward gaze. "I would like to live forgotten on a forgotten place somewhere and never to open more a newspaper," Zweig cried to a writer friend at one point that summer.

Perhaps most confusing of all, as many émigrés noted, for all its alien qualities, New York in fact harbored a split identity in relation to Europe. A character in a novel by Hilde Spiel, a Viennese writer and acquaintance of Zweig's, remarks to an Upper West Side gathering of exiles: "I have nothing against America. Only you don't live in it . . . America is Pittsburgh and the swamps of Louisiana and the cornfields of Kentucky and the bay of Monterey. It isn't even the charming English-Colonial of Boston and Washington. But least of all, as you shouldn't need me to tell you, is it New York. Someone—I can't think of his name either—called it a European city of no particular country. The truth is: none of you have ever left Europe."

This strange, displaced aura of home, borne out by New York's emigrant character if not its physical atmosphere, may have been the final paradox that overwhelmed Zweig. He was reduced, at last, to blanket condemnations of the city. And as he blocked out everything around him, Zweig's thoughts began floating deeper and deeper into the past. For this reason, ironically, it may be that Zweig's memoir could only have been launched in New York. "All the bridges are destroyed between today, yesterday, and the day before yesterday," he wrote in the book's introduction. But *The World of Yesterday* itself was intended as a bridge between the generations, to inform the young about a world that now loomed only in Zweig's imagination, and might never have been reachable beyond the pages of his writing.

Chapter Three

PEOPLE
OF THE
BOOK

Near the end of that spring of 1941, a top Manhattan photo agency commissioned another well-known émigré, Kurt Severin, to shoot a roll of images of Zweig around New York. The Hanover-born Severin was then a star photographer in his thirties, jaunty and bespectacled, given to wearing fancy scarves and rakish caps. After abandoning life as a typewriter salesman in the 1920s, he'd made his name photographing Central America for a Berlin paper. Indigenous peoples became his great passion, and he reported on everything from machete techniques to the sex lives of the tribes he encountered.

The photos taken of Zweig are clearly intended to show the writer in his habitat, much as Severin had depicted the Sarawak and Yaqui peoples in their native environments. Zweig is posed dictating to Lotte at the typewriter, inside Huebsch's offices, standing and sitting at different iconic spots around the city. But

what's striking is how utterly estranged Zweig appears from each setting. In one photo, Zweig walks down the steps of the New York Public Library holding his hat over his crotch and a book under his arm. He's dwarfed by the institution's massive stone façade; it seems less like he's leaving a library than escaping the shadow of an ancient mausoleum. In another shot, Zweig browses a sidewalk bookstall. His right hand closes over the spines of several volumes while a rough-looking stranger lurches back from the table, glaring at Zweig with an expression of indignation that Zweig appears to be straining not to notice.

This alienation stands out all the more in contrast to Zweig's image in the photos taken of him before he left Europe. Once his writing career began to take off, Zweig was photographed wherever he went. Between the countless cameras and his thirty thousand letters, Zweig was forever displaying his face to the lens or exposing his thoughts to a correspondent. He was obsessed with the sanctity of the individual's private inner life, but couldn't stop externalizing whatever was inside him—moods, ideas, feelings about everyone and everything. In photographs taken up until the war, Zweig revealed a chameleon-like capacity to blend into any setting he was posed against. As a young dramatist with plays packing theaters across Europe, he regards the camera with a cultivated, sensual melancholy that seems made for the stage. In early middle age, on his estate in Salzburg, in fancy knee breeches and a billowy white shirt, beside his high-cheekboned first wife and his hounds, he becomes the epitome of the noble country squire. Hunched next to Joseph Roth at a café in Ostend, Belgium, in 1936, Stefan's tie is crumpled and askew precisely as is Roth's, while his hair plasters his brow with a stringy splay of negligence identical to Roth's coiffure at this late stage of his alcoholic decline. Posing in a black suit among figures of Brazilian high society at a party given by President Vargas, Zweig, swarthy and jubilant, pinches his espresso cup with a kind of samba snap that steals the picture from the bureaucrats and beauties clustered around him. His ability to make himself at home in these

disparate scenes brings to mind inevitable clichés about the Jewish appetite for assimilation.

But by the time he is photographed in New York, in 1941, Zweig appears fatally disassociated from his surroundings. The only thing that seems to connect him to these environments is that wherever he's shown, he's always touching books, gripping them like ballast that will keep him from floating away.

Zweig had always treasured the refuge of reading. His parents remembered him locking himself inside his room with a book to escape the disturbance of their socially active family life. Friderike recalled the sight of him seated in an old red leather chair at their home in Salzburg, "his legs hanging in elastic abandon over the side: so immersed in a book that his surroundings seemed to have vanished."

It's no wonder that in the Americas Zweig turned more than ever to what remained of his library as an antidote to the tumult of the era, and to the spirit of New York, which typified that disarray. When he retreated to New Haven, he complained endlessly. He derided the city's cultural pretentions. He couldn't get over the fact that there was virtually no public transportation, so that anywhere he was invited he had to impose on his host to be ferried home again. He bemoaned the disgusting weather—"sharp winds blowing with ice and rain, the streets so muddy that I who hates this since childhood has to buy rubbers." And yet there were *books.* Zweig's thrill at being given free run of the university library is touching. "I can take as many books at home as I want and go to the shelfs myself," he informed Lotte's family in England. "Books are better company than humans just now and I have had to do without them for a long time," he exclaimed in another letter.

The pain of being separated from books is a recurrent motif among the émigré authors. (In a poignant twist, the literary scholar Victor Klemperer wrote of how Jews such as himself who managed to survive inside Germany during the war became psychologically detached from the books around them, since so many of these had been left behind by someone dispatched to the camps. Books were chilling reminders of the fate that could overtake them at any moment.) No one reverts to the problem of separation anxiety from books so insistently as Zweig. His pining for their presence reflected the way books served him both as sensual objects that could be held and stroked and as vehicles of sublimation—physical entities that mediated between this world and a higher realm.

In an essay written near the end of his life in Austria, Zweig describes books in language the opposite of that he used to convey the blustering commotion of exile: "They are there, waiting and silent," he writes. "They neither urge, nor press their claims. Mutely they are ranged along the wall . . . If you direct your glances their way or move your hands over them, they do not call out to you in supplication . . . They wait until you are receptive to them; only then do they open up. First, there has to be quiet about us, peace within us; then we are ready for them." The process of finding the right book for the hour Zweig likens to the way the finger gropes along the piano to find the key for an inner melody. At last, a book is chosen: "Gently it nestles against the hand . . . this closed violin; in it all the voices of God are locked up." And as you "sink down into them; you experience repose and contemplation, a relaxed floating in their melody in a world beyond this world."

As Zweig retreated more and more into the world of yesterday, his thoughts returned to the early years of his bibliophilia, the era in which he'd published *Silver Strings*, his own first book, a collection of poems. Even more enviably in the eyes of many Viennese, he'd had an essay accepted for publication by Theodor Herzl, the feuilleton editor of the *Neue Freie Presse*, the city's foremost newspaper, which Zweig's father considered "an oracle and the abode of the Lord's anointed." In his youth, as well, Zweig had embraced books as vehicles of transcendence, but at the beginning of the twentieth century, the world he was fleeing was his childhood home.

Victor Fleischer, an ambitious young Austrian playwright, bounded up the narrow, dingy staircase of an apartment house in Vienna's 8th District—the city's student quarter—with surprise. He knew that Stefan Zweig, whom he was about to meet for the first time and who, at the age of twenty-one, was already a well-known author, came from an immensely rich family. His father, Moritz, had patiently built a solitary weaving mill in Bohemia into a textile industry empire. Moreover, everyone in Stefan's orbit knew, the way that everyone in Vienna knew everything about everyone, that Stefan had ample funds at his private disposal thanks to an inheritance from his maternal grandmother, whose wealth came from banking and trade. He was reputed to be on the best of terms with his parents. He was *seen* going to their large apartment on the stodgy Rathausstrasse for lunch every day of the week, for God's sake. Why was Stefan Zweig living like thousands of his broke classmates at Vienna University?

It was autumn in 1902, eleven in the morning. Fleischer gave a sharp rap to the door knocker. And then he waited, and waited. When the door at last opened, surprise mounted to astonishment. Stefan was only half dressed, and entirely unshaven. Walking into the humble room, Fleischer confronted a scene of utter dissipation. Cigar ends and cigarette butts were strewn about everywhere. Heaps of ash filled the trays and saucers. Dirty cups lay all over. The bed was a tangled mess—clearly Stefan had only just struggled out of the covers to answer the door.

Fleischer had entered the belly of the young Stefan Zweig's freewheeling, hedonist Viennese arcadia. "When I think back to the years between the ages of eighteen and thirty-three and try to recall what I was doing back then, it seems to me that I spent the whole time traveling around the world, sitting in cafés and dallying with women," Stefan reminisced twenty years later. "Try as I might I cannot remember ever doing any work or ever learning anything."

Zweig had only recently returned from Berlin, where he was allegedly taking a semester of university studies but had spent every free moment at motley bars and cafés squeezed between "heavy drinkers, homosexuals and morphine addicts," he later wrote. "The worse someone's reputation was the more I wanted to know him personally." Obviously Zweig had now secreted himself away in the 8th District to pursue his raunchy pleasures unobserved by the eye of respectable society.

And yet, along with the unmade bed, the unwashed crockery, and the residue of Zweig's binge smoking, numerous books, manuscripts, and notes were also scattered about. Fleischer quickly learned that all was not quite as it had seemed. Far from having just gotten up, Zweig already had several hours of hard labor behind him, Fleischer reported. And the reason he hadn't shaved or finished dressing was "only by way of compelling himself to stay in and not let himself be disturbed in his work by social contacts." His relations with friends, Fleischer would discover, followed a similar pattern. Just as he'd managed to distance himself from all nonessential duties at his family home without missing out on the regular meals served there, so he consorted genially with a gang of contemporaries, chatting for hours in cafés, only to vanish for weeks on end if some literary project made distraction unwelcome. Within a few months, Fleischer came to know a Zweig just the opposite of the one he thought he'd met. "I am working like a wild thing," Stefan wrote him in the summer of 1903. "I was in Paris, etc, now I'm on an enchanting little island in Brittany and working like crazy in a small arbour, when I am not eating or—don't be alarmed!—swimming. I'm working on (a) my dissertation, (b) a novella, (c) a translation of Emile Verhaeren, (d) the foreword to the Lilien book. So that's four things I'm trying to get ready for publication in the next three weeks."

Fleischer came to realize that the reason Zweig had sequestered himself in modest lodgings was not a wish to be economical or a disdain for comfort—let alone a desire for debauchery—but an ironclad sense of priorities: this single furnished room minimized the demands on his time, giving him license to live as he pleased. Here Zweig was free from the smothering comforts and protocols of his family's bourgeois lifestyle to follow his own strict discipline. Zweig's brother, Alfred, reported that Stefan was not in the least romantic and never had a proper girlfriend in his youth. But the rapture with which he wrote of beloved books suggests that even then he knew the feeling he later articulated of spreading their pages to sense his breath mingling with another's breath, "as though the warm, naked body of a woman were lying next to yours." It's consistent that when Zweig began to publish he often seemed more concerned with the smell, look, and feel of his work than with the actual words. Printer's ink struck him as the most fragrant odor on earth—"sweeter than attar of roses from Shiraz." He obsessed over the typeface and layout for his first book—shunning the publisher recommended by an editor friend because he thought its productions mundane, and demanding from the house he eventually settled on ornate graphic flourishes, thick paper, and the trendiest jacket design. When Zweig went between the covers of a book, he made a very physical entry.

In 1907, Zweig set up a new bachelor flat at 8 Kochgasse with a design scheme that might have been drawn from the pages of a book-mad Gothic novel. Outside of several crimson leather armchairs and a lush scarlet carpet, the apartment's only notable furnishings were plentiful bookshelves filled with beautiful volumes and cabinets for his burgeoning autograph collection. The entire kitchen had been converted into an archive containing numerous boxes filled with letters, crammed with clippings of stories from newspapers and a huge collection of autograph catalogs. After the artist Gustinus Ambrosi—a close friend of Zweig's who would later mold his bust in bronze—saw this residence, he rhapsodized, "Oh! in your room, dark red like the dried blood of 4000 beheaded Saxons . . . how good it is there to create and to be alone." It sounds like just the place to have inspired one of Zweig's more lurid bibliophiliac reveries. Describing the experience of stepping toward bookcases in sweet anticipation of sampling their contents,

Zweig exclaimed, "A hundred names meet your searching glance silently and patiently, the way the slave women of a seraglio greet their master, humbly awaiting the call and yet blissful to be chosen, to be enjoyed."

Zweig's sexuality sometimes appears so carefully disguised as to operate in the realm of espionage more than the erotic. He drifted in and out of the sheets with any number of young women, and quite possibly a few young men as well. Yet the riddling clues left in his journal and correspondence give the impression of relations that often remained ethereal—more gasp than clasp. Any homosexual encounters he did consummate probably occurred more in the spirit of polymorphous curiosity than as the ventilation of a repressed identity. His sexual appetite seems to have been catholic, but light; he kept himself on a dancer's diet. In one anguished poem Zweig gives hints of some mysterious vice and dark deeds locked up, casket-like, in the depths of his hidden self. But it's all so masked—so woefully literary—that it's hard to get past the thought that he's playing with emotional registers to test-run poetic effects. Of one encounter with a girl he met in the Paris Metro, Zweig noted in his diary that she came to his room "without anything serious happening. I'm not greedy in these affairs, only curious."

The absence of greed may be a cover for fear: Zweig once noted that the erotic skill he did possess scared him, "as it masters me rather than I mastering it." Carl Zuckmayer observed that Zweig "loved women, revered women, liked talking about women, but he rather avoided them in the flesh." Having tea at Zuckmayer's home,

Zweig would shy away whenever a woman started a conversation. The result, Zuckmayer concludes, "was that after a while they tactfully left us alone, whereupon he thawed immediately; among men he was always intensely and stimulatingly talkative."

Asked by an interviewer what had prevented their having children together, Friderike once cagily remarked that Zweig "was no Don Juan." On another occasion she said that fear of insanity lay behind his refusal to become a father. Zweig himself wrote his brother in the 1920s that he considered it "a piece of good fortune" that neither of them had children, since he required nothing to be happy but two rooms, "a few cigars and a daily visit to the café."

Whatever transpired when Zweig became intimate with a woman, his most passionate relationships were, like those of Freud, Hofmannsthal, and a host of other illustrious Viennese, invariably close male friendships. Was this preference engendered by father, mother, society, genes? All of the above and everything in between. Early-twentieth-century Vienna struck almost everyone as a city where hypersensitivity, meager career opportunities—especially for Jews—and high-priestly devotion to aesthetic ideals made routine relations between lovers a challenge. Karl Kraus described Vienna as a research laboratory for world destruction. Freud certainly found there a laboratory for sexual self-destruction.

The high incidence of suicides over "love trouble" recounted in books by Zweig, Arthur Schnitzler, and other Viennese writers had its corollary in what, by the mid-1920s, was being called a suicide epidemic among German and Austrian Jews, especially women. A B'nai B'rith meeting in Berlin in 1926 that filled a large hall to capacity was devoted to this topic. The gathering had been preceded by a slew of newspaper articles, such as one headlined,

"Shattering Suicide Figures: The Fairy Tale of the Rich Jews."
Eighty recent suicides had been counted among Vienna's Jewish
community alone. Often such statistics were suppressed, however,
since Jews were afraid anti-Semites might read the accelerating suicide rate as evidence of endemic mental degeneracy, proof that Jewish devotion to *Bildung* had not been sufficient to truly assimilate
them. Hans Rost, a Catholic theologian and suicidologist writing
about this wave of self-murder, declared, "The modern Jew has
fallen prey to skepticism, materialism, the rage for wealth . . . an
addiction to enjoyment and the tickling of the senses . . . especially
affected are Jewish women, who have fallen victim to an extreme
fashion luxury."

Returning to Vienna from London in 1946, Hilde Spiel remarked how coming from a country "where cricket is a cure for
melancholy, I shudder at the thought of the febrile, hysterical climate in which we grew up." Recalling Zweig's wish to make himself out as a latter-day Erasmus, Klaus Mann noted that while
the sixteenth-century humanist's indecision and loyalty bore simi-
larities to Zweig's character, there was also in Zweig "something
bland and iridescent, seducible and seductive . . . Stefan Zweig
came from Vienna—not Rotterdam." The deliquescence of Viennese sensuality moved it along the spectrum toward the death drive
Freud explored.

Mann's portrait of Zweig as a kind of predatory peacock recalls a rumor spread by his old friend Benno Geiger. According to
Geiger, when Zweig was a young man he used to hide in the bushes
by the monkey cage of the Schönbrunn Zoo waiting for young
girls he could pop out and flash. Zweig had his own name for
the habit—a made-up German word that denotes self-punishment

through public humiliation. Capping the weirdness, Zweig ostensibly carried with him a note from Freud identifying him as a mental patient in Freud's care, as a kind of get-out-of-jail-free card should he ever be nabbed by police. The story is at once so strange that it's hard to believe and so specific in details that Zweig's old pal would appear to be a psychopath if it were pure fabrication. Perhaps Zweig at least recounted something like this to Geiger as a fantasy, which would say plenty in itself. Exhibitionism as a route not just to being stared at but to self-mortification—toying with his fears of himself and the law under the safe protection of father Freud—it all suggests someone who can't bear to be seen for what he really is and craves precisely this exposure as the ultimate orgasmic release. The story reads as an allegory for how profoundly Zweig failed to feel at home even inside his own flesh.

It also resonates with remarks made about Zweig's social character by Oskar Maurus Fontana, another, more reliable café chum. Fontana remembered an evening when Zweig and a pack of young men went off to one of the suburban dance parties that had become popular among the privileged Viennese. While everyone else leapt out onto the dance floor, Zweig stayed frozen on the sidelines, watching. In a break in the music the group sat down with some of the dancing girls to carouse. Zweig, Fontana wrote, "joined in with gusto, but his bright, beady eyes never left us for a moment, they drank us in, every one of us, the girls, the swaying mass of dancers, the waiters running back and forth, the strolling couples, the flower girls begging for trade." Along with the hunger in Zweig's gaze, Fontana detected something melancholy. "He remained the detached voyeur."

Freud paired up opposite erotic drives such as sadism and masochism—and exhibitionism and voyeurism—as expressions of the ambivalence at the heart of sexuality. In Zweig's case, both the impulse to greedily watch and the urge to rip open his clothing suggest how cut off he felt from the world around him. As a voyeur he stood with his face pressed to the glass; as an exhibitionist (imaginary or actual), he longed to punch out and shatter the pane. Either way, he felt unnatural, which is partly why he—like many of his Viennese peers—was given to wildly romanticizing nature. Zweig gushed over the rustic simplicity of the life enjoyed by rural friends such as Herman Hesse, who lived in an old farmhouse on Lake Constance. In one letter he lamented the fact that his own childhood—spent in Vienna, his birthplace—had lacked the pristine radiance nature bestowed on Hesse's youth. "The lot of a city dweller can be just as tragic but never as great!" Zweig cried. When Zweig finally went on a pilgrimage to visit Hesse in 1904, he was so excited to meet the pastoral sage that, bursting through the doorway, he immediately slammed his head on the house's low beams and knocked himself cold.

The sexual embraces that seemed to please Zweig himself best were those that contributed to his education as an artist but left few tracks on his heart. After one Parisian adventure Zweig carefully recorded the realization that he didn't know the name of the person he'd just been to bed with. Jules Romains wrote of how Zweig's intense curiosity about other human beings "in their authentic diversity" had about it the quality of "a deeply personal interrogation." To Romains, Zweig always seemed to be asking, "In what way do those men resemble me? In what way do I resemble those men, those women? Isn't their life, their destiny, one of the satisfactions that I myself wanted to acquire? Was I wrong or right not to live as they have done? Have they or have I made the better choice?" On the one hand, this kind of self-questioning conjures the writer seeking to understand and identify with the world around him in pursuit of literary material. On the other hand, it can be read as symptomatic of someone who has no idea how to be himself.

Otto Zarek, a German writer friend of Zweig's who identified openly as a Jew and a homosexual, once observed that Zweig was very conscious of the artificiality endemic to Viennese character. Zweig spoke with Zarek about how the gaiety of life in old Austria, which had proven so beguiling to foreigners, had "always been mistaken as the self-expression of a vivacious, life-loving people, while, in fact, it was but a mask behind which the people were hiding their *Schwermut*—hopelessness, despair, and a feeling of insecurity and abandonment—the true Austrian philosophy of fatalism." Zweig attributed this fatalism to the unnaturalness of Austria's geopolitical stature as "a weak country, a rather artificial construction of an Empire, unsound perhaps in its set-up, and doomed to fall when the first fierce onslaught was launched." This "national disease" had spread from Vienna, Zweig opined, because notwithstanding Austria's weakness, Vienna had for centuries been home to many of the world's foremost musicians, eminent poets, and superb theater. The Viennese "grew up in the delusion that, as the cultural centre of Europe, Austria would be the most respected and beloved of all countries," Zweig declared. The entire nation had a bad case of hurt feelings. Austrian fatalism reflected the discovery that making great art did not translate into wielding political clout.

Given Zweig's ambivalences about who he was, and what he wanted to become, it's true to form that he reports in his memoir having had no natural inclination to be a writer. The process whereby he latched onto books was completely dictated by environment. Vienna's school system was a miserable prison that did its best to stifle all "intellectual, artistic and sensuous curiosity" among Zweig and his friends. So they turned avidly to everything outside the schoolroom. At first, Zweig states, just one or two of his friends found they had artistic, musical, or literary interests. Then it was a dozen, and at last just about everyone caught the bug of artistic ambition.

Enthusiasms among young people are infectious, "like scarlet fever or measles," he argued. "It is therefore merely a matter of chance which direction these passions take: if there is a stamp collector in one class he will soon make a dozen as foolish as himself, and if three rave about dancers, the others will daily stand before the stagedoor of the Opera. Three years after us came a class which was possessed with a passion for football . . . By chance I entered a class in which my comrades were art enthusiasts; and this may possibly have been decisive for the development of my life."

Why would Zweig so downplay the role of intrinsic aptitude in determining vocation? For one thing, he thereby foregrounds the primacy of education in character formation. The craze for all things aesthetic among his friends was not in fact random, he explains, since theater, literature, and art were on display everywhere in Vienna. Newspapers overflowed with reports of the city's cultural events, "and wherever we went, right and left, we heard the grown-ups discuss the opera or the Burgtheater . . . Sport was still considered to be a brutal affair of which a student of the Gymnasium should rightly be ashamed, and the cinema with its mass ideals had not yet been invented."

Zweig was writing this in 1941, when his need to believe that youth might once again be directed away from militarism toward cultured pursuits was urgent. Make a town where art is everywhere, and children will grow up inspired by beauty and eager to become artists, Zweig said. Stud a city with athletic fields and valorize physical competitions, and they will grow up gung ho for battle. Young people, like chameleons, take on the color of their surroundings. Zweig wasn't just being prissy about physical contests. Nazism made sports into the cornerstone of all education, and athletic victory coequal with military heroism. Goebbels stuffed his speeches with metaphors from boxing, football, and racing. He defended this practice by invoking Martin Luther—archrival of Zweig's hero Erasmus—who'd preached that to communicate with the people you must listen to the man on the street.

In Zweig's view, had the atmosphere around his school friends been different, he'd have ended up in football shorts. But the Vienna of yesterday, bursting at the seams with books, taught him instead to become an author. He wrote in order to fit in, just as, when he began to succeed, what mattered to him was the creation of a community. Success enabled him to make himself at home anywhere in the world.

As for *what* he was writing, in his youth Zweig comes across as not just modest, but almost dismissive. To an editor friend he describes being "completely convinced that at best my talent is a small one, for the sketch or the lyric." Zweig never outgrew an endearing humility about the stature of his work. Ever quick to label other authors greater than himself—both friends like Joseph Roth and rivals like Hugo von Hofmannsthal—Zweig's sense of his literary mission was gently tutorial rather than magisterial. Klaus Mann captured this quality when, likening Zweig to his mentor, Freud, he wrote that with his "odd blend of detachment and sympathy" Zweig had neither the hope nor the pretention of changing the world with his books. "His sole ambition is to mitigate the bitterness of human suffering by amplifying our awareness of its roots and causes." Commenting on the burning of his books in 1933, Zweig pronounced it more "an honor than a disgrace to be permitted to share this fate of the complete destruction of literary existence in Germany with such eminent contemporaries as Thomas Mann, Heinrich Mann, Franz Werfel . . . and many others whose work I consider incomparably more important than my own." It's sad to think of Zweig finding himself ranked with the German literary giants only when their work was being jointly immolated.

Regarding the subject matter of Zweig's early work, his letters suggest that he was nearly as casual in deciding what to write about as he was fatalistic about accepting the work's limited power. But the topic choices he made, unconscious or not, were telling. Among the first novellas he tried to get published was one about a working-class poet taken up by fashionable society who discovers that he's unable to bear the switch in milieu and retreats back into his old humble environment. Another early work, entitled *In the Snow*, tells the story of a medieval Jewish community hounded out of their homes by a band of flagellants and ultimately caught in a blizzard, which frees them from worldly suffering by burying them. While the first novella portrays an individual who couldn't fit in to new social circumstances; the second depicts a whole people made to realize they have no home on earth.

When Zweig's writing began to be published, the theme of isolation remained a constant; the alienated condition just became predominantly psychological, rather than explicitly driven by class or religion. Zweig wrote in order to belong, but what he wrote *about* was the experience of not belonging. His portrayal of people who couldn't fit in anywhere earned him his international citizenship.

He wrote of men running amok through the tropics, unraveling inside casinos, chasing dreams around the Prater amusement park; of women who jeopardized a lifetime of respectability to follow the flame of a momentary passion—or who devoted their whole lives to a passion that ought to have been momentary. Of men and women who commit a crime just to see how it feels. Of men, women, and children who obsessively spy on one another's erotic lives, until surveillance becomes their chief form of eroticism. Of ecstatic confessions, and equally ecstatic secrets. Of people who sacrifice everything for one cosmic instant of unity with everything. And, in one novella, *Buchmendel*, of a man whose immersion in books is so consuming that he actually becomes a "magical walking book catalogue"—until "the blood-red comet" of the First World War bursts into his remote life at a Viennese café and reduces him to a bundle of rags.

Zweig himself explained his taste for characters who "squandered their lives, their times, their money, their health and reputation— passionate monomaniacs" as a literary rebellion against his own "solidly established background." His autobiography documents the touchingly deluded sense of security defining his Viennese home life, making it a stand-in for the minutely regulated, magnificently static condition of the empire at large. Critics have taken Zweig to task for the naiveté of this portrait of the old Vienna, where people lived comfortably and easily, where "rich and poor, Czechs and Germans, Jews and Christians, lived peaceably together in spite of occasional chafing." In fact, Zweig is very careful to say that this world of security was always illusory. His point, rather, is that one might do well to hold on to illusions, given the realities exposed by Hitler.

But if the world of security was, in truth, a fantasy, then perhaps what Zweig restlessly hunted for wasn't some exotic contrast to reality on the Ringstrasse, but environments that felt psychologically familiar, however much they may have differed in externals. "You know, fundamentally I have terribly strong passions and I am full of every kind of violence," Zweig once remarked to Romains. Only by exerting intense control over himself could he manage "anything like reasonableness," he said.

I know of no one who meted out to himself a scantier measure of the customary pleasures," Friderike said of Zweig. Theater and cinema held little attraction for him. When he went to a concert, this music lover who kept talking about wanting to resume his own piano studies quickly grew fidgety. Friderike could hardly remember a single program he listened to through to the end. "Perhaps he wished to light his inevitable cigar; perhaps to avoid by an early departure, boring conversations that might have disturbed the melodies still sounding inside him." Most likely, however, she said, was that music just stimulated him to take up his own work again as swiftly as possible. To Friderike, Zweig was himself a "passionate monomaniac" who couldn't sit still.

Friderike and Stefan became involved on the eve of the First World War. They'd first exchanged flirtatious glances in 1908 during a recital by a celebrity folk singer at a village wine tavern that drew a fleet of fancy carriages from Vienna. Four years later they spotted each other again in a restaurant garden. Friderike happened to be holding a copy of Zweig's translation of Emile Verhaeren's poetry. He cast her a beguiling smile. She wrote him a long, admiring letter. He answered that the evening had been "winged and magical," and expressed the hope that he would see her again soon. "For the first time she saw his beautiful rounded handwriting, clearly belonging, despite its firmness and determination, to a lyric poet," Friderike recounted in her third-person account of their courtship. "The letter was written, with the violet ink he generally used, on a heavy paper marked with the initials designed for him by a friend, and destined to become so familiar."

Along with a copy of Stefan's book, Friderike also had with her that night her first husband, Felix von Winternitz, to whom she was still married. She and Felix had united when still in "a child-like stage of development," Friderike later explained; yet while Felix was content with his stock of general culture, everything in her yearned "for maturity and depth." In portraits at the time, Friderike appears self-confidently exquisite. With hyper high cheekbones, a narrow black gaze, thin lips, and a dark bob, she's no less feline than Stefan, but a harder cat: Egyptian onyx to his Sèvres porcelain.

Their relationship progressed fitfully. Not only was Friderike married and a young mother, but Stefan claimed an embroilment with a Parisian woman. And his initial response to the affair was hardly euphoric. While still in the first blush of their romance, he recorded in his diary, "The mood in which I am living is flat and dull." The only things he professed to find meaningful were his random sexual adventures, and these only because of their risk factor. But Friderike clung fast, and Stefan didn't detach her. She accepted the unrestrictive terms he dictated for their liaison. Over the next few years, ties deepened. In 1916, when Stefan went into self-imposed exile from the war climate of the capital, first to Zurich, then to a little Alpine retreat, she followed him and they rented a discreet pair of rococo pavilions in the same garden.

Friderike came from a Jewish family but chose to convert to Catholicism before her first marriage, which made getting a divorce especially onerous. By the time her dispensation finally came through in 1920, they were already settled in the home where they'd remain the whole of their married life. On a chance visit to Salzburg during the war, they'd glimpsed a large yellow house on a thickly wooded hill that rose above the clutch of Salzburg's medieval lanes like a giant's hunchback. The dreamy, elevated situation gave the place the aura of an enchanted castle. Salzburg itself struck Zweig as a masterpiece of mediation—integrating modernity with the anachronistic, north with south, mountain with valley, and art with nature above all. After the Armistice, Stefan spotted a real-estate advertisement for that same bewitching castle. The couple leapt on the property, which proved to be a seventeenth-century archbishop's hunting lodge inhabited by squatters and belonging to an industrialist who'd needed somewhere discreet to invest war profits.

In addition to overlooking the rooftops, gables, and twenty-three church towers of Salzburg, the Kapuzinerberg hill provided views onto the dramatic Alpine chains beyond, including the range nestling in Berchtesgaden, where Freud wrote most of *The Interpretation of Dreams* and Hitler built his vacation home. Friderike boasted of their house having an "extraterritorial," pan-European character. It was also a hermitage in its own right—at least an aerie intended to discourage all but their select circle of artists and global humanitarians from making the trek. Shortly after they moved in, Stefan purchased a sundial for a wisteria-draped balcony, which he wanted to inscribe with an epigram of his own composition: "The sun stops here for but a short rest, / May you do likewise, very dear guest."

As matters turned out, the effort required to reach the Zweigs' home only made it a more satisfying pilgrimage destination for the growing waves of Stefan's fans. Throughout the summer months, benches lining the calvary path leading to their house were packed with people hoping to meet the famous author. Autograph hunters and budding artists—elderly people, young students hoping to cadge money for their return journey, and women of all ages and nationalities carrying dog-eared copies of his books and sometimes love letters—trudged up the steep hill. He could never bear to turn away admirers when they arrived at his garden gate, regardless of the labors they interrupted. The friction between his urge to sociably accommodate everyone and his sense of having his creative powers dissipated by a hyperactive sympathy was already apparent in the 1920s. Zweig was an extrovert who liked to fantasize about being an introvert.

Friderike, at least in her own estimation, was the supreme guardian of Zweig's inner peace. There were daily challenges—problems with the help and with portaging goods from the town below—and endless difficulties keeping everyone quiet while Stefan was working. His sensitivity to noise was notorious. The opera he selected to collaborate on with Richard Strauss was an adaptation of Ben Jonson's *Volpone*—renamed by Zweig *The Silent Woman*—and he took relish in writing an aria based on the torture he experienced from the din of Salzburg's pealing church bells. Radios were not admitted in their home for years. Friderike's daughters were forbidden any disruptive pleasures, confined to resentful sulking over his proscriptions against everything from gramophones to loudly shut doors.

Over time, however, no amount of quiet could assuage tensions on the Kapuzinerberg as Zweig aged, wearied of domesticity, and watched Europe edge closer to catastrophe. When Charles Baudouin visited in 1926, Zweig led him at once into his library, "a long room, with sliding glass doors and grills, where nothing has been neglected to make his books, in their dark and light dress, feel at home," Baudouin wrote. Zweig's books were made to feel at home even when he himself no longer could. By then he was telling friends that he felt perpetually exhausted and "played out," aware that he was living in a lull between disasters, part of a "beaten generation . . . fed with hatred, purged again with terror, attacked by stupidity, our spirit distracted by the senseless fireworks of money games. How can we create something complete . . . based on peace, when our powers are so obsessed with externals?" His words echo those of Hans Rost, the theologian cited earlier, only where Zweig diagnosed a blight on his generation, the cleric blamed the era's cultural decadence on the Jews.

It was around this time that Zweig had his picture painted by his friend the Belgian artist Frans Masereel. Friderike cried out in horror at the portrait, claiming it made Zweig look like an American whose mother had been ravaged in Chinatown. His beautiful rarified hands appeared brutish and bony, like the hands of a butcher. But Zweig loved the painting, seeming to feel that it captured some truth about the mongrel nature and savagery at his inner core. He traveled away from home constantly now, in desperate pursuit, as he put it, of his old sense of inner freedom through the mediums of French wine and blue southern seas. By 1931, Zweig's agitation and protracted absences had driven Friderike to the brink of despair. "The house isn't enough my home anymore," she wrote him on the last day of the year, after he'd skipped off to Paris for the holidays. "I don't own it; it is too big for me, a too ample cloak for a sometimes chilled and shivering soul."

The next day she wrote again to report that everything around her was glazed in sleet. At Christmastime he'd left her shivering hardest of all.

Salzburg ought to have been a glorious place for them to celebrate Christ's Nativity. "What other house could have harbored a more festive spirit than ours on top of the Kapuzinerberg, approached by a Calvary path that ended at the church?" Friderike mused. Deep snow drifted all around, glistening with light cast by the adjacent church. Thirty people received presents, and the cook prepared a table heaped with Stefan's favorite holiday dishes. "Even our dogs . . . and the many cats received sausages as gifts, and were happily excited," Friderike recalled. At first Stefan too "would enter into this joyful spirit." Then, out of nowhere, he would suddenly announce that he was leaving. He would rapidly pack a small suitcase and depart—usually to somewhere near Munich, where celebrations were less overwhelming. In time, he began avoiding the entire Salzburg Christmas season, spending the holidays with his mother in Vienna. It was a sad fact, Friderike later observed, that due to Stefan's depressive tendencies, "cheerful people and innocent children at play could make him shudder."

But it was only after Friderike joined Stefan one December at his family home in Vienna that she grasped the deeper reason why her own magical Christmases so distressed her husband. The couple sat together watching Stefan's mother, Ida, trim a small tree for the maids, when he suddenly flared up, "It would have been nice if she'd done the same for her children." All the while he was growing up, Stefan revealed, he and his brother had stared out their windows on Christmas Eve, seeing other children's homes shining brilliantly with holiday lights, while the two of them enjoyed no celebration whatsoever—no tree, not a single gift. More and more pent-up anger gushed out as Stefan confessed to jealousy of present-day youth who enjoyed themselves so freely, while he'd spent his childhood buttoned up in velvet suits with giant bows, leading a vacuous existence of family socializing—or locked in a bedroom that, for all the family wealth, he'd always had to share.

The Christmas tree functioned as a kind of anti-madeleine for Zweig—reminding him of everything that had *not* been part of his childhood: a secure, nurturing home before all. Throughout his youth, summer holidays had consisted of one long migration from watering hole to watering hole in an ungainly parade of relatives, servants, and trunks beyond number. The endless switching of trains became a slapstick exercise in stress and excitement. After leaving one seaside resort, the Zweigs found they'd somehow left behind a Bohemian maid with a tongue-twister name, and had to circle back and send out the town crier to call for her as best he could until she finally turned up again. These vacations managed the trick of simultaneously being occasions for claustrophobic engulfment in family *and* for being excluded by family. Once, when Friderike and Stefan were in Marienbad, he began pointing out the humble taverns where the children had to eat with their nannies, while the adults feasted at the town's flashiest restaurants. Even when it came to nature, Stefan was shut out from all but voyeuristic pleasures. When they went to visit beautiful mountains, he and his brother were permitted to gaze at the peaks, but not climb them. When they went to the sea, his mother's anxieties restricted the boys from playing in the waves. Everything they did reinforced the pattern of exclusion from life's best treats.

In Friderike's estimation, Stefan Zweig had remained stranded in this childhood: a spoiled sissy in the eyes of some less fortunate, but in reality a child who'd been cruelly deprived. He couldn't bear *her* happy Christmases because they were reminders of the Christmases his mother had not given him. Ida looms as the chief villain of Zweig's unsentimental education. "Extremely self-willed," in Friderike's words, she had an "uncurbed, unrestrained vitality, undiminished even in old age," which "often caused much suffering to her son." No wonder "Stefan always longed for the 'Silent Woman' . . . his mother's opposite. The silent, devoted Lotte so tragically fulfilled this idealized conception during his last years!" Friderike lamented.

But this stirring indictment slips in one tricky move. At first, Friderike acknowledges, she imagined that Stefan's flight from Christmas might be the result of "a subconscious antipathy to a Christian festival, but had not the tree been universally adopted by non-Gentile families?" she asks. Well—not quite. Certainly my father's family—who were far from orthodoxy—never had a Christmas tree. My father remembers about half his Viennese Jewish friends having Yuletide trees. We have a habit of overstating the sense of assimilation enjoyed by Vienna's Jews as a way of throwing into relief the terrible irony of their dispossession and destruction. My grandfather was typical among his Jewish peers for believing that the medals he'd received from the Kaiser for distinguished service during the Great War guaranteed him immunity from Nazi persecution. But faith in the state's commitment to your protection is not the same as the dream of integrating harmoniously with the majority population, or even of being cheerfully embraced in the people's traditional celebrations. The latter misapprehension was rare, even in Vienna. The art historian Ernst Gombrich recalled there being only one Viennese pastime untainted by anti-Jewish feeling: "In musical circles no one ever asked about a person's origins," Gombrich wrote; "naturally there were Jews and non-Jews, and they made music together; that's all there was to it." The sanctuary from race consciousness offered by music helps explain Zweig's idealization of the medium, even though he lacked patience to sit through performances.

Resentment of Jewish economic activities permeated Austrian discourse long before Hitler's rise, and often worsened at holiday times. "The Christian Yule festivities would be desecrated if a present bought from a Jew lay beneath the Christmas tree," remarked one follower of Vienna's openly anti-Semitic mayor Karl Lueger at the turn of the century. When Nazism made its first show of power in Vienna in 1932, Christmas shoppers patronizing stores owned by Jews were teargassed. In the countryside, where Catholicism was stronger and politics more reactionary, some priests still taught parishioners that Jews sprouted horns and were not really human. Demonization intensified around major

Christian holidays. Year-round boycotts of Jewish businesses were also organized by Vienna's numerous anti-Semitic organizations. Jewish career advancement, even in professions where they had a strong presence, such as medicine, was impeded by individual anti-Semites even when official policy forbade such measures. And then there were just everyday incidents of anti-Semitic meanness in the city's public sphere. My father still recalls having asked another boy what time it was in a park by his house and having that boy's father snatch away his child's hand before he could answer. "We don't tell time to Jews," the man told his son. My father was all of six years old when he had to process that encounter.

In the halls of government, anti-Semitic outbursts were so numerous that they took on the character of a game. Once, when a member of Parliament proposed discussion of a new anti-Jewish measure ahead of some mundane piece of legislation, the House speaker denied the request with the remark, "No, my good sir, business before pleasure." One anti-Jewish bill near the end of the nineteenth century proposed that all Austria's Jews be jammed onto a ship, which would then be sailed out to sea and sunk.

However, if virulent anti-Semitism saturated Vienna for so long, doesn't this leave us with an equally vexing puzzle? If we're not to imagine that anti-Semitism erupted out of nowhere to destroy the symbiosis achieved between Jews and non-Jews in Vienna, then we have the opposite problem: How could the Jews in Austria have been so willfully blind to their impending fate? What degree of pathological denial had allowed them to ignore the toxic signs of hatred everywhere?

Zweig confesses in his memoir that he cannot remember when he first heard of Hitler. At some point an acquaintance from

Bavaria mentioned a violent agitator named Hitler who opposed the Republic, staged meetings that became crazy brawls, and stoked anti-Semitic feeling. Zweig didn't give the news a second thought. "Hundreds of these little bubbles of discontent were bobbing about in the general fermentation of the time, leaving nothing behind when they burst but a bad smell which clearly showed how Germany's still open wounds were festering and rotting," he wrote.

Similarly, the very prevalence of anti-Semitism in Vienna, rather than raising a red flag that things were about to turn dark, may have just anesthetized people to the notion that anti-Jewish sentiment could ever become dangerous. Viennese anti-Semitism signaled that it was business as usual in the Austrian capital. However, though Jews had no way of anticipating that routine anti-Semitism might eventually usher in a whole new paradigm, a sense of things being out of alignment pervaded the city. "It's unjust always to blame Vienna for its faults, since its advantages also deserve blame," Karl Kraus once quipped. Analyzing the difference between the situation at home and in Germany, he remarked, "Prussia: freedom of movement with a muzzle. Austria: an isolation cell in which screaming is allowed." In time, another epigram comparing the two states gained currency: "The Germans make terrific Nazis but lousy anti-Semites; the Austrians make lousy Nazis but terrific anti-Semites." Austrian anti-Semitic thought had always inspired the National Socialist leadership, Hitler above all. And the Austrians' swift and thorough translation of anti-Semitic theory into violent action after the Anschluss startled even some of the German Nazi ideologues, who thought their Austrian comrades should be reigned in a bit. The truth behind Vienna's mordant witticisms played into the city's spiritual malaise.

Perhaps Zweig's bitterness at the sight of the Christmas tree was grounded in a deeper sense of exclusion from the ritual so rapturously celebrated in Vienna and on the Kapuzinerberg than he could articulate even to himself. Perhaps it had less to do with what his mother didn't do for him than with his complex relationship to what she *was*—and the identity he inherited through her. And perhaps Zweig fled Salzburg to be with his mother in Vienna because he didn't want Ida to be alone on a holiday that brought home to her the fact that she still didn't fully belong in the city.

As more of Zweig's family background has come to light, it's emerged that not only his paternal grandparents but also his maternal Brettauer grandparents were religiously observant for much of their lives. Ida's mother, Josefine, came to live with the family when Stefan was born. Josefine and Stefan became close over the years when he was growing up, and on her death she left him a legacy that enabled him to rent rooms of his own and begin the pursuit of his own cultural passions. Zweig's relationship to this woman—who quite possibly did not find it so easy to trim a Yuletide tree and whom Zweig's mother might well have wished not to disrespect—surely played into the abiding concerns with Jewish themes in his writing. There are hints of Ida's own lingering attachment to her ancestral past as well. "I often accompanied my mother-in-law to her parents' grave in the Vienna cemetery," Friderike wrote. Indeed, it was precisely in this vast graveyard that she liked to talk about her youth in Italy. For all that Friderike insisted on Ida's indifference to religious identity, Zweig and his brother were bar mitzvahed. The family appears to have fasted on Yom Kippur. And one of the most distraught letters Zweig wrote to Friderike was one penned in the mid-1920s in which he described his poor mother in Vienna surrounded by "vermin," who viciously sought to upset her by claiming he had joined a Christian church. "Now she has secretly asked Alfred *when* I was baptised, if it was a long time ago or has only just happened," Stefan cried out. Remarking to an interviewer in 1931 that he'd been "vitally interested in Jewish problems all my life, vitally aware of the Jewish blood that is in me ever since I became conscious of it," Zweig asked, "What human problem can be so important as that of the race to which one is born?"

Between his sense of insecurity at his parents' house and Vienna at large, his estrangement from the home he and Friderike had made in Salzburg, and the self-alienation that made him itch to fly out of his skin, it's possible to see Zweig's entire life in Austria as a kind of trial exile.

When he showed up in Salzburg for the last time in 1936, shortly before leaving his homeland for good, "chaos broke out in the old house on the Kapuzinerberg," Friderike wrote. "For two days the incinerator smoked from an auto-da-fé of letters and innumerable papers. Stefan stood there watching the flames which seemed to liberate something inside him." Thousands of volumes of his books were carted away, some to the Austrian National Library, others to the Hebrew University in Jerusalem, while his collection of autograph catalogs "and God knows what else" vanished, never to be seen again. After the great fire was finished, Zweig walked off alone from the house. An old friend who ran into him on his way down the mountain found the look on Zweig's face so intense that it frightened him.

Little wonder that, as world-historical events caged him more tightly, Zweig's yearning for release inside the covers of books became only more acute. "When a hand frees you," he cried in his hymn to books, "when a heart touches you, you imperceptibly break through our mundane surroundings and, as in a fiery chariot, your words lead us upward from narrowness into eternity." Zweig's ultimate metaphor for the emancipation books offer derived straight from the Book of Books: the scene from Kings of the blazing chariot on which Elijah ascends into heaven.

Chapter Four

TRAVELING WOMB

In 1938, at the age of eighty-four, Ida Zweig still observed her daily constitutional—around the spiderweb of the Ringstrasse, through a nearby park such as the Rathauspark or the elegant Burggarten, former private palace garden of the Habsburgs, which had been opened to the public after the Empire's fall. As she became more elderly, her legs grew a little shaky, and she was grateful for the way the city planners had provided benches where a person could pause a moment to rest. She stopped every five or ten minutes to gather her strength and look around at the changing scenes of this city she had lived in since she was a sixteen-year-old schoolgirl. Many of the buildings she saw were new. For decades, the city had been a massive construction site—huge pits everywhere with jumbles of wooden boards and trestles at the bottom. Ida had watched Vienna "being demolished into a big city," in Karl Kraus's phrase.

Much of the imposing architecture built in the center of the city over the course of her life there had reflected the aspirations toward political and cultural enfranchisement of families precisely like the ones she and her husband grew up in. The Zweigs' apartment was situated just behind the giant neo-Gothic Rathaus—seat of the city council. Moritz's family, who had moved to Vienna from Prossnitz in Moravia when he was five, was even more typical in this regard than her own Brettauer clan. In his autobiography, Zweig characterizes the Moravian Jewish community as prime stock for populating the city in its era of expansionist liberalism, which lasted from the 1860s up until the beginning of the twentieth century. The Moravians had been emancipated from orthodoxy at an early age. They were "passionate supporters of the contemporary cult of 'progress,'" he notes. "When they moved from their places of origin to Vienna, they adapted with remarkable speed to a higher cultural sphere, and their personal rise was closely linked to the general economic upswing of the times."

As for the city's new architecture, Zweig recalls, it "reared itself proudly and grandly with glittering avenues and sparkling shops," amid the old palaces and religious monuments. "But the old quarreled as little with the new as the chiseled stone with untouched nature. It was wonderful to live here, in this city which hospitably took up everything foreign and gave itself so gladly." The variety of historical styles on display in the buildings of the Ringstrasse, still under construction in Zweig's own youth, was the most striking architectural testament to the ascendancy of the new middle class, with its liberalizing political mission and almost religious veneration of the arts. A statue of Athena, spear in hand, stands on a high pedestal before the neoclassical Parliament. The young

Klimt's murals for the new Burgtheater give a panoramic, densely allusive vision of the history of drama, stretching back in time to erotic gatherings around the altar of Dionysus. The Renaissance motifs in the university building celebrate the marriage between, in the historian Carl Schorske's words, "modern, rational culture and the revival of secular learning after the long night of medieval superstition." Whether deemed kitsch or sublime, the Ringstrasse buildings present a carefully orchestrated parade of bourgeois cultural ideals as applied to the spheres of politics, education, and the arts. "In Vienna, the streets are paved with culture!" Kraus observed. "In other cities they manage to pave them with asphalt."

None of this democracy-laden symbolism prevented the young Adolf Hitler from discovering his own strain of enchantment in Vienna on his first visit to the city in 1906. "For hours on end I would stand in front of the Opera or admire the Parliament Building; the entire Ringstrasse affected me like a fairy tale out of the Arabian Nights," he recalled in *Mein Kampf*. On his second trip to the city he found so beautiful, Hitler took his entrance examination to the Academy of Fine Arts. He'd always been dead set against his father's plans for him to become a state employee. The thought of sitting in some government office spending his whole life filling out various forms made him yawn himself sick, he wrote. When he was twelve years old the knowledge that he would become an artist burst into his head. Ever since that moment he'd worked to hone his skills as a painter and draftsman.

While he waited for the results of his submission with a mix of "excitement, impatience and proud confidence," Hitler once more feasted on the fairy-tale sights of Vienna. And when rejection came, he wrote, it struck "like a bolt from the blue. And yet, that was it, period." Hitler's failure to be admitted into Vienna's great art school has been much commented on, but the pure shock of the refusal is equally important. His experience with the Academy showed Hitler that the world was not what he'd believed it to be. The glittering vision of the Ringstrasse *was* a fantasy from *The Arabian Nights*. Vienna, it seems, did not give itself gladly to everyone. This was the moment when, realizing he was unlikely to be given the chance to develop his art in the city, Hitler began to think about transforming Vienna into the vision incubating inside him.

Hitler returned to the city after his mother's death in 1908, intending to reapply to the academy. But this time his preliminary drawing submission was judged substandard, and he was not allowed to take the exams. He stayed on in Vienna for five years, struggling to launch a career as an architect. In *Mein Kampf,* he thanked the Goddess of Trouble "for snatching me from the emptiness of a comfortable life and for pulling this mamma's boy out of the comfortable, cozy bed." Vienna, he observed, "was and has remained the hardest and most thorough school of my life." And the result of this hardness was to make him strong—to make him *hard,* he explains repeatedly.

Soon drained of his meager savings, Hitler was thrown into the world of misery and poverty, "which introduced me to those I would later fight for," he wrote. Vienna's population had quadrupled between 1850 and 1900, and now at more than two million the city was the fourth largest in Europe. Most of Vienna's furious new building activity had in fact been slums and tenement houses beyond the inner rings. Hitler ate at soup kitchens. He slept on park benches—sometimes, perhaps, the very benches where Ida would later pause to gather her strength.

Hitler's return to Vienna in the year of Ida's eighty-fourth birthday after a long sojourn in Germany heralded the enactment of the city's first racial hygiene laws. Nowhere else in *The World of Yesterday* does Zweig's voice radiate fury the way it does when he describes how Hitler had not been master of the city a week before he gave the order forbidding Jews to sit on public benches. Appropriate Jewish businesses; rob them of their art—these crimes at least could be made sense of by the logic of personal greed and the need to buy the loyalty of one's henchmen. After all, Hermann Goering had built his splendid picture gallery this way. "But to deny an aged woman or an exhausted old man a few minutes on a park bench to catch his breath—this remained reserved to the twentieth century and to the man whom millions worshipped as the greatest of our day."

One by one, the elements of Ida's Vienna were whisked from her grasp like props in a children's game: benches, cinema houses, restaurants, theaters, opera, streetcars, playgrounds. For a time it may have seemed as though the city were vanishing around her, but people streamed in and out of the doors and through the gates she could no longer enter. It was Ida herself who was disappearing, shrinking, effacing, turning into a phantom—exiled from Vienna while still in her home.

"Fortunately my mother was spared long experience of such brutal humiliation," Stefan wrote. "She died a few months after the occupation of Vienna." The fact that his mother's death and the Anschluss occurred almost together resonated powerfully. Indeed, Zweig's inability to return to Vienna to be at Ida's bedside when she was dying—since his crossing the border into Austria as a Jew now could mean arrest and deportation to a concentration camp—drove home to him that he was no longer a voluntary nomad, but a true exile. A friend who was with Zweig in London shortly after he received the telegram announcing her death described Zweig sitting, staring in front of him for a full hour without speaking or listening to anything being said, all the while "rubbing the palms of his hands in utter nervousness."

A portrait of Ida taken around the time of Stefan's birth depicts her in a close-fitting black dress with delicate flowers at the breast and a single blossom woven into her plume of dark hair. She is seated; her left hand rests in her lap holding a closed black fan; her right fingers curl beneath her cheek, which tilts to meet them. She gazes out with a dreamy, slightly wistful smile from sealed lips. Shapely and with an intense gaze, she appears elegant and seductive—but hardly ostentatious. Indeed, it was rare for Ida to adorn herself with anything beyond a simple brooch or necklace. With her inquisitive dark eyes, slight plumpness in the cheeks, and ambivalent expression playing over her lips, Ida so strongly resembles those photographic portraits of Stefan in which he appears lost in sensuous melancholy that he might have been modeling himself on his mother's look.

The family apartment was often full of people—crowded with the voluble fraternizing of relatives and friends from the spheres of law, commerce, and finance appropriate to Moritz Zweig's professional station. Zweig's brother, Alfred, later characterized their social circle as "Jewish bourgeoisie of the first rank throughout." All at once, Ida would burst up and with barely a word of apology announce that she was going off to the cinema. All alone, she would dash out from beneath the heroic stone maidens ornamenting the façade of their apartment house and make her way to the dark cavern of one of Vienna's new movie theaters, where she would sit for hours on end, rapt in the black-and-white flickering.

Only many years later did it emerge that Ida's impulsive passion for film had been driven by a disability. In the wake of Stefan's birth, she was discovered to have a hormonal imbalance that progressed to sclerosis of the middle ear. The symptoms were misread by her doctors, and a short time later she descended into severe deafness, resorting to an ear trumpet to make out conversation. Like many people suffering hearing loss, she found noise torturous. In the theaters of that era's silent cinema Ida found peace from the din of her home—a sanctuary otherwise elusive in congested, combustive Vienna. Instead of the musical performances and plays she could no longer follow, she had the motion pictures. The image of this refined, solitary woman, often dressed in black, sitting through film after film, year after year, as she aged and the world outside metamorphosized beyond recognition, is haunting. It finds its echo in a cry Zweig gave from the depths of his exile when he told a friend that art had become purely a refuge for him. "Will you think me ungracious that I use it now as opium and hashish?" he asked.

Perhaps Stefan had feelings of guilt about the connection between his birth and the onset of his mother's deafness. Regardless, Ida's difficulties in hearing and her related vulnerability to loud sounds were part of Stefan's most intimate childhood experiences. Given the norms of the age, her deafness would have been both socially isolating and embarrassing; she was known for being a temperamental, peculiar creature. When Stefan was a child, the cinemas where she would later find refuge were not yet built, and the absence of escape outlets may have been part of what lent her an air of perpetual restlessness. Stefan made the same impression on others. The biographer Antonina Vallentin remarked that when one met Zweig there was always the feeling that a half-packed suitcase stood ready in the next room. And Stefan's own hypersensitivity to sound must be looked at in the context of his mother's deafness. The anguishing sense of not being able to hear what one needs to hear and the sense of being forced to hear more than one can bear are deeply linked.

It's true, as Friderike asserted, that Zweig was obsessed with silence and the ideal of the silent woman. But silence was a much more complicated notion for him than she implies in the crude reduction of the concept to a quiet house and a woman who knows when to shut up. Silence was constellated in Zweig's mind with a whole series of profound notions. First there were his beloved books, which he once defined as "handfuls of silence, assuaging torment and unrest." Then there were the deep ties between silence and ideas of inner freedom; silence and secrets; silence and interiority as such. However much Zweig's mother did or did not speak, there's no question that her deafness both locked her into a kind of silence and led to her cultivating a rich inner life. What we know about her conversation suggests an ardor for poetic reminiscence. Having spent her childhood in Ancona, Ida never lost her preference for speaking in Italian and loved to conjure the nocturnal fetes in colorfully lit boats she'd enjoyed from the family gondola. Among her contemporaries in Vienna she was viewed as exotic because of her fondness for cooking risotto and artichokes, which had been favorite dishes in her childhood home. (Later, Stefan drew an analogy between historical truth and an artichoke: layer after layer could be stripped from our stories of the past, he wrote, without ever reaching the inner core; for this reason, history, he declared, must always consist to some extent of artistic fabrication.) Friderike cast Ida as one who "took joy in fables," in contrast to the sober realism of Stefan, who'd followed in his father's footsteps. Yet the conscious elisions, reframings, and questionable interpolations that characterize his telling of his own personal history in *The World of Yesterday*—and which he defends as integral to the nature of history itself—show the degree to which, on this count also, Stefan was his mother's child.

Rather than just thinking about what Zweig idealized in the notion of the silent woman in terms of the volume of words that left her lips, we might consider the idea of a person for whom much invariably remains unspoken—even incommunicable—because the scale of yearning and anguish always exceeds the dimensions of language. Over and over in Zweig's fiction—in *Twenty-four Hours in the Life of a Woman*, *Fear*, and *Letter from an Unknown Woman*, to name just three examples—readers discover sympathetic female protagonists who have been forced by male obtuseness, social convention, or both to close off their impassioned inner life from the world—to live in a compulsory silence regarding emotions at once tragic and incomparably more intense than the feelings shading the lives of those around them. Zweig's acute sympathy for characters both male and female who harbor complex, turbulent inner existences that society cannot fathom, and that render them effectually mute, is one of the most powerful strands of his work.

With the social circle occupying their home either snickering at Ida's moodiness or shrugging it off as symptomatic of her general eccentricity, how could the young Zweig not have wondered what really transpired behind his mother's wandering gaze? He too was continually disturbed by the noisy entertaining in their home—and learned to flee into daydreams at first, and then, as he grew older, into creative labors. How could he not have felt confusion, shame, and compassion for what Ida could not say, notwithstanding whatever was said? All the more so because relationships between them *were* strained. There are sinister hints of how he began to turn this sense of exclusion back around on his mother as he grew up: locking himself into hotel rooms when he wished to refuse her the right to doll him up in fancy clothes; locking her into her own bedroom when he was older and wanted to be left in peace to do his own work. (He would later lock himself away from Friderike and her daughters, refusing to speak to them for days at a time, which became formal grounds for the divorce granted on Christmas Eve 1938.)

And where was his calm, industrialist papa during these harsh battles? Some describe him as a taciturn figure hovering in the background of the family melodrama with a tinge of cynical amusement. From his father, perhaps, Zweig inherited not just a measure of sobriety but also the quiet, sometimes cruel titillation of the voyeur.

Whatever dangers Zweig sought in the underside of Berlin had some counterpart in the emotional violence of his home. And it was Paris, which he discovered several years later, and which he called in his memoir both "the city of eternal youth" and his "home away from home," where Zweig found something he'd genuinely never tasted in Vienna: tolerance. "No one felt shy with anyone," he wrote of the French capital of his youth; "the prettiest girls didn't shrink from going into the nearest *petit hôtel* with a black man—who cared about the bogies that were to be made much of later on, race, class, and birth? One walked, one talked, one slept with whomever one pleased, and cared not a hoot about others." The streets propelled one's steps, always revealing something new. Paris was a return of a very different sort for Zweig. Seeing the city in reality, he wrote, was a case of what Aristotle called anagnorisis: recognition, the most enigmatic of all aesthetic delights—for he had encountered almost every feature of the city before arriving, in the pages of beloved books.

Finally—and bound up with the relationship between outward silence and inner life—there is the silence that underlay Zweig's concept of ethical integrity. Even after the "Action against the Un-German Spirit," the Nazi book burnings of May 1933, Zweig wrote a friend that it was crucial now to "wait, wait, keep silent, and silent again . . . For my part I would gladly have done without such publicity. You know I am a man who prizes nothing more highly than peace and quiet."

There is an off-putting sense of political disengagement in such a passage. But informing his disgust for the contemporary blowhards was Zweig's long study of the historical link between demagoguery and noisemaking on the one hand, and the quiet, calm forces of reason on the other. These reflections culminated in his Erasmus study, which was published in 1934.

It's remarkable in retrospect that with *Erasmus* Zweig succeeded in writing something that Thomas Mann would consider flawed for being *too* obvious an allegory for the present—with Luther caricatured as Hitler's fanatical precursor—and yet managed to blind the Nazi censors sufficiently that it could continue to be sold in Germany up until 1936. Joseph Roth took lengthy quotes from *Erasmus* as epigraphs for chapter headings in *The Antichrist*, his own apocalyptic jeremiad. ("Ah for whom should one write in the midst of political clamour and shouting that deafen the ears to more moderate sounds," reads the first citation.) E. M. Forster recommended Zweig's *Erasmus* to his English audience as a "brilliant and true" historical study—as well as a personal meditation by a writer who was himself consumed by an eternal theme: "Thought and Understanding" or "Passion and Power"? Though Zweig didn't hide the faults of Erasmus, who "was not brave" and "disliked defining his attitude," or vilify Luther, he showed why, in the long term, tolerance was the "major instrument in the upward movement" of humanity. "It is the power to understand people not the power to boss them that distinguishes us from the apes," Forster wrote, adding that Stefan Zweig himself had lived by this principle.

The New York Times chose Zweig's *Erasmus* for its 1934 Christmas book list as a "penetrating study of the great humanist whose tragedy was that of the Middle-of-the-Roader in turbulent times." One *Times* reviewer noted Zweig's acknowledgment of the responsibility born by the humanists themselves for Luther's ascendancy. Erasmus and other early humanists, Zweig wrote, believed that broad human progress could be achieved through enlightenment alone. In words that anticipate critiques of Zweig himself, Zweig declared how, in "their overvaluation of the effects of civilization, the humanists failed to take account of the basic impulses and their untamable strength; in their facile optimism they overlooked the terrible and well-nigh insoluble problem of mass hatred and passionate psychoses of mankind . . . This noble company of idealists would fight against the boorish impact of the folk revolutionaries with the no less effective weapon of beauty." By the time he composed *Erasmus*, Zweig saw the way misplaced hopes and overrefined sensibilities had doomed humanism in the past, even as similar hopes and sensitivities undermined him and his fellow cosmopolitan pacifists in the present. If judgment is due, it must be on the grounds of Zweig's conviction that sometimes the right choice is *not* to prevail—that failure may achieve a redemptive moral beauty. It's not incidental that Zweig chose Nietzsche's line, "I love those who know not how to live, except by going under, for they are those who cross over," as the epigraph to his principal study of German literature.

Such notions of failure and surrender find so little resonance in the American dream that they may have contributed to Zweig's sense of alienation in the United States. They're also ideas with a deep Jewish lineage. As such, they help explain the recurrent theme in Zweig's writing of what's glorified in Yiddish literature as "the virtue of powerlessness, the power of helplessness, the company of the dispossessed, the sanctity of the insulted and the injured." The sculptor Gustinus Ambrosi once said of Zweig, whom he called "an eternal pilgrim in the human psyche," that his greatest mistake was the shunning of strength, motivated by his chronic sense of being "overwhelmed by the mighty." But when we see how passionately Zweig resisted the idea that the Nazis could be fought on their own terms, it's clear that something more than just weakness was at work. Zweig believed that silent withdrawal could render a form of moral judgment, and that such stereotypically female attributes as softness, receptivity, and even oversensitive nerves could serve an ethical purpose. Franz Werfel described a moment when, after some Nazi outrage in the early 1930s, he and some friends eagerly invoked war. Zweig "only went white to the lips and turned away," Werfel recalled. It was a striking act of passive protest. Such qualities of hypersensitivity also turned a person into a human bellwether. "My nose for political disaster tortures me like an inflamed nerve," Zweig told Joseph Roth in 1936.

Hitler had made a fetish of the notions of hardness and strength. (German terms for these concepts appear more than two hundred times in *Mein Kampf*.) The obsession with education that permeates Nazi rhetoric elevated physical education above all else. Victor Klemperer wrote of how passionately Hitler loved the official phrase for physical training, *körperliche Ertüchtigung*, with its bang and crash of hard consonants. Erika Mann, Thomas Mann's daughter and an activist-artist in her own right, reported how boys who were members of the Jungvolk and Hitler Youth were taught to rebel against tenderness with all their might—even a mother's kiss might inculcate mushy affection. Mothers' boys, they were told, cry when they are hit. "They don't know what a night march or war play is . . . Mothers' boys rest their heads on soft pillows and sleep under silk covers. *Jungvolk* youngsters are hardy."

Zweig—characterized so frequently by others as soft and feminine in his manners—saw the Nazis as having already taken over the position of hardness. Even if it meant doom, a counter-position had to be staked out. Trying to explain his stance to the German-French writer René Schickele in the summer of 1934, Zweig wrote, "Everything I do I try to do *quietly* . . . There is nothing of the so-called heroic in me. I was born a conciliator, and must act according to my nature." He said that the only way he could work was by making connections and offering explanations. "I cannot be a hammer, nor will I be an anvil," he wrote, characterizing himself as one of those whose "post is the most thankless and most dangerous of all—in the middle, the no-man's-land between the trenches: those whose hand is not on the trigger."

One day in the spring of 1904, after having just returned from a trip abroad, Zweig was passing through Vienna's Stadtpark when he glimpsed a familiar figure. Advancing slowly alongside the sculptures of great artists and politicians that lined the swirling walkways, in between nursemaids and governesses, knitting, reading, gossiping—while children spun in the sand and ducks quacked on the pond—came none other than Zweig's first editor, Theodor Herzl.

Herzl must have been just leaving his nearby offices at the *Neue Freie Presse*, Zweig realized. But the change in this man whom Zweig remembered bursting with vitality only a few years before was frightening. His beard may still have been nearly blue-black—he was only forty-four years old, after all—but gone was the swinging step, the light ease of manner. Herzl inched painfully along, hunched over.

Zweig greeted him from a distance and began to move on. However, Herzl managed to straighten his back and walk up to Zweig, extending his hand. "Now why are you hiding away?" Herzl asked. "There's no call for that."

The reproach in his voice was understandable. Ever since their first meeting in Herzl's dingy, cramped office at the newspaper, the two men had felt drawn to each other. Herzl's school friends remembered him in terms similar to those with which Zweig was later recalled by youthful comrades, "a dark, slim, always elegantly clothed youth, always good-humored," an enthusiastic conversationalist whose dandyish aura of superiority remained genially graceful. In his memoir, Zweig says that Herzl "was the first man of international stature I met in my life"; his was "the most cultivated kind of journalism," delighting a city that had "trained itself to appreciate subtlety." (He uses similar terms to characterize his mother: "Hers was an international family," with "international contacts that gave the family more sophistication, a wider vision.")

On the occasion of that first meeting, when Zweig was a brash nineteen-year-old filled with a sense of his own pluck at broaching the inner sanctum of the Viennese literary world, clutching an essay on poetry he'd written, Herzl rose up from a desk heaped with papers, his dark beard rippling down his high white collar between the lapels of his elegant black morning coat, his forehead clear and high, his dark, melancholy gaze meeting Zweig's own. Herzl's eloquent gestures were simultaneously natural and dramatic, Zweig wrote—managing this trick by virtue of their great dignity, learned from countless evenings at the Burgtheater, where Herzl had even seen a few of his own sentimental plays produced. It was rumored that if he'd been a more successful playwright, Herzl might never have developed Zionism.

Herzl took Zweig on, accepting submission after submission to the newspaper, making him an anointed disciple. Before long, Herzl announced to his coterie that Vienna had no reason to be afraid of decadence in art, for there was a whole army of gifted young talent in the city, and Stefan Zweig stood at its head. Other writers began to discern a resemblance between the two men that went far beyond their shared Francophile feuilleton style. No doubt this was partly attributable to the fact that, for all his enviable fluency, Zweig, like Herzl, viewed literature not as an ultimate task, but as a bridge to some hazy, higher mission on humanity's behalf. When Zweig and Herzl first met, Zweig later recalled, the older man was still at odds with himself, not yet believing in the future of his own movement sufficiently to give up the position at the paper from which he made his living, yet tormented by the conviction that without his full commitment the Zionist project would fail.

Along with the literary pursuits for which Herzl served as a mentor, Zweig started following Herzl's movement to create a Jewish homeland. He attended meetings of those interested in Herzl's ideas in the basements of different coffeehouses. He began to be acquainted with Zionists at the University. Martin Buber, in particular, became an admired friend. Zweig was impressed with the courage of Herzl's insistence on the need for a Jewish homeland, notwithstanding the astonishment his ideas provoked among Jewish bourgeois circles in Vienna who thought the cosmopolitan Austro-liberal editor had gone soft in the head. "Why would we want to go to Palestine?" they lashed out. "We speak German, not Hebrew; our home is in beautiful Austria." Even beyond the specific Zionist project, Zweig was attracted to Herzl's position that—in Zweig's paraphrase—"if humiliation is always to be our fate, let us meet it with pride."

However, for all Zweig's attraction to Herzl himself, he felt disturbed by almost every aspect of how the Zionist movement was developing. Later explaining his failure to have become a Zionist, he commented, "The right relation never presented itself." On the one hand, the Zionist students, who were completely submissive to Herzl and to whom "the ability to defend themselves was somehow still the nucleus of Judaism," were "alien" to him, he wrote in a 1929 essay. And Zweig felt even more estranged by the disrespect shown Herzl at the basement meetings of more mature Zionists that he attended at Herzl's prompting. There was a level of savagery and dishonesty to their opposition "of a kind hardly comprehensible today," Zweig wrote. Jews from the East, whose background was more religious, accused Herzl of not understanding Judaism, while the economists condescended to him as a journalist. Everyone had their own objection to Herzl, and to one another: some were orthodox, some freethinkers; some socialists, some capitalists; everyone spoke different languages, hailed from different places, had different histories. They all tore into Herzl for different reasons—and always for the wrong reasons.

Zweig studied Zionism almost literally at Herzl's feet. And he took Herzl's teachings to heart, meditating on them for years afterward. Yet the conclusions he drew from the early Zionist scene were precisely the opposite of those Herzl sought to disseminate. In a fascinating letter Zweig wrote to Martin Buber in 1917—at the very moment Zweig felt he was discovering his own higher life-task in the cause of pan-European pacifism—Zweig asserted that he had "never wanted the Jews to become a nation again and thus to lower itself to taking part with the others in the rivalry of reality. I love the Diaspora and affirm it as the meaning of Jewish idealism, as Jewry's cosmopolitan human mission." Expanding on this position as the exchange with Buber grew more heated, Zweig announced that ten years of avid foreign travel had confirmed for him "the value of absolute freedom to choose among nations, to feel oneself a guest everywhere, to be both participant and mediator. This supranational feeling of freedom from the madness of a fanatical world has saved me psychologically during these trying times, and I feel with gratitude that it is Judaism that has made this supranational feeling possible for me."

When Buber parried these thrusts with a recital of his Zionist ideals, Zweig grew only more unequivocal. "I am quite clear in my mind," he wrote, that "the more the dream threatens to become a reality, the dangerous dream of a Jewish state with cannons, flags, medals, the more than ever am I resolved to love the painful idea of the Diaspora, to cherish the Jewish destiny more than the Jewish well-being. In well-being, in fulfillment, the Jews were never with anything."

The satirist Karl Kraus, who exerted an overwhelming influence on the Viennese intelligentsia through his journal *Die Fackel*, shared many of Zweig's reservations about Zionism but took what was, finally, a more conventional bourgeois approach to the Jewish question. Kraus saw the Zionists' decision to glorify stereotypical Jewish traits as a regressive move that artificially divided educated Jews from their non-Jewish peers—while riling up vulgar anti-Semitism. He thought it risible that big noses and other characteristics identified as signs of Jewish inferiority by anti-Semites should now be elevated into objects of pride by the Zionists. And he mocked the assimilated coffeehouse idlers who'd taken up the cause for its fashionable backwardness. "It took narrow-minded Zionism . . . to enable these gentlemen, who have hitherto been occupied only with their nerves, to feel that they too are of this day and age," Kraus wrote, alluding to the vogue for nationalism. Jews ought to remain where they were and become socialists, he argued: "Where a down-to-earth settlement project is involved, messianic rapture is entirely dispensable." The true Jewish mission ought to be total assimilation. "Through dissolution to salvation," he quipped.

Zweig resisted this binary prescription, arguing not for the disappearance of the Jews but for their global scattering, rather in the manner of heirloom seeds, sown to propagate universal cultural values instead of prize vegetables. "Through dispersion to salvation" would have been his riff on Kraus's epigram. No doubt Zweig's horror at all the quarreling dogmatism on display at Herzl's coffeehouse Zionist meetings contributed to his conviction that the Jews' future did not lie in mass congregation.

And still, this was not quite the same thing as preaching, like Kraus, that adaptability was the most memorable feature of Jewish identity. Zweig wrote with pride in his autobiography that "nine-tenths of what the world celebrated as Viennese culture was promoted, nourished, or even created by Viennese Jewry." The problem, he explained to Buber, was that in the professions of Jewishness he encountered, "everything that bespeaks pride seems to me to be an exposure of insecurity, a reversed anxiety, a twisted inferiority feeling. What we lack is *security, composure.*" While he acknowledged having these feelings himself, he concluded, "Being a Jew does not burden me, does not uplift me, does not torment me, and does not separate me. I feel it as part of my being, like my heartbeat, feel it when I think of it and do not feel when I do not think of it." In this sense, Zweig opposed what some scholars view as a Freudian strain bolstering the Zionist narrative of exile and return: the belief that a national trauma can be repaired only by going backward in time to the childhood of the nation, the time and place where the trauma began. Zweig didn't believe a literal return could heal anything. His analogy of Judaism and the heartbeat instead recalls what the mother leaves behind with us, what remains inside after the dyad has been outgrown.

Finally, Zweig makes the roles of Vienna, his mother, and Judaism in his development remarkably akin: they compose a trinity of muses in the art of letting go. In his autobiography, he segues from a description of learning to be a polyglot cosmopolitan with a taste for travel from his mother and the Brettauer family to an account of Vienna as a city that allowed him to become a "supernational, cosmopolitan, citizen of the world." His correspondence with Buber reveals that he saw Judaism's exemplary role not in its promotion of adaptability, but in the call to empathy. Individual Jews were enjoined by their historical Jewish consciousness to identify beyond Judaism with a spectrum of the world's people. The present condition of the Jews, he wrote Buber, was for this reason "the most glorious in all of mankind: this oneness without language, without ties, without a homeland, solely out of the essence of our beings . . . And the one point where we have to strengthen ourselves is to feel this condition not as a humiliation, but with love and awareness as I do." It was the Jews' sacred mission, in their capacity as eternal foreigners, to serve as "the gadfly which plagues the 'mangy beast of nationalism'" until nationalism lost its intellectual composure. The dissolution of nationalist tendencies thus "helps us to rid ourselves of the dead past, of the 'eternal yesterday,'" Zweig wrote. "These Jews without a country are the best assistants of the 'good Europeans' of the future."

On that day early in the spring of 1904 when Zweig began to duck off from Herzl in the Stadtpark and Herzl insisted on taking his hand, telling him there was no need to shy away, Zweig must have braced himself for Herzl's next words. How could Herzl *not* have seen Zweig's increasingly consuming travel schedule as symptomatic of his alienation from the movement? The less time he was in Vienna, the less time he had for Herzl or for Zionism. Zweig had gone on the lam.

Amid the sounds of birds and playing children—the hushed conversation of promenaders in elegant dress, and perhaps the murmuring of some less fortunate in shabbier garb—the two men stood breast to breast on the Stadtpark path. At last, Herzl broke into speech. I *approve* of your going away from Vienna and Austria so often, he abruptly declared. "It's our only way . . . Everything I know I learned abroad. Only there do you get accustomed to thinking on a wide scale." It would have been impossible, he went on, to nurture the growth of Zionism in Vienna. He would never have been able to muster the courage. The movement would have been nipped in the bud. "But thank God, when I came up with it, it was all ready, and they couldn't do anything but try tripping me up."

Herzl went on to speak with extraordinary bitterness about Vienna. It was in Vienna, he said, that he'd encountered greater opposition than anywhere else in Europe. When he entered the theater, Jews would titter and whisper, "Here comes the King!" invoking the nickname Kraus bestowed on Herzl in his pamphlet *A Crown for Zion* and the ridicule Kraus heaped on Herzl for imagining he could transform "hooked noses into badges of merit." Vienna's chief rabbi, who'd seemed receptive to the Zionist idea before Herzl published *The Jewish State*, recanted his support once the book appeared, labeling Herzl's project a *Kuckucksei*—a cuckoo's egg—that would end up leaving the Jews friendless and driven back to the ghetto. The *Neue Freie Presse* simply ignored Zionism, denying all Herzl's entreaties to grant even a few columns of space to the subject. Had not invitations come to him from outside Austria's borders, from the East and now from America as well, he would have been worn out by the struggle, Herzl said. "If my health were as strong as my will, then all would still be well, but you can't buy back the past."

Zweig walked Herzl back to his house. The two men shook hands at his door at number 9 Türkenstrasse. "Why do you never come to see me?" Herzl asked as they took their farewell. "You've never visited me at home. Telephone first and I'll make sure I am free."

Zweig promised to do so, and promised himself to break this promise, "for the more I love someone the more I respect his time."

Thus, Zweig claims, in what proved to be their last encounter, the prophet of the Jewish homeland endorsed Zweig's wanderlust as the only solution to the Jewish predicament. But the scene also conveys, beyond any philosophical debate, the pang of sheer human loneliness as Herzl reached out his hand. And Zweig's failure to keep his promise left Herzl in his solitude. Perhaps Zweig couldn't bear to let his old friend discover how far away from him he'd actually traveled.

A few months after their chance meeting in the Vienna Stadtpark, Herzl died. And on the eerie July day of his funeral, Zweig saw a sight such as he'd never seen before and would never see again. From all corners of the globe, from every province and country, Jews poured into Vienna's railway stations. Day and night, thousands upon thousands: "Western, Eastern, Russian, Turkish . . . they suddenly stormed in, the shock of the news of his death still showing on their faces." Zweig describes a colossal, miraculous ingathering of the Jews of the world such as the biblical prophets and Herzl himself had dreamed of. Only the site of this great convocation was not Jerusalem, but the central cemetery of Vienna. And as they reached their destination, instead of the rapture the prophets had fantasized for the long-awaited hour of return, there was a horrible screaming, howling, weeping, "a wild explosion of despair."

Some years later, in his biography of Joseph Fouché, Zweig would actually call for a "Hymn to Exile." "Has any poet ever sung the glories of this power which moulds destinies, which uplifts those who have been cast down, which under the harsh stresses of loneliness reassembles in a new order the dispersed energies of the soul?" he asked in a ringing apostrophe, adding that the most important messages humanity ever received were delivered from exile, those of Moses, Christ, Muhammad, Buddha, Dante, and Nietzsche among them. And yet, as his friend the essayist Alfred Polgar remarked, "Oh foreign land how beautiful you are—for one who still has a home." With all the ideological bravado of Zweig's embrace of a sort of preemptive exile, there were moments, even before leaving Salzburg, when he trembled before the implications of perpetual migration.

Zweig's opposition to Zionism was insurmountable. He couldn't make the leap from recognizing the Jews' endangered status in Europe to calling for a Jewish homeland in Palestine when that project seemed bound to repeat the disastrous choices made in European nationalist movements. He balked at Herzl's romantic propaganda and the efforts to make Zionist political events into charismatic spectacles that would trigger mass enthusiasm. But Zweig also identified with Herzl as a tormented, utopian dreamer—respected his self-sacrifice, felt deeply for and with him. Moreover, Zweig knew in his heart that he had no alternative to propose.

One day in the 1920s when Zweig happened to be traveling in Germany with Otto Zarek, the two men stopped off to visit an exhibition of antique furniture at a museum in Munich. After some desultory meandering around the galleries, Zweig stopped short before a display of enormous medieval wooden chests.

"Can you tell me," he abruptly asked, "which of these chests belonged to Jews?" Zarek stared uncertainly—they all looked of equally high quality and bore no apparent marks of ownership.

Zweig smiled. "Do you see these two here? They are mounted *on wheels. They* belonged to Jews. In those days—as indeed always!—the Jewish people were never sure when the whistle would blow, when the rattles of pogrom would creak. They had to be ready to flee at a moment's notice . . . Yes, these chests on wheels are striking symbols of the Jewish Fate!"

Chapter Five

THE REUNION

Lotte blinked. Youthful wonder for once got the better of her resignation to Stefan's mood. An Italian garden floated in the sky above Vanderbilt Avenue. Along with this aerial extravaganza, the Biltmore Hotel adjoining Grand Central Terminal had nine hundred rooms, was shaped like a horseshoe, and smelled like marshmallows. It had its own exclusive arrival chamber dubbed "the Kissing Room" for the smooches that took place there underneath the famous bronze clock, and a private elevator shooting up from the station to the presidential suite. F. Scott Fitzgerald portrayed the hotel's Palm Court lounge as a kind of spatial quintessence of Jazz Age glamour. He and Zelda were chucked out of their rooms once while the bathtub was still running, on account of the raucous honeymoon bash they threw there. Headquarters of the National Democratic Party, the Biltmore had now been turned over to the inaugural dinner of European PEN in America.

Zweig's presence at this event in May 1941 reflected his feeling that there were still certain obligations one could not avoid. To be sure, he grumbled to Lotte's family about the fact that the gala promised to be precisely "one of this enormous dinners with 1000 persons which I have avoided all my life long." But I like to think that Stefan mustered a little stoicism on the night itself—enough at least to prevent Lotte from feeling too guilty about her pleasure in attending. Perhaps the two even took a little whirl around the establishment before filing into the grand Cascades ballroom, which had a hand-cranked sliding roof that enabled guests to stargaze while dining.

The Zweigs were seated at the high table, with other literary notables. Lotte expressed the hope that "it was not disappointing for the thousand people who paid 3 dollars each for this privilege to see that writers really do not look different from other people." She found her name card between that of Count Carlo Sforza, the eminent former Italian foreign minister who'd been exiled by Mussolini, and Somerset Maugham, arguably the most famous writer of the age—the "old, old parrot," as Christopher Isherwood dubbed him, with "flat black eyes, blinking and attentive, his courtly politeness and his hypnotic stammer." So far from being "stiff," as she'd imagined him to be, she happily reported to her family that Maugham was "very nice." In truth, the whole evening was "quite interesting and entertaining," Lotte wrote to her family. Stefan noted with pride that Lotte had proven to be "a brilliant conversationalist." Friderike's casting of her as the passive "Silent Woman" in the drama of Zweig's last years apparently did not fully capture her character. It was Lotte's first large-scale public dinner, and she was brightly voluble. Having been holed up for months in hotel rooms doing nothing but working and worrying, she was ready to break out a little.

The dinner's organizers had been stringent about holding speakers to brief time-slots to accommodate the needs of the shortwave radio operators who were transmitting the event all across Europe. Dorothy Thompson, the journalist who was called the second most influential woman in America after Eleanor Roosevelt, spoke of "the weapon of the word of truth" proving more potent in Hitler's eyes than "airplanes, bombs and machine-guns." Jules Romains, who'd instigated the founding of the European PEN Club in Exile, declared that European writers refused to "accept the material defeat inflicted in Europe." Maugham averred that the real battle of the war was to determine whether truth was better than falsehood— "whether the only means of right is might."

But none of them struck the popular chord so resoundingly as Zweig. In a surprising, counterintuitive move, Stefan devoted his ten minutes to apologizing for the wrongs inflicted on humanity by the Nazis. "We writers of the German language feel a secret and tormenting shame because these decrees of oppression are conceived and drafted in the German language, the same language in which we write and think," he admitted. And though he acknowledged that he was no longer considered German by the Germans themselves, he insisted, "I feel it is my duty publicly to ask forgiveness of each of you for everything which today is inflicted on your peoples in the name of the German spirit."

The diners were moved, and the reporters were galvanized. Stefan's remarks, which had been delivered in English, were quoted in the headlines and cited at greatest length in the *New York Times* article about the event. "Zweig Apologizes for Wrongs in Germany's

Name," trumpeted *The Christian Science Monitor*, adding that his remarks were "cheered loud and long."

When Thomas Mann was asked, shortly after his own emigration to America, about the Nazification of Germany, he remarked, "Where I am there is German culture." Europe's immolation notwithstanding, Mann assured his public, the exalted tradition lay snug inside his gigantic brain. Zweig's address at the Biltmore revealed that he too believed that where he was, there was German culture—except for that very reason he was a shambles of his former self. Like German culture, Zweig was a wreck.

The German language held a special allure for Central European Jews, the Viennese dialect perhaps most of all with its unique cultural and spiritual resonances and its soft, rich, slightly nasal drawl. As a child I felt the allure of that tongue. On very special occasions, my grandmother would bake an exquisite dessert she called simply "Viennese layer cake." Bands of mocha cream alternated with apricot jam, almond paste, and the darkest chocolate frosting. I remember being inside her dreary high-rise apartment in northern Virginia watching the gleam of her knife swishing through those layers, and then the taste of all the different flavors mingling in my mouth. When I was still very young, the German that Mutti spoke with my father became identified in my mind with those extraordinary confections. There was a sensual congruence between them such that I still see those cakes when I remember the sound of her speaking.

The special affection the Jews had felt for Viennese German played into the anguish of their exile, especially because the question of what the true German language consisted in—to whom it belonged and who belonged within its linguistic-territorial fold—had been contested for so long. The relationship between

Germany and Austria is confoundingly tangled. During the Iron Age, Germanic tribes had spread through large parts of Central Europe. By the time of the Romans, they had earned a reputation for being formidable warriors; the writings of Tacitus on the character of the Teutons became popular in Germany as the idea of the master race was being articulated. One of the more sober German historians in the generation preceding Zweig's chose to isolate a scene from Tacitus that generally received less attention, however. Wilhelm Scherer recounted Tacitus's description of a Teuton who lost all his possessions in a dice game, then staked his own freedom on the final throw, lost this round also, and immediately stepped forward to be sold as a slave. This, Tacitus remarked, indicates "the extent of Teutonic tenacity, even for a bad cause." The refugees wisecracked that when a German wants to make an impression at a party he dives out of the window. "A lack of moderation seems to be the bane of our intellectual development," lamented Scherer.

The Austrians in general and the Austrian Jews in particular saw themselves as able to temper that enduring strain of Germanism in ways that would allow the strengths of German intellectual achievement to translate to the rest of civilization. "We formed the bridge from Germany to the world," Zweig remarked of Austrian culture to a New York writer in 1938. "This bridge has now been completely destroyed with the Iron Ax." Jules Romains understood Zweig's attachment to Germany as natural, since it was "his intellectual fatherland in the broad sense," but Zweig's fatherland, as Romains characterized it, was "an eternal Germany, bounded not by frontiers but by its culture and its great men—the German of Goethe, Beethoven, and Heine." Zweig told Romains that he had always found the atmosphere of Vienna "infinitely pleasanter than in Berlin." And still, he acknowledged, the Viennese were nearer to the Germans than any of the other subjects of the Dual Empire. "All that we ask is that we may not be bothered by politics," Zweig concluded. Gershom Scholem, the German-born scholar who himself emigrated to Jerusalem early on, described this perception of belonging to the German people even on purely cultural terms as "a lurid and tragic illusion" to which Zweig, Schnitzler, and other Jewish authors were especially susceptible. But Scholem also acknowledged that the few German-speaking Jews who avoided this delusion—he singled out Freud, Kafka, and Benjamin—would not have been at home in the land of Israel either. These superior artists, even while being tied to the German language, "never succumbed to the illusion of being at home," Scholem wrote, because they were not of this world at all.

Zweig himself clearly suspected that something didn't quite work in this formula of serving as Germany's benign, rather priestly cultural brokers, exempt from all political bother. Up until the very end of his life he was still worrying over the question, and in his last conversation with a German-Jewish exile friend who'd joined him in Petrópolis, Zweig suddenly began talking about Austria, remarking that there'd been "much reasonableness" in the country's admixture of Slavic character—more than he had recognized. "We Austrians never appreciated that," Zweig said. "What admiration we had for the Germans!"

The National Socialists, rather than trying to mediate the German's singular tenacity "even in a bad cause" identified

1100. The partition of Charlemagne's vast empire. Germany was obliged to fight against marauding Hungarians, Wends and Danes. The Normans attacked France and England. Spain defended itself against the Arabs. Hungarian and Arab campaigns against Italy

1100—1300. German Emperors against German Princes. Rivalry with the Pope. Campaigns in Italy. The wars against the Albigenses in France. English campaign against Ireland. Spanish victories over the Arabs. Mongols in Silesia. Normans in Southern Italy

1300—1500. Wars of the Confederacy. The Hansa against Denmark. Teutonic Knights against Poles and Lithuanians. Wars on the Hussites. Peasant revolts in France and England. England against France. Wars in England itself. The Turks in the Balkans

1500—1650. The Turks advanced as far as Vienna. Peasants and knights at war in Germany. French campaigns in Italy and Flanders. The Wars of the Huguenots. Sweden fought in Germany during the 30 Years' War. Cromwell's campaigns in England and Ireland

1650—1780. The War of the Spanish Succession in North France, Belgium, North Italy and the Main region. Turks expelled from Hungary. War in Scandinavia. Prussia against Austria. England and France at war overseas. War between Sweden and Poland

1780—1900. The Napoleonic Wars in Italy, Germany, Belgium, Holland, Spain, Portugal and Russia. Greece fought against the Turks. German and Italian wars of unification. Franco-Prussian and Russo-Turkish wars

What we are fighting for:

For Europe's liberty and the end of its continual fratricidal warfare

For many centuries past Europe has been torn by the wars of its peoples. Actually there have never been any long periods of peace on our Continent. An unfortunate policy of coalitions resulted in the European peoples taking up arms against one another and mutually slaughtering the flower of their youth at frequent intervals. An end must be put to that now and an end can be put to it.

Europe is no longer today the uncontested centre of world power as it was a century ago. Vast power complexes have developed outside Europe in the Soviet Union, in the United States and also in Asia. Were the peoples of Europe to continue annihilating one another, they would in turn finally fall an easy prey to these powers outside Europe. Until now there has not been any real opportunity to put an end to these internal European wars because the destiny of whole continents outside Europe also depended upon their outcome. Today the situation is simply that either Europe unites in combating these extra-European power complexes or that it is gradually undermined country by country and destroyed by them. "Hereditary enmities" dating from former centuries cannot and must not be of any importance in view of this world situation.

In former epochs nobody would have believed that a time would come in which one town would no longer fight against another and one small principality against another. It did nevertheless come about on the formation of the various national states in Europe. Today we are faced by the necessity of reaching the next stage, that of the unification of Europe.

The establishment of this final European peace is our greatest and most important war aim and it is combined with Germany's struggle against the extra-European powers.

→

Transferred to a map, the adjoining sketches show where the centres of European warfare lay during the period from 1100 to 1900. Whilst the world was being partitioned, Central Europe served throughout the centuries as a Continental battlefield

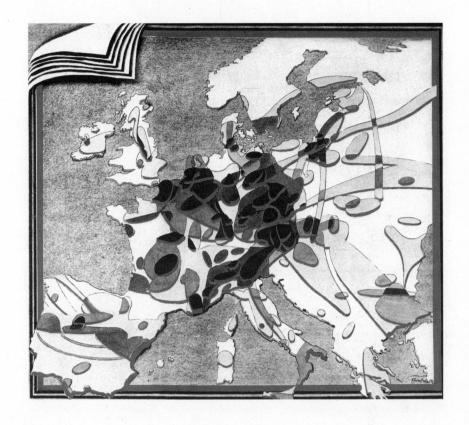

by Tacitus, sought to magnify that quality. Inspired by Wagner's operatic interpretations of Nordic mythology and theories of Aryanism developed from multiple strands of European racist philosophy, they sought to reincarnate ancient Germanic nature. But the Nazis enhanced the emotional power of their superman archetype by fitting that figure into a larger historical sequence entwined with the growth and decline of imperial Austria. The establishment of the Holy Roman Empire, "the First Reich," which yoked together not just the lands of modern-day Germany and Austria but also the Low Countries, was one of the early milestones cited by National Socialist historians. From early in the fifteenth century until its collapse during the Napoleonic Wars, the Holy Roman Empire was ruled by the Habsburg dynasty, so that Austria, the center of Habsburg power, presided (weakly) over the other German states. Prussia's ascendance within the German principalities over the course of the nineteenth century marked another key passage in the nationalist version of events. The seven-week-long Austro-Prussian War of 1866 that resulted from tensions between the Austrian Empire and the rising Kingdom of Prussia ended with the decisive defeat of the Habsburgs at Königgrätz. (In the 1930s some Germans joked that Hitler was Austria's revenge for Königgrätz.) The unification of Germany in 1871, establishing the Second Reich under the leadership of Bismarck, made yet another milestone. But more than any other historical event invoked to legitimate the Nazi cause, the Treaty of Versailles became a rallying cry to inspire zealous support for Hitler.

The terms of surrender dictated by the Allies after the First World War recut the board of Europe. Some German populations were left divided among other nations; most goadingly of all, the treaty forbade Austria and Germany from merging, despite those countries' wish to do so. Hitler attacked this twentieth-century settlement with arguments that harkened back to the tribal definition of Germanism, and then spiked that rhetorical brew with more recent historical resentments and racial blood theory.

Years before the Anschluss, the curriculum in Austrian schools had been recalibrated to reflect pan-German sentiments. Textbooks were revised to teach students that Austria had been a German land from time immemorial populated almost exclusively by Germans. My father's education in Vienna took place after these changes were instituted. He escaped Austria halfway through the equivalent of an American elementary school education. When I asked him whether he could recall being taught anything as a schoolboy in Vienna about why Austria and Germany should unite, he answered reflexively, as though his knee had been struck with a hammer: "They formed a community of German-speaking people." Okay, I said, but beyond that? "Well, the Nazis felt they had a common heritage," my father said. I pushed him for more. "They spoke the same language," he said. And he shrugged a bit helplessly. That was all he could remember being told. The German language was the verbal expression of German blood.

The language problem confronting Zweig began with the very word *"Deutschtum"*—Germanness—which meant one thing in Berlin, where the mythic fundament of a German *Volk* underlay the discourse, and quite another in polyglot, ethnically diverse Vienna. Even before the focus on the magical element of the German people, however, as Prussia sought to unify the German states under its own rule, Prussian military leaders had developed a habit of justifying naked aggression with metaphysical bombast. "The trouble with Germans is not that they fire shells, but that they engrave them with quotations from Kant," Karl Kraus once quipped. The language became Prussianized, with florid platitudes as camouflage for brutality, and Hitler layered the bureaucratic Prussian-German with mystical, incantatory elements. One early follower in the 1930s likened the hypnotic effect of Hitler's voice to being "within the field of a powerful magnet. Whether one was repelled or attracted one was electrified." Ernst Kris, a refugee Viennese psychoanalyst, noted in 1940 that Hitler once said the masses were so dumb and so feminine, they would take anything you told them, so long as it was expressed in the manner of advertising catchphrases. "Truth is of no avail, but there must be an ideology behind it, something to inspire the imagination," Kris explained.

To the Jews who were forced to hear Hitler's speeches only over the wireless, or to read them in newspapers, Hitler's language seemed almost comically impoverished, while his delivery amounted to a convulsion of fury. Zweig wrote of the horror he experienced on a train somewhere outside Houston in the course of his 1938 lecture tour when he suddenly heard a "loud, mad shouting in German." A fellow passenger had innocently turned on the radio, and, while Zweig sat frozen and his Pullman car rolled along the endless flat expanse of the Texan plains, Hitler's voice raged through the compartment.

But when individuals opposed to Hitler actually attended his speeches, they often left feeling they'd experienced something beyond a shrill torrent of anger from this character who, it was rumored, worked himself into such a lather while speaking that, after chewing his handkerchief, he would dig his teeth into a cushion and then throw himself down on the ground and start gnashing the carpet fringe. An American journalist commented in 1933 that Goebbels had supplied Hitler with words that "transposed the German language into a mystic music, which sounds harmonious, and almost religious, to the citizens of the Third Reich." Another spoke of Hitler's "pleasant baritone, drawing out vowels in the true Austrian manner . . . The voice of an orator has often been likened to a musical instrument, but Hitler's resonant voice seems to be an entire orchestra."

What was the nature of this symphonic sound, I wonder, relative to the music some heard in Zweig's voice—a speech one listener characterized as "extraordinarily soft, and yet so richly expressive"? The Austrian film director Berthold Viertel declared that Zweig's style was "essentially Latin. His German lacked the Gothic element." A German journalist told me that her own passion for Zweig's written language derived from its "Bach-like" range of resonances. In one of the few surviving recordings of Zweig reading his own work, Zweig's voice rises and falls through countless registers, quavering and fluting; crisscrossed with *ooos* and richly rolling *r*'s, drawn-out vowels and clipped, percussive consonants. It's a dramatic recitation, yet communicates something beyond the cadences of performance. Zweig sounds supple, exuberant, and world-weary all at once.

Clearly not everyone responded to this mélange in the same way. Along with Zweig's legions of fans, there were others who were turned off by his voice both in person and on the page— castigating him for being at once unctuously fluent and sloppy. Responding to a devotee of Zweig's work who stated that with his novellas Zweig had mastered every language on earth, Karl Kraus remarked: "Except one." That pretty well sums up the critical view of Zweig's German.

In *Mein Kampf*, Hitler is obsessively concerned with preserving the authentic German language from the threat of contamination posed by Slavs and Jews. People in Germany didn't understand the degree to which German was under siege in Austria and especially in Vienna, Hitler wrote. He boasted of never having been able to learn the Viennese dialect despite years of living in that city, precisely because the language was layered with so many non-German influences. Even sympathetic observers before the First World War saw the city as irredeemably ambiguous. Vienna was at once "intellectual and sentimental, sophisticated and naïve, over-refined in its tastes and primitive in its instincts"—so ethnically and psychologically hybrid that one might speak of "a Viennese race," opined the essayist Amelia von Ende.

The dream of belonging haunted Zweig's era in ways that many of us now, never having had even the illusion of a permanent home, find difficult to fathom. The shock of discovering one might *not* belong wherever one found oneself was still fresh then. Stateless-ness as a large-scale phenomenon began in the West only after the First World War, when events such as the Russian Revolution, the reshuffling of boundaries in the Balkans, and widespread persecu-tion of Armenians and Assyrians in Turkey left millions without a homeland or governmental protection. And this was also, concur-rently, the moment when a well-documented state identity became imperative for traveling across borders.

Vienna, long a magnet for migrants, with a population that was Slavic, Hungarian, German, and Italian, for starters—a place where "belonging" always implied that one also belonged else-where, if anywhere—had an edge on this condition of modernity. The French Catholic poet Charles Péguy saw in this character a specifically Jewish element: "Being elsewhere, the great vice of this race, the great secret virtue, the great vocation of this people," Péguy wrote. The Viennese aptitude for being and belonging else-where, whatever its ethnic roots, made the city a place where ques-tions of people's national allegiance were thrown into high relief. And these issues often played out in savage disputes over the right to use languages other than German in schools and bureaucratic contexts.

Hitler wrote that he was not an anti-Semite as a young man, and in fact viewed the Church's demonization of Jews as distastefully archaic. But he adds that in Linz, where he grew up, there were virtually no Jews to be seen. This situation changed radically after he got to Vienna, and he pinpoints the moment when he first realized he was mistaken to have made no effort to learn what anti-Semitism was all about.

One day, while strolling about the Inner City, he suddenly met a man in a long caftan with black curls. "'Is that a Jew?' was my first thought," Hitler recalled. "Jews did not look like that in Linz. I covertly observed the man, but the longer I stared at that alien face, scrutinizing feature after feature, my question changed from, 'Is that a Jew?' to 'Is that a German?'" Hitler eventually came to focus on language questions because, he argued, the ability of the Jew, "who can speak a thousand languages," to pretend to have a German identity "depends on his ability to emulate the language alone." Language alone let Jews "pass" as real members of the *Volk*. And if they got into power they would force everyone to speak an international tongue such as Esperanto. *Mein Kampf* opens with a call for the reunion of Austria and Germany, and it swells into a hysterical hymn *against* exile: "I speak to all those who are separated from the mother country and must fight for even the sacred possession of their native language, those who are pursued and tormented for their faithfulness to the Fatherland and who long in anguish for the moment that will bring them back to the heart of the beloved mother, and I know that they will understand me!"

The scene of Hitler encountering the Jew in Vienna's Inner City provides an eerie counterpoint to a scene involving Zweig and Otto Zarek in London, not long after Zweig had gone into exile. The two men went off together for a night at the Yiddish theater to see a performance of the *Dybbuk*. It was an impressive staging that brought to life the reality of Jewish ghetto existence in Russia, Zarek reported. But after the show Zarek was struck by Zweig's state of acute nervous agitation. He could not contain his inner excitement. "These old Jews," Zweig said, "in their grotesque dresses, their beards unshorn, their eyes flaming, these adherents to Chassidism . . . they are *our brethren*." It was only the measures toward assimilation taken by their great-grandparents that had kept them from looking just like those Jews did, Zweig told Zarek. Had it not been for their near forebears, the two of them would have ended up "believing in what they believe," considering "our life in the midst of the Western world as just a transitory period—we, too, would harbour in our very hearts, the dreams of our eventual 'return to the land of our forefathers.'" Zweig comes within a hair of saying, "There but for the grace of God." But Zarek said that Zweig's voice took on a note of despair and resignation as he registered that he hadn't, after all, quite dodged the bullet. Here he was, despite everything: one more Central European Jewish émigré in London. And in a kindred phenomenon, for all that Zweig sought to emulate the spirit of Schiller when the poet declared, "I write as a citizen of the world. Early did I exchange my fatherland for mankind," Zweig was able neither to shake his attachment to the German language, nor to shed his conviction that the language was permanently lost to him with Hitler's accession to power. When

Hannah Arendt was asked after the war what she missed from Europe before the rise of the Nazis and what survived from that era, she famously responded, "The Europe of the pre-Hitler period? I do not long for that, I can tell you. What remains? The language remains." Her interlocutor pressed her to explain whether she'd kept this allegiance even in the most bitter time. "Always," Arendt answered. "I thought to myself, What is one to do? It wasn't the German language that went crazy. And second, there is no substitution for the mother tongue."

It's a powerful counter-position to set up against Zweig's linguistic despair, but I'm not sure it wins the day. Perhaps parts of a language *can* go mad. Zweig continued to read his Goethe and Rilke up until the end, but as a living tongue on the world-historical stage, Zweig had strong evidence that the German language, if it had not gone crazy, had at least been hijacked—stripped for parts and reconfigured in the linguistic equivalent of a chop shop. Victor Klemperer analyzed the fate of "*fanatisch*," the German term for fanatical. Before Hitler, this was a strictly negative term denoting detachment from reality and reason. During the Third Reich, "*fanatisch*" became conflated with courage, devotion, and the refusal to ever surrender. On Hitler's birthday, Germany's newspapers were studded with congratulatory messages that repeated "fanatical vows," "fanatical declarations," and expressions of "fanatical belief" in the immortality of the Reich. Late in the war, as the Nazis' position grew increasingly hopeless, declarations of a "fanatical faith in final victory" became ubiquitous in the media. One could say that the commonly held sense of "*fanatisch*" was forced into exile. By 1936, Zweig was writing Rolland that it

was essential to develop "a fanaticism of anti-fanaticism"—a for-
mulation that indicates he'd fallen prey to the same syndrome.

Nothing made Zweig feel so estranged from the world as the
sense that his language had been split off from its meaning—a
metaphysical problem wrapped in the physical one of how he could
continue to identify with his native tongue when he was barred
from setting foot in the principal German-speaking lands. His
dilemma was all the more grim because he also believed that there
was no replacing one's first language. In recounting his shame at
the Biltmore for the Nazi brutalities being committed "in the
name of the same German culture which we are trying to serve
with our work," he acknowledged that it might be surprising to his
audience that he and his fellow exiles continued laboring in German. However, he declared, "An author may leave his country but
will never be able to detach from the language in which he thinks
and works."

Martin Gumpert described how coming to New York as a
refugee who was less than fluent in English meant arriving "deaf
and mute." One was transformed into a state both "truly undignified and pathological." Where voices had been melodies, suddenly
everything became just "sounds." To a person "on an advanced
intellectual level" this loss of language amounted to "an almost in-
superable shock." Apart from all the nuances of Zweig's dilemma,
as a Jew, an Austrian, and a European, I think the sheer shock of
this deprivation must have fueled the surprising moment in his
PEN speech when he broke from his traditional restraint into a
crude, desperate lament: "This is the language in which we have
fought our whole life against the self-deification of nationalism!
And it is the only weapon we have left to keep on fighting against

the criminal demon who is destroying our world and kicking the dignity of humankind into feces!"

The only weapon the German and Austrian Jews had was being twisted back against them by their archenemies.

Listening to her husband speak and to the swelling rounds of applause, Lotte experienced her own moments of recognition. She'd played an intimate role in the process of composing Zweig's speech for PEN, so busy "preparing, translating, altering, correcting, shortening, retranslating," she told her brother and sister-in-law, Manfred and Hanna, that she'd seen nothing of their daughter, Eva, for days on end. Beyond just hearing the sentences she'd helped to shape spoken aloud, there was another element of déja vu to that night. "Most of the European writers whom we ever read were present," she marveled—Thomas Mann, André Maurois, Sigrid Undset, Lion Feuchtwanger, Franz Werfel. Suddenly, in the Cascades ballroom, all these names she'd so often seen stamped in ink on the pages of her family's books leapt into fully dimensional flesh and blood.

The beginning of Lotte's relationship with Stefan, seven years earlier, must have been flush with such moments of recognition as well. I think of words Zweig himself wrote in his novella *Letter from an Unknown Woman*, long before meeting Lotte, in which he described a famous novelist's affair with a young, innocent, ardent soul who writes in her confession of love: "Even before you actually came into my life, there was a prestige about you, an aura of opulence, of being special and mysterious." Watching the novelist's belongings being moved into a flat near hers, the story's protagonist muses about what the man must be like "who owned and read all those wonderful books, who knew all those languages, and was so wealthy and knowledgeable at the same time."

Exposed to the wide circles of Zweig's acquaintances, Lotte suddenly found herself actually meeting people who'd long represented cultural reference points. Some degree of vertigo must have been induced by being with Zweig himself. This figure whose name was in every bookshop and so many newspapers and literary journals—whose work aspired to be a microcosm of the whole of European literature—there now, breathing before her, relaxing in her company during interludes between impossibly glamorous travel itineraries, making plans to rendezvous with her in railway stations, exquisite restaurants and hotels, folding her coolly into his over-packed existence.

Her own family's achievements were also significant, but on a less extravagantly cosmopolitan scale. Lotte, who was born in 1908, grew up in Frankfurt, where her great-grandfather, the renowned rabbi Samson Raphael Hirsch, had established himself as a founding spirit of modern orthodoxy. Though opposed to the innovations of the reform movement, Hirsch had defended his exacting faith in elegant, classical German, rather than Hebrew or Yiddish, as his ancestors would have done. He was also a pioneering force for progressive social welfare within the Jewish community. Lotte's grandfather Mendel Hirsch became the head of one of Frankfurt's leading Jewish schools. Her mother, Therese, who was religiously observant, taught in this school, while her father, Josef, who became a merchant, had always been an insatiable autodidact, teaching himself many languages and becoming a fine pianist.

Friderike's introduction of Lotte in her biography of her former husband is a masterpiece of damning less by faint praise than by bold pity. She claims to have made the connection between Stefan and Lotte in the course of hunting for a competent secretary for her husband in England. "After a pretty girl recommended by our consul had proved to be too pleasure-loving, I turned to the solemn precincts of Woburn House, the excellent institution of Jewish refugees," Friderike writes with a quick double twist of the knife. "From among their number I engaged a girl whose especially serious and even melancholy mien, seemingly a symbol of the fate endured by herself and innumerable fellow-sufferers, induced me to choose her." (Friderike's story of having made this introduction has since been determined to be a fabrication.) "Miss Lotte Altmann," she continues, "whose sedateness belied her youthful years, had been obliged to discontinue her university studies, and was now extremely happy to find interesting, even though temporary, work." We're left with the impression that poor health, dullness of mind, or both led to the decision by this stolid, doleful Jewess to withdraw from university. Friderike's émigré audience might well also have heard echoes in this sketch of a deftly wicked caricature by the German satirist Kurt Tucholsky: "Mrs. Steiner was from Frankfurt, not terribly young, alone and with black hair. She wore a different dress each night and sat quietly to read cultured books. She was a devoted follower of Stefan Zweig. With that, everything has been said."

Correspondence from Lotte's father, Josef, reveals that in fact Lotte had been compelled to break off her studies because of anti-Semitic policies that were implemented long before the start of Hitler's chancellorship. By the latter half of the 1920s, when she would begin her higher education, the subject of Germany's lost glory and the injustice perpetrated on the German people at Versailles had infected many academic disciplines—none more so than the philological studies in which Lotte had been interested.

At the PEN meeting, Lotte's encounter with the literary icons she'd studied before going into exile became yet more resonant upon learning that the congress had fulfilled its higher mission on behalf of those still trapped in Europe. "We were surprised that really a number of people publicly donated three and four hundred dollars each," she wrote to her family afterward. Yet even though thousands of dollars were ultimately raised, she noted that it would be "just sufficient to pay the travelling expenses of 10 people as they can only get out by the most phantastic routes—via Russia and Japan or via Africa and Martinique and only a few local people in Lisbon direct to the USA." A thousand paying guests—among them people who contributed real money—and only ten lives spirited out of Europe!

Still, the occasion should have been poignant for Zweig as well. Along with all the prominent figures from his adopted homeland of France, there were dozens of Viennese and German émigrés present, a number of whom he'd known since he was a young man. For this one evening, at least, a fragment of his world of yesterday was restored.

Yet in anticipation Zweig expressed only disgust with all the "pettiness authors develop on such occasions." These egoists, he wrote to Lotte's family, could not understand people like Lotte and him, "who would be happy <u>not</u> to sit for show and prefer to leave to them all these little things which seem so ridiculous in a time where houses are smashed, innocent people murdered and the greatest decision of mankind is at stake. Sometimes one wonders that these are the same people who really wrote beautiful verses and show in their books wisdom and psychology." After the event he assured Hanna and Manfred, who'd been unable to listen to his speech via radio, "You have nothing missed, all these lectures are without importance."

Zweig's discomfort with the PEN gathering points toward another of the great paradoxes of exile: as well as being a forcible separation from loved ones, exile can also have the quality of a macabre reunion. Already the previous winter Zweig described to Lotte's family attending a concert conducted by Bruno Walter and sitting in Walter's box "with a lot of ghosts from another life." Hilde Spiel nailed this experience in a description of an Upper West Side party. Of the guests, she wrote, "They were, with few exceptions, relics from the past and the far-away, ciphers for something that was dead and gone, lemurs haunting a graveyard, yet more alive, in their cadaverous way, than the visitors to [those] other parties I had witnessed. At times . . . it occurred to me that they were held together, as a social as well as in their individual body, merely by their malice, their melancholia and their memories. But held together they were." Gumpert remarked simply that "emigration creates a sad fellowship, consisting to a large extent of disunity and hostility."

Zweig addressed this notion of exile as an obligatory cofraternizing in a passage from his memoir about the mystery of modern anti-Semitism. After describing his happiness at finding Sigmund Freud in London following his own emigration there, Zweig declared that the single most tragic aspect of the Nazi attacks on the Jews lay in the total inability of the Jews to understand why they were being thrown together for persecution. At least, he writes, their ancestors in medieval times knew what they were suffering for: their shared "faith and their laws." But the Jews of the twentieth century were no longer a community and had not been one for a long time. They had no law. They did not want to speak Hebrew together. Only exile swept them all together, like dirt in the street: "bankers from their grand homes in Berlin, synagogue servers from the Orthodox communities, Parisian professors of philosophy, Romanian cabbies, layers-out of the dead and Nobel prize winners, operatic divas, women hired as mourners at funerals, writers and distillers, men of property and men of none, the great and small, observant Jews and followers of the Enlightenment." In a heartfelt cry, Zweig apostrophized, "Why I? Why you? How do you and I who do not know each other, who speak different languages, whose thinking takes different forms and who have nothing in common happen to be here together?" If Shylock's famous question—"If you prick us, do we not bleed?"—was intended to show that the Jews share a common humanity with all mankind, Zweig approached the injustice of anti-Semitism by revealing the total absence of common ground between the Jews themselves.

Even Freud, Zweig wrote, "the most lucid intellect of the time," with whom he frequently spoke about such issues in the last years of his life, was bewildered by this phenomenon and saw "no way out of it." By the time Zweig held his last conversations with Freud in London, his sense of being forced to identify with people who bore no relation to him had come to seem—along with nomadism—the defining experience of exile.

At the very moment when he began to grapple with the notion that the Germans who administered his "intellectual fatherland" no longer considered him German, he found himself identified precisely as German by those among whom he'd taken refuge from National Socialism. In consequence of the British Aliens Act passed after the

Armistice, upon the declaration of war all German and Austrian refugees were immediately classified as "enemy aliens." They were subjected to curfews, strict travel restrictions, and sometimes long detentions in internment camps. Even before the outbreak of war, exiles had been warned by the leading refugee aid society in London to avoid calling attention to themselves by any kinds of conspicuous behavior, to speak quietly, and—just as would later be the case in the United States—to refrain from speaking German in public. These cautions reflected concerns not only that the refugees might be apprehended as potential saboteurs, but that English anti-Semitism would be awakened by the sound of German—a fear that the established Anglo-Jewish community was especially sensitive to.

Finding himself designated an "enemy alien" in September 1939, Zweig seemed to become more incensed by the fact that the English deemed him a German citizen than by the label itself. "I who have never been anything but Austrian," he protested to his publisher, Huebsch. "I believe that the new Ministry for Information should be informed a little at least about German Literature and know that I am not an 'enemy alien' but perhaps the man who (with Thomas Mann) could be more useful than all others . . . Don't forget me, old friend, and don't be ashamed of me, because they have stamped 'German' here!"

Zweig was compelled to remain within five miles of the center of Bath, except on receipt of special permission. He told Huebsch, "You will understand . . . that I do not like to sit in waiting rooms with 58 years and a somewhat substantial work behind these years . . . I will avoid from now on as much as I can any 'favour.'"

The one occasion on which Zweig chose to petition for the right to travel was when Freud died, a few weeks after the British declared war on Germany. Zweig was asked to deliver the eulogy at the intimate memorial service in Golders Green on the twenty-sixth of September. The trip from Bath to London through the blackout was harrowing, with long hours of empty waiting in dark train stations. A steady rain fell on the day of the ceremony.

"In our youth we desired nothing more fervently than to lead a heroic life," Zweig declaimed, in German, to the small crowd of Freud's international allies, among whom were many Central European exiles. "We entertained dreams of meeting such a spiritual hero in the flesh, a hero who would help us better ourselves, a man who was oblivious to the temptations of fame and vanity, who possessed a complete and responsible soul, dedicated to his mission, a mission that reaps not its own benefits but enriches all of mankind. Our dear departed Freud fulfilled this enthusiastic dream of our youth."

Anna Freud stood beside Miriam Beer-Hofmann Lens, the daughter of a famous Austrian playwright, and the two of them marveled together at the beauty of Zweig's German prose. Ernst Jones rather bitterly acknowledged that Zweig's language had no doubt soared to amazing heights. But in English Zweig's eulogy reads as a flat, empty procession of abstractions. The oration just doesn't translate. "Words you have heard and learned and remembered from childhood have all the sweet or terrifying melody of symbols," Gumpert wrote. "To me 'dead' means something else than 'Tod,' 'mother' will never be 'Mutter,' 'war' cannot be 'Krieg.'"

The moment war was declared, all Zweig's ambivalence about being a Jew fused with linguistic despair. To a friend he declared that he'd become an impossible anomaly, "speaking and thinking in a language that has been taken away from us, living in a country . . . in which we are only tolerated. Jews without religious faith and the will to be Jews." Language, which had always been his means of taking flight from the world, was turning into a trap, as he worried that the new tongue he was immersed in would only end by corroding his German. "Now begins an other life for me, being no more free and independent," Zweig noted, in English, in his diary on the third of September 1939. "I regret only to have no opportunity to write as I am unable to do it in English and have nobody here to rectify my mistakes and to give more colour to what I want to say; that's what me oppresses most, that I am so imprisoned in a language, which I cannot use."

Chapter Six

TO THE COFFEEHOUSE!

One privation Zweig could never adjust to in New York was the absence of proper coffeehouses. There were spots that called themselves cafés where you could get a cup of coffee, but this had nothing to do with what defined the coffeehouse. The classic Viennese café had been an institution unique on the planet, Zweig maintained: at once office, home away from home, and democratic club, open to all for the price of a cup of coffee. "I cannot understand why they have no cafés in America when they are otherwise so civilized," another Austrian refugee lamented. There was just no such thing in the USA as the classic European "café-dwelling individual," who could remain at one small table all day contemplating other patrons and the universe at large.

You could draw a map of all of Europe tracing "the *Stammcafes* [favorite coffeehouses] where, at one time or another you would find Stefan Zweig, reading his newspapers or playing chess, and

always willing, nay eager, to meet friends and strangers," declared
Otto Zarek. "The 'Beethoven' and the 'Herrenhof' in Vienna, or the
'Hangli' on the Danube in Budapest, the 'Terrace' in Zurich or the
'Café du Dome' in Paris." Even in London, Zweig managed to trans-
form one of the quieter cafés off Regent Street into his headquarters
in exile. "There he would sit and wait for those whom the wave
of emigration had thrown on to the shores of this free country,"
Zarek recalled. Men whom Zweig had thought dead or imprisoned

in concentration camps would suddenly appear at his "round table" across from the Palladium theater. After their escape from Dachau or Buchenwald, they'd known how to find Zweig. Cafés became, at the outset of exile, more important than ever as transnational oases. Zweig wasn't alone in recognizing their new stature. "If one lives in exile," remarked his friend Hermann Kesten, "the café becomes at once the family home, the nation, church and parliament, a desert and a place of pilgrimage, cradle of illusions and their cemetery . . . In exile, the café is the one place where life goes on."

But in New York no such haven could be created. Nothing in that city was organized for stillness or attention. Even when people were eating in New York, they were invariably doing something else at the same time—reading their papers, making business deals. "In New York, the hobo has no right to exist—he's jerked into the constant flow of the city like a chunk of wood in a flood!" Zweig declared. Even the unoccupied women of luxury were constantly busy. Sports and fashion hounded them back and forth. In the museums there was endless activity—lectures being held, no room for quiet contemplation. On boats and trains you saw men suffering terribly from being constrained to a couple of hours of compulsory inactivity. They all seemed hopelessly inexperienced at the art of doing nothing, racing off at every station to buy a paper, to gamble, to smoke, to do anything at all rather than stay coolly perched above a cup of "black fire," in the classic pose of the café intellectual.

The psychoanalyst Fritz Wittels observed that the Viennese coffeehouse could never thrive in America. "They say it would not pay here and they are right," he wrote. "One cannot transplant the spirit of the coffee-house, which comes from the Near East and is the spirit of the Oriental Bazaar. There a man does his business, meets his friends, listens to gossip, fairy tales and music, sits down for his innumerable little cups of black coffee. The indescribable and inimitable loveliness of the coffee-house must be linked to the Arabian nights. The Prussian goose-step and the Viennese coffee-house are mutually exclusive."

When plans were being laid for the 1939 World's Fair in New York, one committee proposed a "Freedom Pavilion" to celebrate pre-Nazi culture under the name "Germany Yesterday & Tomorrow." The works of Stefan Zweig were to be prominently displayed there, alongside books by figures such as Thomas Mann, Albert Einstein, and Sigmund Freud.

The moment the Nazis got wind of the undertaking, they unleashed a huge propaganda campaign against what they labeled the "freedom pavilion for Jewish 'jetsam.'" The project was ultimately scrapped—partly because, despite strong support from many of the fair organizers and the State Department, it was seen as so "loaded with dynamite" as to risk drawing America into war with Hitler.

Nonetheless, despite all the controversy, there'd been a consensus among the planners that to achieve its aim of "bolstering every free German spirit," the pavilion would have to feature a scrupulously reproduced Viennese coffeehouse, complete with café mélange, waiters in Viennese costume—and perhaps an orchestra playing waltzes. The classic Viennese café was seen to epitomize the values of Austrian and German culture imperiled by the National Socialists.

Zweig's life in Vienna's coffeehouses began at the Café Griensteidl in the late nineteenth century, where he became one of the younger members of the so-called Young Vienna circle, which spawned Austrian literary modernism. He moved on from there to the Café Central, the Café Herrenhof (where one of his companions was Trotsky, who appeared to him a rather "stern-looking Russian émigré"), and countless other coffeehouses around the Inner City. Filled with newspapers, art magazines, literary periodicals, and vibrant conversation, the Vienna coffeehouses were, as Zweig described them in his memoir, "the best place to keep up with everything new." They were incubators of new movements of every sort—the only place where, "thanks to the collectivity of our interests, we followed the *orbis pictus* of artistic events not with two, but with twenty and forty eyes."

Zweig was back in the coffeehouses of Vienna in 1935. By this time, he had already gone into exile in England, and this visit was his last extended spell in the city of his birth. He checked into the Hotel Regina, a benevolent old hulk near his childhood home, just across from the Votive Church, at the site where, in 1853, Emperor Franz Joseph had been stabbed in the neck by a Hungarian nationalist, only to be saved by the thick material of his ceremonial high collar.

Zweig intended to remain in Vienna just long enough to see his new biography of Mary Stuart through the printer. But his mother had been very ill, and he didn't feel he could abandon her. Then he learned to his dismay that a course of extensive dental work could no longer be put off. What was meant to be a stay of a few weeks drew out for several months. At times it was almost as if he was living in the metropolis of his past again. *Mary Stuart* appeared in the bookstores, and notwithstanding the book burnings and a slew of new publishing restrictions, the biography became yet another Zweig smash hit. Almost everywhere, Zweig found, the Viennese frolicked away with a madcap abandon that struck him as deranged. "Austria Cheerful Despite Her Woes," announced a *New York Times* headline that fall. The currency had stabilized. Tourist traffic had shot up

25 percent. Beyond specific economic data, the *Times* reporter declared, one could not leave out of consideration "the character of the Austrian people, their charm, culture gayety—and *laissez faire*. They are fully aware of the shadow that hangs over Europe, but today they feel that their own particular patch of sky is lighter than it was."

Not Zweig. He was besieged by writers in financial distress and felt repulsed by Vienna's make-believe optimism. "You can have no idea . . . how badly off authors are here," he wrote Roth, "how much even small sums mean to them, nor again how *many* of them get in touch, including a few I would never have expected. It's ghastly, and I'll be glad when the book is printed and I can leave." His old friend the German novelist Erich Ebermayer visited him at the hotel and made the case for remaining on the scene in Austria, describing the anti-Nazi activities he and his friends were involved in. "I can't sit forever staring at the wall of Germany looming over Salzburg," Zweig responded. Right in front of the Hotel Regina there'd been "occasional coquettish, confetti-like showers from the air, gilded paper swastikas and narrow strips of printed paper" inscribed with mottoes that "were short and bright and to the point," recalled the poet Hilda Doolittle, who stayed at the hotel while being analyzed by Sigmund Freud. "One read in clear primer-book German, 'Hitler gives bread,' 'Hitler gives work,' and so on."

Zweig's sense of dissonance between Vienna's actual prospects and the surface luster only intensified in the brief trips he made there over the next two years. On his last trip, in 1937, there were moments when the split gave him vertigo. Bomb explosions and rabid protests had become regular occurrences by the end of that year. Everywhere one saw young Austrians sporting the tight white knee socks that signaled membership in the Nazi Party. Swastikas multiplied on

walls, on doors, in chalk marks on sidewalks. Public gatherings
of every sort became excuses for violence. When Germany played
Austria in a handball match that spring, forty-two thousand people
attended—and ten thousand people went on a rampage after Germany won, singing Nazi songs, attacking Jewish-looking people, invading the coffeehouses and assaulting their customers.

The politics of Austria from 1933 to 1938 as the state tried to
position itself as advantageously as possible in relation to Germany
and Europe at large, when Austria had almost no chips to play
beyond its strategic location, lurched from bad to worse, and then
worse still. Zweig wrote of how the Austrian chancellor Engel-
bert Dollfuss, who came to power in late 1932, seeking to preserve
Austria's independence, turned to Italy as the most likely protec-
tor state, given French and English indifference. But Mussolini's
price for this alliance was that Austria become a Fascist state in its
own right—one that would prove its loyalty by neutering Austria's
powerful Social Democratic party. The move wasn't only Mussolini's idea. There was plenty of impetus from within the Dollfuss
administration and the larger Austrian populace to establish a dictatorship under Fascist principles. Few people believed that enough
of Austria remained after World War I to survive on its own. The
truncation of empire inspired many Viennese to retreat further
into fantasy. "I shall live on with the torso, and imagine that it is
the whole," Freud wrote in a 1918 letter, capturing the mood in the
former imperial capital. The general sense of physical inadequacy
was expressed in an anecdote involving two Tyroleans who decide
to take a hike together. "Let's walk around Austria," one of them
suggests. "No," says the other. "I don't want to get back before
lunch." The practical consequence of this weakness was reliance

on other, more powerful states for survival. A joke from Germany in the late 1930s described Hitler, Goering, and Goebbels sitting around deciding what to do if the Third Reich collapsed. Goering remarks, "I will wear civilian clothes, and no one will recognize me." Goebbels says, "I will keep my mouth shut, and people will not know who I am." Hitler shrugs: "I don't have to do anything. I am an Austrian, and therefore the powers will have to protect me."

If one had to choose the two decisive shifts in the Austrian political scene after Hitler's rise to power and before the Anschluss, the first would be in 1933, when Dollfuss stripped the Austrian Parliament of its power and established an Austro-Fascist state. With this move, the arch-Catholic, pan-Germanic Austrian countryside gained a lasting grip over Vienna. The second landmark event was the brief, bloody Austrian civil war of February 1934, when Dollfuss—falling in line with Mussolini's priorities, pressure from Hitler, and Austria's own right-wing militias—gutted the Austrian Socialist movement. After the violence was over, many hundreds of workers lay dead and thousands were injured, while most of the Socialist leaders had either fled or been hanged. Hilde Spiel recalled hearing a broadcast of Verdi's *Requiem* on the radio at this time. "We felt it as a lament for our companions, and the events of the past week as the end of our world," she wrote in her memoir. To those who challenged her claim that February 1934 marked a more dreadful turning point than the Anschluss, Spiel rejoined: "When, after years of fighting in Spain, Madrid fell to Franco, a woman in a group of exiles in London was reproached for not weeping. She said: 'I wept for Barcelona.' We wept that February."

Yet radiant parties with guests attired in evening dress still went whirling on behind the heavy doors of palaces and bourgeois apartment houses all across Vienna's Inner City. Zweig warned old friends and acquaintances that the end was near. He told them that he'd seen what was coming from Salzburg years earlier. In his auto-biography, Zweig remembered being laughed at for these admoni-tions by his old crowd. "I was still the same old 'Jeremiah,' they mocked," alluding to the allegorical drama he'd written during the First World War about the biblical prophet. How they laughed, he wrote, as they extended invitations for the next fete and jammed into fancy stores to do their Christmas shopping. He wanted to say to them: "Don't you understand? All this will be gone in a few months' time. Your homes will be plundered. Your clothes will be changed for prison garb." But everywhere he went, he seemed to hear a line in Viennese dialect that epitomized the city's lighthearted air, which he always used to love so much: *"Es kann dir nix g'schehn*—nothing can go wrong for you." And perhaps, he mused four years later from Ossin-ing, they'd all finally been wiser than him. Why upset people who don't want to be upset? he asked, in his own version of that sweet Viennese laissez-faire. Klaus Mann, visiting that same year, saw a city in which "everything stagnated and waned."

But in 1935 matters had not gone quite so far. Notwithstanding his pessimism, Zweig was still circulating. And one of the people he saw a good deal of in those months, someone who did not need handouts—whose large fortune came from a family that, like Zweig's, owned a textile factory, which would be seized three years later—was Hermann Broch. Everyone agreed that Broch was the soul of kind-ness. He was that rare case of a Viennese high artist who did not feel that his own status depended on maintaining a scorched-earth policy toward any sign of talent in others. Large-boned, gentle-eyed, a pipe jutting from his lips, he liked to deliberate with Zweig about cultivating a spiritual democracy that would somehow enfranchise the masses without empowering the herd.

The name of James Joyce was often on Broch's lips in those days. Zweig knew him also. The two had met in Zurich, when Zweig went there to sit out the end of the First World War and Joyce too was living in self-imposed exile. Zweig had studied the unsmiling young man with a little brown beard and thick-lensed glasses where he perched by himself in a corner of the Café Odeon. When they were introduced, Zweig was struck by Joyce's denial that there was any English in him.

"I would like," Joyce declared, "a language above other languages, a language serving them all. I can't express myself completely in English without making myself part of a certain tradition." At the time, Zweig couldn't fully understand Joyce, but the words haunted him later when he confronted his own split between attachment to and alienation from the German language. Zweig was touched when Joyce lent him his only copy of *Portrait of the Artist as a Young Man*, along with his play *Exiles*, which Zweig wanted to translate. Zweig was later responsible for arranging the first production of Joyce's only drama. Joyce's facility with languages dazzled Zweig. He seemed to have "all the words of every idiom," archived behind a convex, sculpted brow, which "shone as smoothly as porcelain in electric light," Zweig wrote.

By the 1930s, Joyce had made his mark and Broch was fascinated by the elegant self-assurance with which he carried off his fame. He and Zweig talked about the writers in Vienna striving to be noticed, struggling to survive. Broch brought up the name of Elias Canetti, the young author who'd recently returned to Vienna from Switzerland, where he'd had the fortune to meet Joyce. Broch frankly envied Canetti this encounter, in which Canetti read aloud at a fancy house party in Zurich from his play *The Comedy of Vanity*. Joyce had noticed Canetti. Canetti was gifted, Broch told Zweig. He'd written a book, *Kant Catches Fire*, that, despite his many literary connections, had yet to find a publisher. It was not an easy book. But it would find its way once published, Broch told Canetti. "It's too intense, too gruesome perhaps to be forgotten." Broch made clear to Zweig that Canetti could use a helping hand.

Zweig had always dedicated himself to promoting young talents. When he was only twenty-five years old, living in his Vienna bachelor apartment, he nurtured a group of a dozen or so still younger writers in the elegant, glassy chamber of the Café Beethoven. And at the Café Pucher, next to a little cactus shop, he went patiently through the verses of René Fülöp-Miller when that writer was a fourteen-year-old runaway, half-starved, struggling, as Fülöp-Miller recalled, with "a hopeless, cosmic poem." Zweig's investment in youth only intensified after the war. The German poet Walter Bauer wrote to him when Zweig was at the height of his fame and Bauer was a humble elementary school teacher. To Bauer's amazement, only a few days later he received a letter back from Zweig, "with its easy flowing handwriting in violet ink," in which Zweig assured him, " 'It's me and I shall always be behind you; rely on me, I shall keep an eye on you—if you need help. What are we here for if not to help each other?'" From that moment, Bauer writes, he felt himself to be "in the shelter" of Zweig's friendship. He speculates that Zweig saw in his first verses "a youthful spirit which yearned across the frontiers, seeking clumsily but eagerly the word that afterwards became its motto: Europe." Zweig's embrace had a maternal quality, but also reflected his larger commitment to promulgating cosmopolitan tolerance among the rising generation.

Zweig had all sorts of business with his new publisher, Herbert Reichner, that spring of 1935 as Reichner was transferring his hub of operations to Vienna from the Insel in Germany. The two talked on the phone all the time. Beyond his own work, Zweig was helping Reichner get the new house going with the right kind of authors.

One day, after a particularly brutal encounter with his dentist, Zweig wandered over to the Café Imperial, in a wing of the massive hotel of that name. The Imperial, formerly the haunt of Gustav Mahler, Sigmund Freud, and Karl Kraus, was just down the street from the opera house. Zweig made his way to a back room of the establishment and sat down alone at a table, holding his hand over his mouth. He was suffering. Teeth had been extracted. He was ashamed of how he looked. Yet he sought out the familiar repose of the coffeehouse anyway. At the Hotel Regina there were forty phone calls he had to make. He had no secretary. He was in no hurry to go back to all of that. He paged through a newspaper. He tried to be anonymous while remaining, inevitably, the famous author on display, in that popular, expansive, multichambered café.

The American correspondent John Gunther could be found there as well almost every day that year, news gathering. He liked the Imperial because it carried twenty Viennese papers and between forty and fifty foreign ones, all neatly bound on rattan frames filed in a large cabinet under the jurisdiction of a special waiter who could never find just the one you wanted. But still, for the price of a cup of coffee, you could sit and read the lot of them. He began with the *Neue Freie Presse*, and worked through the whole array—all physically "similar as tenpins," Gunther wrote. His job was to collect local impressions. On a typical day in the spring of 1935, the *Neue Freie Presse* had a meditative piece about the nitrate industry in Chile above a feuilleton piece about the colonization of Manhattan Island by the Dutch. On page one, there were four cable pieces about developments in Washington, Paris, Brussels, and Peking. Page two carried news of Germany. Page three had datelines from London, Budapest, and Sofia. On page four came the first mention of Austria—a run-of-the-mill report of a speech by the chancellor. The Viennese press was far more serious than the American papers, Gunther wrote, but what he cared about was news of Austria, "and I don't find it." He went from paper to paper, searching for the real news of the day. "And I don't get it." Twenty newspapers from Vienna alone, and not a single one able to report what was actually happening. It was, as Hilde Spiel wrote, a time of "blurs and smudges."

As Zweig sat alone in the Imperial, hand over his mouth, Elias Canetti happened by. Zweig knew him slightly, and Broch's report of his struggles to get his novel out was fresh in Zweig's mind. Despite his dislike of being seen in his condition, Zweig gestured for Canetti to come over to his table and bade him sit down.

Zweig's hand came gingerly away from his mouth. "I've heard the whole story from Broch," he said. "You've met Joyce. If you have someone who will guarantee your book, I can recommend it to my friend Reichner. Get Joyce to write a preface. Then your book will get attention."

Canetti exploded. What Zweig proposed was *out of the question!* I couldn't make such a request of Joyce, he declared. Joyce hasn't seen the manuscript! He's almost blind and couldn't be expected to read such a thing! Even if he could read as easily as anyone else, I would never ask such a favor of him! I would never ask anyone to write a preface! The book should be read for its own sake! *It needs no crutches!*

For a moment, Canetti himself was taken aback by the violence of his outburst.

"I only wanted to help you," Zweig said. "But if you don't wish . . ." His hand floated back up over his lips. That was the end of the conversation.

Canetti marched away, he wrote, "without the least regret that I had turned down his proposal so firmly. I had saved my pride and lost nothing . . . the thought of publishing my book with a preface by Joyce, regardless of what it said, stuck in my craw. I despised Zweig for suggesting it."

Zweig remained alone at the back table of the Café Imperial, clutching his throbbing mouth.

A few days after the scene, Canetti received a letter from Reichner's press, asking him to submit his manuscript and making no mention of a preface. Even after the reception Canetti had given him, Zweig had proceeded to quietly intercede on his behalf. "Fortunately, perhaps, I didn't despise him [Zweig] so very much," Canetti allowed.

There's no indication that it ever crossed Canetti's mind to offer Zweig any thanks for making the connection, let alone to apologize. Why would he? Zweig, he wrote in another context, was one of the pack who owed their reputation to "sheer bustle."

We have a tendency to look back on the feuds among writers and artists of the past with a fond chuckle—to find something cute in the sparring, or perhaps poignant in the testimony such quarreling proffers to the notion that at least the world of ideas *mattered* to those tempestuous creative souls of days gone by.

But to read of the arts and the press in pre-Anschluss Vienna is to glimpse a realm of rage-addled, murderous battle, which had consequences for the disintegrating political sphere as well.

The transition from the idyllic symposium of young aesthetes Zweig describes at the Café Griensteidl in the 1890s to Elias Canetti's ecstasy of spite at the Café Imperial in 1935 incorporates several phases of antagonism. The phases mimicked each other in external features, which helped mask their mounting toxicity.

The first giddy era Zweig writes of—that period dominated by passion for new sensation and fertile comradeship, which expanded his view of the intellectual cosmos—carried its own complexities. Fueling all their artistic pursuits was the overwhelming urge for liberation: freedom from the oppressive school system that had stifled their youthful talents and desires, freedom from authority as such.

Solidarity among the students was more martial than aesthetic. Zweig's depiction of the role of the arts in the Vienna of his youth is riddled with metaphors of revolution and war. He and his friends were "shock troops" of the new, eager participants in the "wild and often rabid struggles for the new art." Seeking to convey the effect of Hofmannsthal and Rilke on his generation, he can only liken them to Napoleon Bonaparte, who "electrified an entire generation." We knew, Zweig declared, that *our time had arrived*—the hour when youth had finally achieved its rights. Their restless blood demanded art that kept pace with "the accelerated tempo of the times." Both the "Young Vienna" writers and the artists of *Jugendstil* (Austrian Art Nouveau—literally "youth style") tapped the *Ver Sacrum* or Sacred Spring—a term tied to an ancient Sabine ritual involving a group of children who, after being exiled, founded their own youth settlement. Youth, Zweig wrote, "like certain animals, possesses an excellent instinct for change of weather," and they recognized before anyone else that radical change was coming—which they would fight for tooth and nail "just because it was new."

No wonder the artistic-intellectual rivalries were so bloody in Zweig's youth: they carried whiffs of the revolts and antipathies that would end by obliterating much of Europe. Today we speak of how the migration of artists into rough neighborhoods often paves the way for gentrification; in the realm of ideas, when artists move in it can be a first step toward *de*-gentrifying—or even re-barbarizing—an area of thought gone overly bourgeois. In both real estate and the cultural sphere, the problem is always who moves in after the artists—who have the artists made the space comfortable for?

Zweig writes in his autobiography that because he and his friends were so fascinated by the aesthetic aspect of life, they didn't notice how the transformations they helped usher in through the arts were "nothing but trends and foreshadowings of more far-reaching changes which were to shake the world of our fathers, the world of security, and finally to destroy it." He places his emphasis on the "nothing but." However, we can reverse the stress: these wild artistic endeavors *were* "trends and foreshadowings" of the unspeakable end. And perhaps they were yet more than this. Brecht's famous epigraph about Kraus—"When the age died by its own hand, he was that hand"—is generally taken as homage to Kraus's campaigns against the irresponsible Viennese press, but the implication that Kraus was also the weapon of the era's self-destruction can't be ignored.

Scrutinizing the other authors gathered around the big round tables at the Café Griensteidl, Kraus ticked off their collective attributes: "Lack of talent, preciousness, poses, megalomania, suburban girls, cravats, mannerism, false datives, monocles and secret nerves." Zweig's friend Hermann Bahr, the leader of the Young Vienna circle, was at the forefront of Kraus's mind when he quipped, "No ideas and the ability to express them, that's the definition of the journalist." Bahr, for his part, allegedly had a couple of pals beat up Kraus inside his favorite coffeehouse not long after *Die Fackel* started slinging punches in print. As for Zweig himself, Kraus declared in the 1920s that without the resistance he'd built up through hard labor it would be impossible for him not to sink down and become lost in the shallowness of Zweig's deep sentences. Like his popular contemporary Emil Ludwig, Zweig managed to flay language of meaning and then regurgitate it back into the public sphere as vacuous cliché, Kraus reported. Worse still, Zweig and Ludwig positioned themselves so that the middle class would read them as exemplars of world literature—and thereby feel spared the obligation to read the real thing. By their crude simplifications, these representative European schmoozers functioned as "elevators of culture," giving their audiences the impression of zooming up into the artistic empyrean, while in truth the masses remained wallowing in the basement, having just been put at ease with their ignorance.

Arthur Schnitzler's famous play *La Ronde* traces the rounds of society through a series of interlocked sexual encounters, but the real Viennese "Round Dance" might follow the infectious circuit of loathing between the city's writers, artists, architects, and musicians. The venereal disease transmitted in the course of Schnitzler's masquerade was like a common cold relative to that malady. I remember having a conversation with a woman who knew Vienna well in the 1930s. When I asked her what she recalled most strongly about the city, she remarked, "Oh, the Viennese! They laugh, and they smile, and then—just as they're leaving"—she squeezed her thumb and forefinger—"they pinch you!"

Zweig devoted many pages to extolling the ways that passion for the arts pervaded every aspect of life in the city. Pictures of great actors were on display in every stationery store. The Burgtheater was "for the Viennese and for the Austrian more than a stage upon which actors enacted parts," it was "the brightly colored reflection in which the city saw itself, the only true *cortigiano* of good taste," in which spectators learned how to dress, walk into a room, and speak. He was hardly alone in suggesting that obsession with art in general and theater in particular in prewar Vienna swung the spotlight away from developments in the political arena. But another consequence of living in a world so saturated with "staged reality" is that everything, including politics, begins to partake of the character of drama. The sense that all social behavior was performative made for a country in which, as the Austrian novelist Robert Musil wrote, "a man always acted differently from how he thought and thought differently from how he acted." (These rife ambiguities made, of course, the ideal staging ground for psychoanalysis as well.) "I'd like to drive myself against myself, only to see who is the stronger, I or me," the satirical playwright Johann Nestroy has his Holofornes say. The line could be cribbed from one of many desperate expressions of inner division riddling Zweig's diaries.

Some observers believed the emperor actively nurtured Viennese indecisiveness as a political move, hoping Vienna's disparate national identities might thereby neutralize each other, just as individuals were paralyzed by contradictory urges. The writer Amelia von Ende attributed the success of this tactic to Vienna's theatrical disposition. The public sought to emulate the "courtly art" of the rulers, whether unconsciously or consciously, she wrote, "until it became a feature of their character. They learned to support repression with a smile, servile at first, then suave, and finally stereotyped into the typical *Wiener Lächeln* [Vienna smile] behind which it concealed the people's real self. Since the paramount aim of Austrian diplomacy in the Empire, which was always on the verge of some unwelcome event, was to prevent anything from *happening*, the people too drifted into this frame of mind which resents action." Impotence and indolence became the low road to tolerance.

The split between what was said and done in Vienna's more privileged social strata also made it easy to miss when language stepped out of bounds into brutality that might be taken at face value by auditors less sophisticated or less scrupulous than Zweig's peers. In his novel *The Road into the Open*, published in 1908, Schnitzler has a character recount a scene based on an actual incident at the Vienna Parliament. As a Jewish member of Parliament makes a speech, another parliamentarian hectors him, repeatedly calling out, "Yid, shut your trap! Shut your trap, Yid!" After the session finishes, the two men go out for a sociable drink together. Hearing the tale, another character in the novel deems it unbelievable. "No. Austrian," responds his interlocutor. "With us indignation is just as insincere as enthusiasm. Only envy and hatred of real talent are genuine here." Elsewhere, Schnitzler cited a well-known joke from the 1880s: "Anti-Semitism only became popular in Vienna after the Jews took it up."

The sense of theatrical disconnects infected many Viennese with angst long before it was clear where or when the blow to the city's fabled mosaic of cultural influences would fall. "With us, there is nothing left but freezing life, stale and bleak reality, broken-winged resignation," the poet and playwright Hugo von Hofmannsthal wrote at the end of the nineteenth century. Narcotic dread infused the outbursts of rage and hysteria that flustered Parliament, the coffeehouse, and the bedchamber alike. Indeed, the eroticism of much Viennese art is most striking not for its explicitness per se, but for the focus on masturbation, ennui, and post-coital exhaustion. The sexuality feels contemporary not because it's liberated, but because it's so lonely.

To his credit, Zweig recoiled from the favorite Viennese parlor games of backstabbing and slow poisoning, seeking out new sources of vigor abroad. Early on, he found in the poetry of the Belgian Emile Verhaeren the touchstone for his own evolving artistic philosophy. "The more a man admires, the more he possesses," Zweig wrote, adopting Verhaeren's Whitmanesque philosophy. Expressing his love for Verhaeren himself, Zweig told a friend, "He is not in any way intellectual. (I mistrust intellectual people because they are too negative and are incapable of the warmth of love.)" For the true artist, Zweig declared in a study he went on to write of the poet, "negation is sterile . . . only assent, acceptance, affection, and enthusiasm can place us in a real relationship with things." In fact, he concludes, "our whole effort must be to overcome what is negative in ourselves, to reject nothing, to kill the critical spirit in ourselves, to strengthen what is positive in us, to assent as much as possible."

If he'd set out to compose a manifesto specifically to infuriate Karl Kraus, he couldn't have done better than with his declaration "Criticism is sterile."

The First World War turned Vienna's artistic discord lethal. A longing for unity and action surely made it easier for many to lose all ethical bearings in the prospect of patriotic bloodshed. In *The World of Yesterday*, Zweig shakes his head over the behavior of the most important Austrian-German writers during the early years of the conflict—all those "poor innocents who spread inflammatory lies about the other side's atrocities and wrote ghastly verses goading Europe's youth on to slaughter, rhyming *Krieg*—war—with *Sieg*—victory—and *Not*—necessity—with *Tod*—death." Zweig proclaimed himself immune to the burst of war fervor on account of all the time he'd spent abroad. After the declaration of war, he wrote, he tucked himself away in Vienna's dozy War Archives as a glorified librarian until the day he could flee to Switzerland and become active in the pacifist movement. "I do not reckon it any particular merit . . . to have recognized from the first moment the ruinous senselessness of Europe's suicide and to have set myself against war with all my moral power," he wrote in a 1922 autobiographical sketch. "For me, the community, the unity of Europe was as self-evident as my own breathing." By the time he penned these words, he'd moved off in disgust to Salzburg—"de-Vienna-ed" himself, as he liked to say. Never could he forget the way dear friends in his hometown, who'd so recently been ardent individualists, had grown drunk with the smell of blood, accusing him to his face of being a false Austrian.

The catch, as Karl Kraus pointed out at the time, is that in the first phase of conflict, Zweig himself was churning out deadly propaganda. He contributed regularly to *Donauland*, a nationalist journal issued by the War Archives. In 1914 Zweig wrote articles celebrating the moral and political renewal of Austria-Hungary, praising the German war effort in general, and championing the invasion of Belgium. For the Christmas issue of the *Neue Freie Presse*, Zweig even wrote a treacly poem entitled "Der Krüppel," romanticizing the vision of a soldier mangled by battle.

To be sure, Zweig's war service was always excruciatingly self-conscious. When war was first declared, he'd been inside Belgium and caught one of the last trains back across the frontier, writing Friderike en route that he would soon be marching into Poland as a private soldier. The prospect saddened him, he remarked, especially for his mother. (Friderike claimed it was the first time she'd ever heard Zweig mention his mother with love.) Friderike jumped on a train at the station in Graz, where she was staying, to intercept him in Vienna. Railway cars streamed by her filled with shouting men headed for the front. She met Stefan ensconced in one of his beloved coffeehouses. To her amusement, he'd grown a beard, making himself appear at once more manly and martyred. She pleaded with him to stop being absurd and realize he wasn't cut out to be a soldier. Fight with the pen, she implored him. He went on to get his physical and was at once pronounced unfit for active duty.

At the same time as he was flattering his German publisher, Kippenberg, by writing that his "great ambition" was "to be an officer over with you in that army, to conquer France," he was lamenting in his journal, "I don't believe in any victory against the whole world—I want to sleep for six months straight, know nothing more, not experience the world going under, the whole horror. This is the worst day of my entire life." Despite knowing better, Zweig did much the same as everyone else—until the second half of the

war. Then, spurred by a trip through "darkest Galicia" on behalf
of the Archives, which exposed him to the suffering of the civilian
population, he wrote the play *Jeremiah*, which really did have an elec-
trifying influence on European pacifist sentiment. "It was the first

drama written by a German playwright that rejected unequivocally the idea of violence," recalled his friend Richard Friedenthal. Most of his comrades never had the courage to speak out against the war. No one so well-known as Zweig did so to any effect.

Almost everyone was guilty in that first wave of enthusiasm. Freud declared that all his libido was given to Austria-Hungary and expressed pride that Austria had displayed its virility to the world. Hermann Bahr turned his journalistic gifts to extolling the virtues of the German-Austrian war machine. Hofmannsthal (whom Bahr depicted in a rhapsodic feuilleton in officer's uniform triumphantly entering the conquered city of Warsaw while reciting Baudelaire to the tattoo of war drums) leaned on influential friends to procure a cozy desk job, while publicly announcing that "the beauty of Austria never shone out so brilliantly as it did in August 1914." Alfred Polgar worked in the War Archives with Zweig, as did Rilke, the sight of whom in uniform, with his hypersensitive intolerance for unpleasant odors, dirt, and noise, sitting stiffly at the neatest desk in the whole of the war office made even Zweig smile. Robert Musil trumpeted his identification with the German war cause in a long newspaper article. The prominent Viennese intellectuals were guilty en masse, with two notable exceptions: Arthur Schnitzler—and Karl Kraus.

But Kraus bears his own heavy burden of guilt. "Long before the dictators, our time produced the worship of intellectual dictators," Musil wrote with Kraus in mind. He was a bully who demanded total subjection from all but a handful of superior souls—taking delight in even petty abuse, calling waiters at his coffeehouse nasty names until someone pointed out that while an offended waiter could not answer back, there was nothing to prevent him spitting in Kraus's soup. So powerful was Kraus's influence on the intellectual elite of Vienna from the period just before the outbreak of the First World War until the early 1930s that Canetti (a Jew himself) confessed that he came to have his own "Jews"—"people whom I snubbed when passing them in restaurants on the street, whom I did not deign to look at, whose lives did not concern me, who were outlawed and banished for me, whose touch would have sullied me, whom I quite earnestly did not count as part of humanity: the victims and enemies of Karl Kraus."

Ultimately Kraus's satiric brilliance coincided with campaigns of personal vengeance so ruthless that he became single-handedly responsible for further fracturing liberal elements in Vienna that, with even a modicum of solidarity, might have mustered more substantial opposition to Austria's burgeoning Fascism.

If Viennese writers and intellectuals never really got along, by 1918 they abominated one another—in part because of the crime they each called to mind: their communal guilt nurturing the war that almost destroyed Europe. "[But] we had returned home, fruitless and inconsolable, crippled, a generation dedicated to death, by death disdained," wrote Joseph Roth. "The verdict of the Commission of Enquiry was without appeal. It read: 'Found unfit for death.'" And precisely because of this festering bad conscience, they also couldn't stop skulking back into one another's company. In those postwar days, the Viennese coffeehouse had about it the air of a primal scene in a myth—perhaps the bloody feast Freud conjures in *Totem and Taboo* when, after killing their father, the young murderers gather to mourn him by consuming his body.

After Hitler was appointed chancellor of Germany, the coffee-house wits were struck dumb; even *Die Fackel* failed to appear. Try-ing later to explain why he'd fallen silent, Karl Kraus remarked, "Hitler brings nothing to mind."

What *is* it that so beguiles us about the dream of the cof-feehouse? Zweig's nostalgia for the Viennese version really harkens back only to the intoxicated first years of his literary ca-reer. And while he made himself a regular at one central London café immediately after going into exile, this was when he still had it in him to hear out the stories of woe from refugees soliciting his help. By the time he got to New York, the last thing he would actu-ally have wanted to find would have been a coffeehouse like those he spent so many hours at in Vienna, where friends and strangers always knew they could corner him. When he finally made it to Rio, Zweig was overjoyed to find that the city harbored countless cafés—there seemed to be one on every street, shadowy rooms ema-nating seductive glows. But I think Zweig was as excited by what Rio's cafés *didn't* contain as much as by what they did. The coffee was splendid; you could sit still for hours—and the odds against anyone from his old Vienna ever turning up were huge. The cafés of Brazil had most of the props and none of the ghosts. They were the perfect stage set for conjuring an imaginary coffeehouse utopia.

In March 1938, the whole of the Hotel Imperial, from the café to the uppermost suite, was requisitioned by Nazi authorities for the reception of Hitler. When the Führer appeared, he paused a moment before the red carpet with a vacant smile swizzling over his lips. He reminisced about how as a young man he used to walk by the Imperial on nights "when there was nothing else to do and I hadn't even enough money to buy a book. I'd watch the automobiles and the coaches drive up to the entrance and be received with a deep bow by the white-mustached porter out in front, who never talked to me if I came near him. I could see the glittering lights and chandeliers in the lobby but I knew it was impossible for me to set foot inside . . . I have waited for this day and to-night I am here." His conquest of Vienna and grand entrance into the Imperial were one, according to a journalist with Hitler; both signified "the wiping of the slate, a settlement of scores." And the Imperial remained the domain of Nazi officials through the war.

Today the chairs, booth backs, and carpets of the Café Imperial are midnight blue and pale gold shades. When I went there in the middle of a Saturday afternoon, there were almost no customers. A businessman sat reading a business book by himself in one corner. A beautiful young woman with a long fall of brown hair sat very straight across the table from two very sober men in dark suits, all of them speaking Russian very rapidly together, ordering course after course of very heavy food. Waiters whisked in and out, zipping from one deserted room to the next. When I asked about the café's history in the 1930s and '40s, waiter after waiter shrugged and made a face as though I'd asked where the bathroom was in too loud a voice.

The extravagant old Viennese opera house just up the street from the Imperial was hit by U.S. bombs near the end of the war; a third of the building took a powder, reduced to a weird nondescript dirt and rubble heap plopped alongside carefully molded arches and sculptures. The stage Zweig described as superseding Dante's paradise now, with its fallen beams, resembled the set of an expressionist horror film, a nightmare from Dr. Caligari. Its meticulous reconstruction hides this interlude. If you go to the Café Central today, a tourist hub in the Inner City, you will read in the promotional literature how the café closed its doors in 1943. No mention is made of the fact that this is because the café was bombed into ruin, as was approximately a quarter of the city by 1945.

At the Historical Museum of the City of Vienna, a few minutes' walk from the opera house and the Imperial, the history of Vienna from the Stone Age onward is showcased on ascending floors. After touring a section on the building of the Ringstrasse and Emperor Franz Joseph's last years, I prepared to climb the steps one last time—but couldn't find a staircase to the story of Vienna post–World War I. I was so sure it had to be there I was practically lifting the sole of my shoe into space. Perhaps Vienna's more recent past was in the basement? With embarrassment, I told the tall, rather stiff balding man in early middle age at the ticket counter that I'd missed the displays of Vienna's more recent history.

"It's not here," he told me. "The history stops with World War One."

"The Museum of the City of Vienna stops with the First World War?" I dumbly repeated.

"Not enough space—yeah." He gave a little shrug and a littler sigh. "It's too bad, because you don't get to see what happened in the war. You know, the bombings and . . ." His voice trailed off. "Yeah. I don't know."

I asked whether there was any other museum in Vienna that told this story. "Not so far as I know," he said. And then he turned away.

I walked out into the September dusk, moving across the sallow Resselpark, heading to the Café Museum. I thought of Stefan

Zweig's last two days in Vienna, when he wandered through every one of the streets he knew so well, "every church, every park, every garden, every old nook and cranny of the city where I had been with a desperate, silent farewell in my mind—'Never again.'"

I walked and wondered about the city's peculiar spell, until Joseph Olbrich's Secession building spangled into view, a meteor of filigreed gilt leaves slamming down into the clean, creamy roof, sending trickles of gold down its façade. *"Der Zeit ihre Kunst, Der Kunst ihre Freiheit,"* read the words beneath that fantastical dome: "To the Age Its Art, to the Art Its Freedom." I stared awhile, then turned into the cool perfection of Adolf Loos's interior at the Café Museum, its celadon walls and wavy red bentwood chairs composing a space his pupil called the birthplace of all modern interior design, and others named the Café Nihilism. The *Wiener Mélange* I drank there—bitter, sweet, concentrating, overstimulating—evoked the jagged contrasts of austerity and ornament all around the café, and the city at large.

In *The Third Man*, a film shot in Vienna in the immediate aftermath of the Second World War (from a script researched by Peter Smolka, the charismatic, mercurial figure who actually introduced Stefan and Lotte), when most of the city is lightless and buildings are pressed against pits and mounds of fallen stone that resemble drifts of dark snow, the archvillain Harry Lime, who conducts a racket in counterfeit pharmaceuticals, tries to comfort his childhood friend Holly Martins when Martins discovers what he's up to in Vienna. "Don't be so gloomy," Lime remarks. "After all, it's not that awful—you know what the fellow said: In Italy for thirty years under the Borgias they had warfare, terror, murder, bloodshed—they produced Michelangelo, Leonardo da Vinci, and the Renaissance. In Switzerland they had brotherly love, five hundred years of democracy and peace, and what did they produce . . . the cuckoo clock."

Near the end of his life, Zweig's thoughts turned constantly to the question of what it means to make art in apocalyptic times. He was haunted by the failure of the myriad artists and intellectuals he'd known to stop *anything*—even their own bitter infighting. "People who make 'literature' today or are able to speak, I cannot fully understand," he wrote to Friderike at the end of 1940; "it seems to me more like a human defect than a virtue (but perhaps art is really always determined by defects)."

Maybe we cling to the myth of the coffeehouse because if we truly surrendered it, we'd lose the dream of there being anywhere to escape when everything else is gone. The café is the last refuge of those exiled by reality itself.

Chapter Seven

GLOBAL
ROULETTE

A fter a time, the only thing that mattered was to get out of New York.

In June 1941, Stefan and Lotte visited Atlantic City, where Stefan had business with a lawyer who helped with their personal affairs. The errand was partly an excuse for their two-day trip; they'd been wanting to survey the town. The couple walked along the boardwalk, between the dolled-up promenaders, past mammoth pavilions of entertainment where acrobats danced manically on high wires and horses were made to perform cruel, heart-stopping leaps from elevated platforms into the sea.

Even here, it seems, Stefan and Lotte bandied back and forth the possibility of coming to rest for a time. It was very pleasant in this "Super-Brighton of the USA," Lotte wrote the family in England. Might Atlantic City be somewhere Stefan could work in peace? Might this place have the elements from which they could compose a life? Where they could find a little house to rent, be left alone, yet not be left too far out of anything? It was good to feel the wind off the sea, and it was essential that they find somewhere away from the heat of Manhattan.

But then they began to imagine what the mobs would be like once the season really got going. That would not be so pleasant. And Stefan could only have scorn for the bombastic grand hotels and tawdry pomp of the casinos. In New York, even though he'd calculated that a hotel with air-conditioning would give him four extra hours of work a day, he declared the few hotels that had such rooms "too expensive and too fashionable for my taste. I could not feel allright in such a Claridges—I never did even in the times when it was possible." Atlantic City would not do. They would have to seek another haven.

On a number of occasions they traveled out to Long Island Sound to visit the jovial Dutch-American historian and illustrator Hendrik van Loon, a huge man whose fleshy nose and enormous hands resembled those of Erasmus, his possible ancestor. Van Loon had been banished from German soil after publication of his 1938 book *Our Battle—Being One Man's Answer to "My Battle" by Adolf Hitler.* The author's prodigious output, commitment to political toler- ance, and unfailing popularity with the broader public placed him on familiar ground with Zweig—as did the indignation his work sometimes provoked from stringent reviewers. The Zweigs and the Van Loons enjoyed many hours of wide-ranging conversation around the latter's cozy hearth in their large white house with blue shutters overlooking the waters of Greenwich Cove. Like Zweig, Van Loon felt that he'd been forced to become a one-man charity society. The previous summer he'd tallied up his contributions in food alone and realized he'd served up an extra 647 breakfasts, luncheons, and dinners in two months. "I've had every damn refugee in America here for a meal," he said, "and half of them came late for the meal. Why can't refugees learn some manners?"

Van Loon's irascibility was good-humored, but it struck a deep chord in Zweig; the two drew closer. Van Loon became convinced that Stefan and Lotte could find refuge in the village of Old Greenwich. He began looking for a house for the Zweigs to rent. Stefan did not dissuade him. Perhaps Van Loon's village *was* the place where he and Lotte could settle. Like Atlantic City, it was cooled by winds off the ocean, but it was less of a draw to the hordes on holiday and far enough from New York to provide some buffer against the refugees.

I picture Stefan and Lotte walking the quiet streets of the little town, gauging distances around the commercial district, tabulating local resources, trying to get the feel of the place. There was a nice little bookstore, but not much of a library. It was appealingly quaint. Yet it was *so* small. And aside from Van Loon, they knew no one. Stefan wavered. Van Loon and his third wife, "Jimmy," former operator of the Mad Hatter tearoom in Greenwich Village, kept trying to convince him to stay. Eventually they did find a house for him. It seemed Zweig would take it. He waffled. They waited.

At an earlier point in their American wanderings, Benjamin Huebsch advised them on the desirability of settling in Cambridge, Massachusetts. The Harvard Library was unexcelled, and yet, Huebsch noted with arch understatement, he'd heard "the Cambridge atmosphere is not over-friendly to strangers." Boston itself might be better. Though it was "somewhat remote," Zweig would there have the Boston Symphony, besides many other musical attractions that visited the city, Huebsch wrote. New England was very agreeable, he insisted—except for the fact that "Winter and early Spring are likely to be cold and moist." The worst conditions imaginable for Lotte's asthma!

They might consider going to Princeton, where Thomas Mann, Einstein, and Broch were. But Huebsch cautioned. "Princeton depends entirely upon the University, and is uncomfortably close to the city."

Then what about Philadelphia? Huebsch ran through the pros and cons. That city's libraries were also first-rate. But the overall atmosphere, he warned Stefan, would be even less desirable than that to be found in Boston. "Philadelphia," he concluded, "is neither one thing nor the other; its principal advantage being that it is two hours away from New York."

There was always the possibility of revisiting Los Angeles. Zweig must have known that his rationale for not following the tide of illustrious refugees west—uncertainties surrounding the extension of his visitor's visa—was flimsy for a figure of his stature. But then again, the question: Did he *want* to be surrounded by those specters from his former existence? And perhaps he knew the observation of his old friend Alfred Polgar, who'd escaped to America on the same Greek steamer that carried Franz Werfel and Friderike: "Hollywood is a Paradise over whose gates are written, '*Abandon All Hope Ye Who Enter.*'"

At some point in his search for a resting place, I'm certain Zweig's mind began riffling through the full deck of American cities he'd visited on his book tour in 1938. This one. That one. That one. This one. He'd gushed to Huebsch over the "marvelous town" of San Francisco—"really, I would like to live there," he announced. They'd enjoyed a glorious drive around the bay that left him "perfectly enchanted." Come to think of it, Salt Lake City had been terrific as well. He'd had the best audience of his entire trip in that town. How revivified he felt in the company of the university students there! Might not the desert air of Utah present therapeutic possibilities for Lotte's asthma? One weekend Stefan and Lotte went to Baltimore. Another time to Washington. They'd tried out New Haven for a couple of months. New York. Atlantic City. San Francisco. Cambridge. LA. Philadelphia. In photographs taken of Stefan and Lotte during this period, Stefan is always in a suit and tie, looking a little heavy—his hair plastered down on his brow, large-featured and sweaty—gazing straight into the camera with a pleading smile. Lotte is invariably stylishly dressed, poised, her face slanted down, eyes averted, one leg advancing tautly before the other. They seem forever caught between places by the camera flash—liminal creatures who would dissolve if they ever stood still.

A story circulating among the exiles told of a Jewish-looking gentleman spotted in a travel agency in Bremen just before all hell broke loose. He was planted before a large globe, apparently undecided about where to emigrate to. The man moved his finger round and round the globe, pausing for a moment on Australia, remaining a little longer above South Africa, revolving on to Shanghai, then spinning all the way around again. At last he shoved the globe away in misery and asked the clerk, "Look here, haven't you got anything else?'"

The rise of Fascism in Italy started the trickle of new refugees. Franco's victory in Spain turned that trickle into a stream. Half a million Spaniards poured into France after the fall of Barcelona. The spread of Nazism turned that stream first to a gush, then to an outright flood. After Hitler took power in Germany, some eight hundred thousand refugees crested over the borders into France. But while Jews left Germany over a number of years, it took just a few months following the Anschluss for Austria to empty out in response to the brutality of Nazi actions there. Between the thousands shipped off to camps and those who fled, the Jewish population dropped by almost 60 percent in less than a year. Sociologists of the era conjectured that the suddenness of this departure may have made Austrian exiles more liable to preserve a rose-tinted picture of their former existence than the Germans, whose lives had grown bitter over a protracted time period.

Zurich became the first stop for most of the intellectual refugees from Austria, since Switzerland was relatively liberal with entry visas. The Austrians hoped to go on to Paris and London, and then to New York; "America was their star of hope," Klaus and Erika Mann remembered. In April and May 1939 on the promenade by the lake, in the Zurich cafés, in the homes of friends, more and more familiar faces began popping up. It was as though a ship of incalculable dimensions full of writers, artists, and musicians had somehow crashed into the Alpine foothills.

Two years later, hundreds of thousands of less illustrious refugees found themselves leaping from frontier to frontier, playing a version of musical chairs with countries. One nation after the next disappeared from the map of plausible stopping points. By the end of 1939, France was overflowing with aliens. Holland, which had taken in thousands of German exiles, now declared anyone who didn't have permission to return to their country of origin an undesirable. Switzerland would grant the homeless permission to reside for a few months, but almost never a visa to work—or license to remain beyond the period stipulated in their temporary visas. In Zurich, Prague, Amsterdam, and Copenhagen, one could see the unfortunates inside the grim "Aliens' Offices," seated on long benches in gloomy waiting rooms, "chattering nervously or sunk in brooding silence, waiting for the summons to the official, for the dreadful interrogation, the upshot of which may always be expulsion," the Manns reported. "Expulsion—but where to? No other country will take the outcasts."

They were writing these words a year before the fall of France— an event that marked the true end of Europe for Zweig, who'd always considered that country his second homeland. When word reached England that the swastika was flying over the Eiffel Tower, Zweig was with Desmond Flowers, his British publisher. "I have never seen . . . a man so completely shattered," Flowers recalled. "He could not speak, and shrank into himself like a mummy." The loss of this crucial refuge plunged everything into chaos, dooming many exiles to ricochet back and forth, from country to country. The ship *St. Louis* left Belgium with almost a thousand passengers for Cuba; when Cuba refused to let the refugees disembark, the boat had to recross the Atlantic, returning to Antwerp, from whence many travelers went on to the camps.

The trickle. The stream. The flood. And then people surging all over the globe, falling from the skies, splashed up by the seas, hurled helter-skelter by the wildly spinning red-and-black wheel. In his memoir Zweig recalled the unforgettable sight of a London travel office jammed with refugees, almost all of them Jewish, seeking to go anywhere, "to the ice of the North Pole or the blazing sands of the Sahara just to get away, move on, because their permits to stay where they were had run out." The sight of a Viennese industrialist he'd known as one of Austria's most brilliant art collectors, now looking wretchedly aged, clinging feebly to the table before him with both hands, inquiring about visas to Haiti, "trembling with the hope of moving to a country he could hardly even have located on the map, just so that he could go on begging his way there," was heartrending, Zweig wrote.

If the United States was the grail for many, the odds of actually getting in were infinitesimal. For all that Americans regularly spoke of their country being overrun with "millions of refugees," the numbers who actually made it were astonishingly small. In fact, the difficulties of reaching America due to the war, the Depression, and bureaucracy-mired visa restrictions combined to make the number of immigrants to the United States between 1931 and 1945 the *lowest* they had been in more than a hundred years. Perhaps most shocking, a committee of social scientists assigned to study the subject after the war discovered that quota fulfillment during these years averaged only 17.5 percent. The total number of quota immigrants admitted between 1931 and 1944 was 377,597, even though existing immigration laws would have allowed for more than two million entries. And out of that group, the estimated number of actual refugees admitted to the States during the core decade of Nazi rule lay somewhere between just two and three hundred thousand people.

Nonetheless, through a combination of intentional propaganda and general paranoia, the perception gained traction that America was being swamped with exiles to the point where millions of jobs and democracy itself were at risk. In one industrial town near New Haven, rumors began spreading that Americans were being forced out of factory jobs right and left to make room for the émigrés. The Department of Labor launched an investigation of the city's six major factories and concluded that "one refugee has been employed in one of the plants as an elevator operator. This job was created for him and no one was displaced." In New York City, a "whispering campaign" begun in 1938 alleged that the hiring of refugees and firing of Americans in major department stores had grown so intense that customers had to carry German dictionaries around with them when shopping. The accusations grew more and more heated until the heads of all the stores felt compelled to issue formal public denials: Bloomingdale's reported that it had exactly one German exile salesperson among its 2,653 employees. "Not a single person has at any time been discharged from our employ in order to make room for a refugee," the store affirmed.

While zealous American patriots decried the way that immigration laws had been ravaged to accommodate refugees, in fact during the entire period of Hitler's reign only two pieces of legislation affecting immigrant numbers were passed: one granting an annual quota of 50 people from the Philippines in 1934 and another permitting an annual quota of 105 persons from China in 1943. After it was understood that children were at particular risk in the new Europe, a bill was introduced into Congress in the spring of 1939 that intended to allow 20,000 refugee children from Germany to come to America, provided they arrived with secure offers of lodging and care, "under conditions that would guarantee they would not become public charges." But even this legislation failed to pass. Until the summer of 1938, because quotas for Germany and Austria never came close to being filled, it had been a relatively easy matter to bring over children who met the immigration requirements and whose parents wanted them to emigrate. But over the course of that year, as conditions in Central Europe deteriorated, adult applications for quota visas ballooned until they far exceed the

allotted number. One of the grimmest sights in the European consular offices of the late 1930s was that of untold numbers of children's
applications piling up higher and higher in those already overstuffed
rooms. We often hear the figure of six million Jews dying in Europe—
approximately one-third of the global Jewish population at the time.
Less familiar is the fact that out of an estimated 1.6 million children
subject to persecution by the Nazis, only 100,000 survived—less than
10 percent. In the end, women and men escaped to America in almost
equal numbers. Hitler got the children.

The arbitrariness of survival came to haunt the refugees. Many
exiles, when asked what had changed most in their new way
of life, rather than singling out any element of the environment
listed their separation from loved ones. Officials taking data from
the immigrants noted the frequency with which, when checking a
box referring to members of their immediate family abroad, the
refugees wrote in "if still alive"—or penciled a question mark after
the entry asking about parents.

The refugees' sense of indignation over American apathy regarding those left behind was exacerbated by guilt that they themselves had made it out. One former Austrian government employee
who'd escaped to find work as a draftsman in Pittsburgh described
how any sensation of enjoyment triggered conscience pangs.
"These thoughts," he declared, "tie us more with the Old Country
than anything else. German culture, science, and literature, which
I enjoyed and loved, starts to pale out, but the bitterness about the
sad fate of my brother, my sister-in-law with her little girl somewhere in Poland, my wife's father and two sisters, digs deeper and

deeper into my being. Why should we be saved and not they? This question is one of the main reasons why I do not enjoy being here."

Zweig became ever more agitated over these questions as his exile continued. By the time he reached the Americas, the idea of the utter randomness of his having been spared corroded his reserves of fortitude even more than fears that the Nazis would find him. The flip-a-coin aspect to his debate about where to go next was made more acute by the moral arbitrariness of his survival. One of the last lectures he ever delivered was for a fund-raiser in Brazil on behalf of Jewish war victims. "You have been kind enough to honor me, to welcome me among you," Zweig proclaimed on that occasion. "I should feel proud and happy. But I must confess to you that at a time like this I am not able to feel happy and still less to feel proud. On the contrary, I feel heavy at heart that you should show me such friendship while countless people, our own and others, are suffering. We as human beings, and especially as Jews, have no right in these days to be happy . . . We must not imagine that we are the few just people who have been saved from the destruction of Sodom and Gomorrah because of our special merits. We are not better, and we are not more worthy than all the others who are being hunted and driven over there in Europe."

I remember my father on one of the only occasions when he talked about the impressions he'd received of the camps from his parents, getting a harrowing gleam in his turquoise eyes and dropping his voice as though imparting a secret to say he'd been told that the better you were as a person, the more certain you were of being exterminated. What could a child do with such a notion? Given his general doubts about the virtue of prevailing, Zweig may have taken such notions to their logical conclusion: the only pattern determining survival was *not* meriting survival. And, how, with this criterion at the back of your mind, could you set about picking where to start a new life?

The necessity of deciding where he might base himself if he could no longer remain in Austria started haunting Zweig with Hitler's assumption of power. Nevertheless, he went back and forth to Vienna and Salzburg repeatedly after going into preemptive exile in England in February 1934. All through the next five years, during which he'd theoretically relocated first to London, then to Bath, he would spring across the channel to Paris whenever a lecturing opportunity arose, or just to lighten the load of sober, stony England with "a touch of Latin gaiety," as he put it to Jules Romains. Paris was only his most familiar escape. He also traveled back and forth to the South of France to spend time amid the German exile communities clustering along the coast there.

Even after 1933, there were hours of revelry in the South of France, especially in Sanary, which became a center for refugees, and where Zweig became friendly with the archpacifist Aldous Huxley, who'd been sojourning there for years. Huxley organized picnics on summer nights in the woods under bright moons, or on beaches by the mild, phosphorescent sea. Guests drank planter's punch made from Huxley's special recipe and played whimsical games in a sun-drunk spirit of serenity and detachment amid bumper crops of grapes and figs.

Not that the Huxleys much liked the German refugees. "Rather a dismal crew . . . already showing the disastrous effects of exile. Let us hope we shall not have to scuttle when Tom Mosley gets into power," Huxley wrote in one letter.

The Manns, Feuchtwanger, Werfel, and Bruno Frank all took villas in Sanary. Heinrich Mann was in Bandol. Brecht, Emil Ludwig, and Stefan Zweig came on visits, trailing wives, secretaries, translators, agents, and fans, the German émigré author Sybille Bedford wrote. There were garden parties, baking afternoons where drinks flowed and petit fours melted in the sun. Once a week, Mann, Frank, or one of the others would read from a work in progress, Bedford remembered. "Thomas Mann sat at the centre of a high table on the terrace, his three colleagues beside him. Behind them were chairs for their wives and Erika Mann. In the grounds below this platform, on steps, cushions, garden bench spread the hoi-polloi." Afterward, the elite were served Riesling and chicken salad; fruit cups and biscuits were dispatched to the groundlings. The Huxleys were struck by the self-regard of the refugees, Bedford recalled. "They threw their weight about; they *were* pompous. Their womenfolk referred to them as *Dictherfürsten*, princes of poetry. And though united in their horror of the Nazis, they were far from being one big happy family."

Zweig went frequently back and forth to Switzerland as well, visiting groups of displaced friends who congregated above Lake Geneva. He traveled to Italy and took expeditions to more far-flung Continental watering holes—in addition to making extended trips to the Americas. The map of Zweig's movements through these years would resemble an airline flight chart traced over by a persistent child with an unsteady hand. There was no one definitive moment when Zweig was actually thrust out of a country. But from 1933 on, his nomadic travels between refugee outposts bore a crepuscular quality—half free, half compulsory; a drawn-out fancy dress rehearsal for the final divorce from Europe.

Though Zweig's affluence distinguished him from the vast majority of exiles, his feeling of being trapped on a continent that had grown ever more claustrophobic even before Hitler's triumph was shared by many of his peers. The mind-set, indeed, became so ingrained that it remained potent even after they left Europe. "Every European suffers from a prison psychosis," declared Martin Gumpert of his fellow émigrés in the New World. "So greatly did we long for the utopian place of freedom that now that we can no longer escape anywhere—because we have escaped—now we look about anxiously for the bars to our cage." Freedom itself, he concluded, had become a source of melancholy and insecurity.

Zweig's freedom from material constraints only made his sense of psychological imprisonment more acute—so that he anticipated the larger European phenomenon Gumpert described. His travels became ever more frantic and less liberating as portents of the future lockdown multiplied. One friend dubbed him "the Flying Salzburger" in the 1920s. "Somehow the headlong tempo of the times has taken possession of us," he wrote an acquaintance in the middle of the decade, and in 1930 he told Victor Fleischer that so far as he was concerned, "there remains only flight." His disorientation was evident in his gross misreading of the German election results that year, when the Nazis made their breakthrough leap from just over 2 percent of the votes in the last contest to winning over 18 percent of the electorate. This outcome prompted Zweig to praise the "perhaps unwise" but basically healthy impulse of German youth to vigorously rebuke the plodding irresolution of conventional democratic politics at the Reichstag. Klaus Mann was stunned by Zweig's error of judgment and wrote an open letter to a newspaper in which he observed that while it might seem paradoxical that he had to remind the elder author of youth's proclivity for making passion an unconditional value, many young people were "now engaged in propagating retrogression and barbarism with all that élan and determination that ought to be reserved for finer purposes." With some embarrassment, given his faith in Zweig's stature as a "mature thinker," Mann chided, "The revolt of youth can be in the service and interest of noble and ignoble forces."

But Zweig had been dedicated for so long to what he called the "ethics of fervor" that he wavered repeatedly in recognizing how thoroughly the terms were transformed in the new Germany. "Our whole evolution can only be to . . . let our feeling have intercourse with as many things as possible," he'd declared in his study of Emile Verhaeren from before the First World War. At that moment, when Europe seemed to be accelerating gloriously away from the stagnation of the previous epoch, Zweig had insisted that true comprehension of the universe was inconceivable "except in the permanently exalted state of the unrest of joy and motion." Indeed enthusiasm, in the sense of what Zweig called "over-estimation," represented a higher form of justice than what was "apparently absolute justice itself."

Knowing Zweig's history of giddy, indiscriminate appreciation, Jules Romains could not resist citing this essay in a valedictory lecture he delivered about Zweig in Paris in 1939, only to point out that at the current moment, "one learns to one's cost that it is dangerous to become excited about anything, to declare one's love, enthusiasm, or devotion to anything." For, he asked, "Of what does human misfortune now consist, and above all what horrible things are threatening mankind? . . . Is it an excess of composure, of reason, or the critical sense? God knows it is not." The chief danger of the times, Romains stated, was precisely "the unbridled proscription of all critical sense, all lucid play of reason." How could Zweig not have blushed when he read his old friend's words and recalled some of the assertions he'd made in the past, such as his declaration, "Criticism is sterile"?

Zweig's idolization of enthusiasm was always meant to be in the service of appreciation, not rage, but the last war should have taught him once and for all how easily the emotion of ecstatic admiration could swivel to an object of evil allure. Instead, he faltered time and again—badly in 1930—and as late as 1939 Romains confessed to a suspicion that Zweig had "to make an effort not to feel sympathetic toward certain great adventurers of today whom he really has a thousand reasons to scorn and to hate." When Zweig argued that through a sweeping embrace "we shall ourselves grow richer than those timid ones who content themselves with choice morsels of life instead of grasping life in its entirety," he was writing in the spirit of his democratic hero Whitman. But Central Europe in the first half of the twentieth century was not the Brooklyn bard's late-nineteenth-century America, and Zweig learned the hard way that cosmic appreciation might also energize the agents of the apocalypse.

Not coincidentally, it was also in the winter of 1930 that Zweig began his biography of Marie Antoinette. In Zweig's telling, the queen's predicament eerily presages his own fate. "With diabolical cunning, history began by making a spoiled darling of Marie Antoinette . . . [who] had charm and grace and wealth in liberal measure," he wrote. "But destiny, having raised her to the pinnacle of good fortune, dragged her down again with the utmost refinements of cruelty . . . Unaccustomed to suffering, she resisted and sought to escape. But with the ruthlessness of an artist who will not desist from his travail until he has wrung the last possibilities from the stubborn clay he is fashioning, the deliberate hand of misfortune continued to mould, to knead, to chisel, and to hammer Marie Antoinette."

To an uncanny extent, after Hitler came to power Zweig's story began to imitate passages from his fiction and biographies, forcing him to confront the implications of the philosophical argument in favor of exile; the potency of youth's urge to remake the world; the exemplary retreat of aging artists into nature. Zweig's claim to prophetic vision with regard to the course of world events was mostly bluster—he had just the luck of the gambler who always bets on black—but he had a weird knack for weaving plot elements from his own future destiny into the stories of his protagonists.

As he sat down to work on the French queen's story in December 1930, Zweig abruptly resolved that he couldn't bear the prospect of shivering through winter in Salzburg. Having heard from a well-traveled friend that the Balearic Islands offered an idyllic refuge where it was possible to write undisturbed, Zweig set about making his travel arrangements. His needs were simple, Zweig always maintained. Outside of the obvious—access to good, authentic local cuisine, complete serenity, and appealing surroundings—a room of ample proportions in which he could walk up and down as he pondered his composition was essential. That and a large table on which he could place all his books and papers. "If the Matterhorn or the Gulf of Naples happened to be outside his windows, that, of course, was a gift of the gods for which he was grateful," Friderike drily observed.

She and Stefan boarded a train for Spain early in the new year of 1931. But when they arrived in Palma de Mallorca, he discovered that the tranquil island was being torn apart by noisy construction projects, on top of which a drop in Spanish currency rates had drawn hordes of loud English people on the dole. Forty-eight hours after their arrival, the Zweigs were back on the slow boat to Barcelona. From there, they boarded a train east, toward the necklace of retreats on the French Riviera, where Stefan had frequently sojourned in the past. But nothing quite suited. Every establishment they passed appeared, precisely, too much like a hotel on the French Riviera. Finally, on the verge of despairing, at the southernmost tip of the Cap d'Antibes, Zweig spotted an elegant white mansion with a black mansard roof situated just above the ocean that didn't look like a hotel at all. They swirled into the long drive, gliding past acres of gardens and Mediterranean pines. It was all promising. On entering and consulting the staff, Zweig learned to his delight that, just as he'd thought, the striking edifice had originally been a private home and bore exactly the kind of pedigree most resonant for him: built by the founder of the newspaper *Le Figaro*, it had become a hotel managed by the family of Guy de Maupassant. The Zweigs strolled the grounds. It was off-season. Essential! There were no athletic bathers. Only people seeking rest. The tasteful balconies of the seafront rooms gave splendid views onto the Côte d'Azur. There was no clatter from the kitchen, because meals were taken in the luxurious Eden-Roc restaurant, designed to resemble a ship's deck protruding out above the deep blue sea. Grottoes and pools had been carved into the cliffs below. Done. The Zweigs checked in.

However, now that Zweig had discovered the ideal sanctuary, he found it unbearable to be without the company of some dear

friend with whom he could share his fortune. He thought of Joseph
Roth, drinking himself into demented furies, shaking with the flu
in Marseilles, having fled there from Paris in the midst of three
lawsuits—two filed by his publishers, one from his father-in-law.
Zweig got in touch with Roth and insisted he join them. Roth did
so, and now, at last, Stefan was content—though he still insisted
on changing his work place at least once a day, moving from his
table at the hotel to a bistro or café. From an elegant luncheon at
the hotel restaurant, the trio would wander into the fortified town
of Antibes and stop at the café Les Rendezvous des Chauffeurs,
where Roth and Zweig took perverse delight in the sight of one
chauffeur after the next politely asking Friderike for a spin on
the dance floor. (How much of Zweig's restlessness might have
been conditioned by a craving not to be left too much alone with
Friderike we can only speculate.) After the café, work and note-
taking resumed, broken up every so often by excited, schoolboyish
visits to the stationery shop, where Zweig and Roth indulged without restraint their passion for pens, notebooks, pencils, and special ink. And when Stefan went quiet, signaling that he was ready
to return to his work on Marie Antoinette, Roth and Friderike
would stroll off together for target practice at a shooting gallery,
where Friderike popped the bull's-eye time and again, while Roth
dreamed of his romantic days in the trenches.

Three years later, when Zweig became involved with Lotte,
his sense of being hunted had intensified to the point where
travel—for so long his greatest delight—had become a torture. Indeed, it's not by chance that his intimacy with her began on the

road, partly in an effort to recapture his old euphoria. Soon after she entered Zweig's employment, he took her with him to Scotland to assist as he followed in the footsteps of Mary Stuart's desperate flight. This may have been the interlude in which the two became romantically entwined. There's no happier photo of Lotte than one he took of her on a windswept coastal path shortly after that trip. She's wearing a light skirt and short-sleeved blouse, twisting toward the camera in partial profile with a sheaf of papers squeezed under her bare arm, clutching her black hair back from her face, a sly, merry grin on her lips. She'd just turned twenty-six and might be taken for five years younger. She looks unbound and in love.

"I have begun to learn again, like a high school kid," Zweig crowed to Joseph Roth at this time. "I am once again uncertain, and full of curiosity. Now, at age fifty-three, I am enjoying the love of a young woman." At the same time he said that his political pessimism was boundless. "I believe in the coming war, the way others believe in God. But merely *because* I believe in it, I am living more intensely now," he wrote. "I have a desire to see this world in the round once more, before it burns."

If their liaison began in northern Europe, it became public in the South of France. Not long after the Scottish research expedition, Lotte joined Stefan and Friderike on a trip to Nice. Despite his infatuation with England's stodgy temperance during the years of Austria's implosion, he found himself in the fall of 1934 beset with a "mortal ennui." Alas, "in the long run the white walls of a sanatorium became insupportable," he declared to Rolland. So he decided it was time for a stint on the Côte d'Azur, where friends like Roth, Toscanini, André Maurois, Jules Romains, H. G. Wells, and Sholem Asch were all staying.

Friderike was so pleased, she reported, when Lotte turned up looking somewhat less "pale and shadowy" than she had in the past. Since her own daughters weren't with her, Friderike rejoiced at the prospect of helping this sickly creature profit from the southern sun. Lotte was given a room on their corridor of the hotel, and Friderike had the inspiration of setting her up with the typewriter on the balcony so that she could reap the full benefit of the ocean breezes.

After each day's work was done, the three of them floated off together to fill the hours in pursuit of beauty and pleasure. A visit to the villa of an illustrious friend. A concert conducted by

Toscanini in Monaco. Drives along the spectacular coastline. On one such motor trip to Monte Carlo, Friderike was happy to find Lotte a little more talkative than usual, for as a rule, the girl seemed utterly impervious to outside impressions. Once, when they were driving along the Corniche, winding above an undulating seam of sapphire, white, and turquoise that bordered the silver-green olive groves, Friderike suggested they stop the car to show the panorama properly to Lotte.

"It's pointless," Stefan said. "She'd be incapable of getting anything out of it." Friderike was shocked at his rudeness, she later remarked. But if the scene actually occurred, it seems likely it was a joke at Friderike's expense, intended to highlight her absurd belittling of Lotte's intelligence.

The date of Stefan's scheduled departure for America in January 1935 drew near. Lotte was about to retire to a mountain resort back in Switzerland, "where she planned to recuperate for a few weeks," Friderike wrote. One day Stefan casually asked Friderike to run down to the U.S. Consulate and pick up his visitor's visa. But when she got there, though she'd brought all sorts of documents, she found she was missing the official proof of Zweig's permanent residence and economic solvency. In a flash she remembered that since the house on the Kapuzinerberg was not yet sold and Stefan was carting around the title to that valuable property, the deed would serve both purposes. She rushed back to the hotel and headed for Stefan's study, which necessitated passing through the bedroom.

"Unfortunately it was an inopportune moment," Friderike noted. Though she presents the ensuing scene in a spirit of high tragedy, it reads more like French farce. However deeply enmeshed Stefan and Lotte were at the moment of Friderike's surprise entrance, Lotte, "roused from a deep trance," was abashed. Stefan was "terribly dismayed." Friderike was mortified. In a trembling voice she explained her errand. And then, she records, six hands, shaking more and less violently, proceeded to search all over the study until the missing Salzburg house title was found, whereupon, clutching the deed, Friderike flew back out the door to the American Consulate.

"Of course I was disappointed in the girl," she confessed afterward. "But perhaps I wronged her. Perhaps this was the first time she had been overcome by the dazzling sun of Nice. I resolved to ignore the whole matter." Possibly this had been an error, she later reflected. Had she remonstrated violently with Stefan, ordering him to cast out the girl, Stefan would have accepted this protest as "an elemental and justified outbreak"—and might have acquiesced to her demand. But this was not the tenor of their relationship, Friderike avowed, for above all she and Stefan were "friends, the best of friends."

Instead, she gave Stefan the silent treatment. Worshipper of quiet though he was, this at once proved unbearable. He burst out to Friderike that the guilt was all his—which only made matters worse. For three days, Lotte and Friderike circled each other in silence, bound together in their gracious Belle Époque hotel, slinking away behind the confectionary pink façade and fringe of palm trees—darting around corners, into shadows, behind doors to avoid the sight of each other. At last, Lotte summoned the courage to write Friderike a letter. It had all been a ridiculous business, she swore; the esteem in which she held Friderike was intact. After this, Friderike reported, the pair had several brief exchanges. "In a few days she would be gone; and I was sorry for the lonely girl. Too bad that the whole thing had to happen— but, as it was all so trifling and silly, we'd wipe it off the slate. My husband would spend a few days alone with me before sailing and, after returning from America, stay only briefly in London before joining me in Austria. These last days, to be devoted to the conclusion of the great biographical work, should remain undisturbed. Lotte departed, reiterating her gratitude, underscored by delivery of a bouquet of roses. My husband was overjoyed that I had not behaved as people do in stage plays and still oftener in life."

But the final scene had yet to be played.

Friderike and Stefan spent a few days together in Nice, and then she traveled with him to Villefranche, where the ocean liner that would transport him to America was docked. He was eager to show her his stateroom, which the shipping firm had specially appointed in his honor. Friderike went on board with a heavy heart. Thirty minutes more and her husband would sail away.

They stepped into Stefan's magnificent quarters—and there, glowing on the table before them, lay a sealed letter from Lotte. "I'm sure it's nothing," Stefan said. "Business matters. Well wishes for the voyage. It's nothing!"

But the mood was broken. When they walked back onto the deck in view of a crowd of friends who sat bobbing in the little boat that ferried between the steamer and the port, waiting to wish Stefan bon voyage, everyone knew all was not right between husband and wife. The horn signaling departure blew. Friderike stepped down into the tiny vessel. The liner began pulling away. And then, as the span of water dividing them widened, Stefan— with his inimitable savoir faire—passed the letter across the waves to a man standing beside Friderike.

The gesture broadcast his complete trust in Friderike's judgment and Lotte's discretion. He was certain, Friderike wrote, "that this timid girl would put nothing on paper suggesting the slightest intimacy." And Friderike herself knew exactly the part she was meant to play. She was now to cast the letter unread into the sea and lift up to Stefan a glance of beatific gratitude. "An angel might have acted this way," Friderike recounted, "but I, a woman like others, read Lotte's words on the lonely shore." Her gaze ran down the page. The harmless note proved to be "a glowing love letter— seemingly the first ever penned by a rigid hand," Friderike wrote.

"'Dearest, I find myself to be a terrible coward but I'm afraid that somebody will be there when you receive this letter,'" Lotte had written. "'I would like to tell you once more that I never told you how much I like you, and how happy you made me through your friendship. If I seem cold on the outside, maybe even toward you without wanting to, I still have a great longing for love and friendship and this you have given me and I'm so thankful for that—more than you might fathom. You don't know how lonely I felt inside before you came. Even though I was content to be in London . . . You gave me so much joy during the time we were together and I was so happy about being in Nice for a longer time with you. It was beautiful despite all the fear and inconvenience, which depressed me because I like your wife also very much . . . the goodbye was hard. I believe you realize that and I wish you could be here—both of us alone. Your acquaintances [here at the spa] are nice, but no substitute for you in any way. Heartfelt greetings. I think a lot about you and our togetherness . . .'"

Or at least that's the typed version Friderike archived with a handwritten note explaining this to be a copy of the letter Stefan presented her en route to America.

Censored? Accurately transcribed with a few passages interpolated? Entirely rewritten? No one knows, since Friderike destroyed the original. But I suspect, given Friderike's mastery of the art of including just enough truth in her machinations to burnish their credibility, that the letter includes at least some of Lotte's actual sentences—where they suited the image Friderike wanted to project of a creature whose gushing devotion and pliant weakness had captivated her husband.

One thing the whole affair was *not*—as Friderike makes plain—was unprecedented as an extramarital sexual escapade. What made the event unique was that always in the past when "the occasional flirtation cropped up outside, he kept me informed with more candor than was necessary or welcome. Never had letters been concealed in the course of a union, a friendship, impregnable to others, were they ever so close." "How then had this happened?" she asks in her memoir of Stefan. *"A hotel was not one's own home: that was the deeper meaning. It was the house which had been broken up."* Friderike linked the loss of their base in Salzburg with the cessation of transparency in their relations. For his dalliances had always been associated with travel—travel, but not nomadism. Fantasies of exile had transformed Stefan from light philanderer into clumsy home-wrecker. He'd become consumed with the impossibility of continuing to live in Salzburg for inflated political reasons, Friderike claimed. She would never forgive the way the fairy castle on the hill, "called *ours* for twenty years," had been sold like "a bit of junk" because of Stefan's impatience once he'd resolved to be done with the place. His anxiety about Salzburg's growing anti-Semitism and Nazi Party members crossing over the border into Austria at night, carrying walking sticks to disguise themselves as hikers, ignored the fact that Stefan himself remained a beloved first citizen of the town—held in reverence by the mayor and merchants alike. "I shall make a new home for myself alone, though God knows where. Stefan is living in an imaginary emigrant's psychosis, and I just enjoy my home," Friderike cried to a friend.

Zweig's early correspondence with Lotte dances with the names of fancy meeting places and his own far-flung appointments. She is to get off at such-and-such a station, where they will find each other at such and such a spot, then board a train to somewhere far away. Backup plans abound. If they miss each other here, they will meet up there. He will be at a hotel in Paris in two days, in Zurich in five, then in Florence, in Rome. In Marienbad. On again back to Paris, then Nice in two weeks for ten days. And then finally London to see her again. London is an awfully nice city. London is lovely, he writes her with a fillip of coquetry. At a certain point in the letters, it's clear, Lotte has become his London, London his Lotte.

How could she not have been intoxicated by finding herself constantly on the verge of being spirited away, from one city, country, continent to the next—or having her lover swept from her side to fulfill some scintillating engagement?

Lotte caught the last breath of Zweig's European idyll—doors opening, walls dissolving; trains, ships, autos, planes slitting through space from harbor to station; gates parting; an endless open sesame; barriers and borders falling before the luminous skeleton key of his literary reputation. But now he was in free fall; and after all the endless searching and indecision about where to tumble next, a deep sense of anticlimax hovered over the abrupt July move to Ossining, New York. Both Stefan and Lotte knew it was a temporary measure at best. After so many months of uncertain wanderings Zweig hardly cared. Perhaps, as he at last signed the deed to the house on Ramapo Road, he heard echoes of a sad little anecdote recounted by Alfred Polgar:

"One émigré asks another, 'Where do you mean to settle?' The other replies, 'In Ecuador.'

"'But that's so *far!*' the first responds.

"'Far from what?' asks the other with a shrug."

Chapter Eight

EDUCATIONAL DEBTS

Insects chittered and hissed in the heavy green leaves. From somewhere down the street came the *clack-clack* of a lawn mower. Wherever you went, that sound formed a background to the voices of neighbors greeting one another. "Looks like a nice day, doesn't it?" When Lotte made the journey to Main Street—the residents of Ossining called their trips along the tree-lined roads to the four blocks of shops "going uptown"—the casual, good-natured air of life felt at once calm and remote. There was no pretense about the town center, with its old two- and three-story brick buildings—the "super," the jeweler, the banks, haberdashers, candy store, barber shop, beauty salon, hotel, and pharmacy. "This is just a warning, in case you're expecting to be shown the eighth wonder of the world," Ossining residents told strangers. On hot days, colored awnings rolled out over the storefronts like floating carpets and the owners sat out front in their shade. Everywhere you went, the *pong* of the check dispenser and the *ping* of the cash register followed you. Americans, the refugees joked, like to hear their money make its own special music.

The size of the "super" was out of all proportion. To see all the *stuff* piled around—meat, butter, canned goods, fresh vegetables, everything conceivably desirable—while knowing how millions lacked even the most basic foods never ceased to give the Zweigs a bad conscience. Like other refugees, they were also appalled by the waste. "There is bread in the streets, paper in them," one fellow exile remarked with shock. "In Germany the poor people would sell that paper, even before the war." Some were astonished by the fact that garbage contained not only surplus food—tabs of butter, rolls, and whatnot—but furniture and radios. The sight of store windows "filled with oysters, lobsters, available to almost anybody at any time, strawberries in January," induced vertigo. It wasn't possible for any middle-class person to have that in Germany, the émigrés noted. The sense of having fallen into a Land of Cockaigne went beyond grocery stores and trash heaps. Many were struck by "the incalculable abundance of restaurants, taverns, cafeterias, milk bars, and soda fountains," as Martin Gumpert wrote. He projected that American workers ate three times as many vegetables as their European counterparts, while also drinking unfathomable quantities of milk and upholding their reputation as dedicated carnivores with an "outstanding passion" for steak done rare. In his book *Heil Hunger! Health Under Hitler,* Gumpert argued that Hitler had failed to solve the problem of feeding the masses and Fascism would be defeated not by the war machines, but by "famine and pestilence, the unholy twins." It was no accident, he wrote, that the real-life model for Uncle Sam had been a meatpacker from Troy on the Hudson who'd been able to turn the War of 1812 to the advantage of American troops by provisioning them with eight thousand slaughtered oxen a week. The current government took the same view. On the cover of *Time* magazine that July was a portrait of the secretary of agriculture against a field of grain with a quote underneath: "Food will win the war and write the peace."

Though the Zweigs lived on Ramapo Road for most of the summer, it's clear from their letters that they left the house rarely; less and less as the weeks passed, working on Stefan's autobiography at an ever more frenzied pace. When they first signed the lease, Lotte's relief at the prospect of at long last settling down trumped everything else, even inciting a flutter of enthusiasm. "We have finally found a house for the summer, which meets all our requirements as 'house-workers' and 'car-less' people, which is nicely situated and even very near Eva," she announced to Hanna at the end of June. The thought of being nearer to her niece and so able to comfort her brother and sister-in-law back in England with regular reports on Eva's well-being clearly assuaged some of Lotte's guilt about being in a country so amply provisioned while her family underwent deprivations back home. "You can imagine that we will be busy, packing, arranging things, seeing some people and trying not to see others and so on," she continued, in a lighthearted vein. But an asterisk above the word "car-less" in Lotte's letter is glossed with a margin note in Stefan's trademark purple pen: "Not 'carefree.'" He'd never expressed pleasure at the idea of their move. Before they left Manhattan he focused on the burden of relocating. Lotte had worked for two days straight, he confessed to her family. They'd already had to abandon a huge number of books in Rio; now another part of his library would be left behind at the

Wyndham. "It is not easy as I have a kind of office to move with me, letters, documents, typewritten copies, addresses, contracts—you can imagine how we are longing to have a kind of home!!" He made clear, however, that he wasn't referring to Ossining. They would never have a home so long as the war continued, he said, adding, "It is possible that I will have to go in the autumn to Cuba and perhaps again the other countries."

Even before he arrives, Zweig is mentally leaving again. The "little house" (he never characterizes it otherwise) is a retreat where he intends to work continuously on his memoir throughout the term of their two-month lease. He has no other expectations. Nor does he have any expectations for the book itself with regard to audience. The only refugee writers who could prosper in the U.S. market were those who gave Americans just what they wanted, he insisted, "exciting stuff or sensational news. Just the best have the smallest chances, those who take responsibility for every word." The very afternoon he and Lotte moved into Ramapo Road, Stefan telephoned Ben Huebsch to try to arrange for him to visit, and when he could only reach the editor's wife begged her at least to come. To tempt Huebsch, he later added that the place reminded him very much of the sites they used to frequent in their old Salzkammergut stays.

To find a semblance between the pristine Alpine resort area north of Salzburg and their new home on its scraggy elevation above Sing Sing seems a bit of wishful thinking bordering on the delusional. But as exile wore on, everything became more and more a game of spotting antecedents, connecting dots to earlier incarnations of their existence. Lotte likened the home above the Hudson to the house of a neighbor in Bath. It was very similar, in certain ways, she said. Well, not the house itself, she confessed, "which is much smaller and altogether different, but its position on a hill with a steep driveway." Their maid, meanwhile, was rather like a woman named Rhoda who'd worked for the family in London. For Stefan, the view overlooking the city of Bath from their home on Lyncombe Hill had been reminiscent of the prospect over Salzburg from his terraced garden on the Kapuzinerberg, while the valleys brought to mind Baden, where he'd lived just before the First World War. Petrópolis, when he moved there, would evoke Semmering, "only more primitive, like the Salzkammergut of anno 1900," he wrote. Tracking the course of many exiles, we find their movement wasn't just over borders, but also across temporal zones, zigzagging from past to present.

A week into his stay, after relaying news to Ben Huebsch of the fantastic rate at which he was writing his memoir—seventy pages in seven days—Stefan added, "Unfortunately it is always a sign of moral depression when I throw myself so deep into work." He never comments on the setting of Ossining. After a few days, he'd seen enough of the place's repetitive vistas and buildings to convince himself that there was nothing there for him. Nothing there, period.

Zweig's response to Ossining evokes the reactions Martin Gumpert heard from other exiles to the whole of America. "'There are no trees here,' say the émigrés in New York. 'There are no clouds here,' they say in California. 'There are no cafés here where one can sit for hours and scribble,' say the writers. 'There are no villages here, no inns, no meadows, no crooked little streets . . . There are no alpine valleys, no real mounts, no real seashore.' The smell of age is lacking . . . Absent are the pine trees, the linden trees, the cornflowers, the steaming dishes, the wine-crocks, the hares and the deer. Gone are the walks at night, chamber music, Lieder, open-air meeting-places in the balmy summer nights. Vanished are the book-shops, the familiar voices, bread and dusk, spring and tender little peas." It was heartbreaking, Gumpert noted—and ridiculous. Many of these things can in fact be found in America, in almost identical form, he wrote, but he and his fellow exiles "in our obstinate love, our senseless nostalgia, we want no part of them."

The problem ran deeper. "Is there anything sadder than a pro-vincial American Main Street?" he continued. "Everywhere there are the same shops, the same products, the same posters, every-where the identical uninspired architecture—the undertaker, the grocer, the movie house, the community center. At ten o'clock the lights go down, a few cars are parked here and there, a few trucks rumble past, otherwise all life is at an end, as in the grave."

Then Gumpert gives the portrait a twist. "This is the way it is—and yet again, that is not the way it is. For this dreariness that so frightens us existed over there too. There were the tenements in the north of Berlin, the workers' quarters in Essen . . . slums in Britain and slums in Vienna, there were small towns in Bran-denburg that left nothing to be desired in dreariness." All of these things that so depress the cultivated exile in America existed in Europe as well. "But we never thought that we should be at the mercy of this backwater of culture that exists everywhere in the world," he wrote. "There are no longer situations against which we are protected, agonies against which we are proof."

Gumpert suggests that the real displacement experienced by the privileged exiles had less to do with the respective physical environ-ments of the Old and New Worlds than with a shift in the landscape of their social circumstances. All at once figures such as Gumpert and Zweig lost their class immunity and had to really *mingle*—not with the romantic underworld Zweig explored in Berlin, but with the dreary shabbiness of ordinary lower-middle-class life everywhere. The New World exposed these exiles to Old World economic truths they'd managed to remain blind to while actually living there.

"Where did our arrogance get us?" Gumpert asked of the hour before they were all forced into exile. "We were suddenly face to face with the silently grown masses of the European continent— an anonymous assemblage of creatures without historical memory, without a traditional picture, whom the scenery and the way of life of the old continent merely serve as a costume and a backdrop. To gratify their rightful claim to existence, they had to be educated, fed, clothed. We thought we were speaking in their name. But we did not understand them, nor did they understand us. All that took place in politics, in public life, in the spiritual or religious sphere, was clothed in an unworldly jargon that had meaning for us, but meant only nonsense to them."

The Ossining train station was always busy in the early evenings when Zweig came back from one of his descents into Manhattan to see a lawyer, a publisher, a dentist, or a friend. You could hear noise from the row of factories by the waterfront and children on vacation shouting down the adjoining streets, playing at Kick the Can and Hit the Curb. Zweig stepped through the milling crowd, always hot, always self-conscious about his perspiring, always aware of his German accent; always concerned that his hair might not be perfectly barbered, always thinking about the gray strands creeping through the dark, always ducking his gaze, always hiding. He slipped into a taxi as soon as he could hail one and rode up the long slope of Croton Avenue. All he wanted was to close himself into the shadows on the porch and summon the genie of the past from the bottle. An autobiography asked something more than a novel, he wrote Huebsch. "Being in the center one does not see so well as another if one has found the right proportions." He'd left aside so much that he had material enough for another book, he realized. The rigid steeples of Ossining vanished behind him. The little dark house waited silent at the crest of its tiny hill.

Sometimes Lotte stepped out of the house's shadows onto the open lawn just to breathe. At least it was quiet and green, Lotte wrote her family. Already by the end of June, New York had become hot, sticky, and smelly. Though not much cooler, the air in Ossining was nice, she told her aunt; "if it smells, it smells of flowers and grass." And when Eva did come to visit, even if there was nothing for them to do there, the sight of the girl curled in their tiny living room reading Paul de Kruif's *Microbe Hunters*—looking, Lotte wrote, "splendid, very brown and strong"—made her feel able to assure Manfred and Hanna that their daughter was thriving. The intimacy between Lotte and Eva had steadily deepened. The girl first came to live with the Zweigs in Bath, when Eva's parents evacuated her from the London Blitz. Later, as the bombing intensified, Manfred and Hanna made the decision to remove Eva from England altogether by sending her to the United States, where they had several contacts. Stefan and Lotte found Eva her first home in America while they were still on their initial trip to Brazil, then helped her find a longer-term residence after returning to New York. Over time, the problem of how best to arrange Eva's education in America became a consuming question for both of them.

Back in Austria, Stefan had complained frequently about what he saw as the idle, self-indulgent existence of Suse and Alix, Friderike's daughters. In a letter Stefan wrote to Friderike following the formalization of their separation in 1937, he tried to assure her that he wished her children "all the luck in the world," while maintaining that his occasional expressions of dissatisfaction had deep roots. "I didn't discern [in them] any of that burning eagerness to learn that both of us know so well and which was the glory of our youth," he wrote. Despite his criticisms of their laziness, Suse and Alix only further aggravated Stefan when—perhaps recognizing that they weren't cut out for a life of higher study—the two sought gainful employment. After one of them managed to land a job with a haberdasher in Salzburg, Stefan promptly wrote the girls' father to object that she was in danger of demeaning the family's reputation by this small-minded employment.

Zweig never looked down on the poor, but he felt contempt for people from any sector of society who sought to better their lot in a strictly material sense. This attitude, more reflective of his own exemption from economic pressures than he seemed able to recognize, could rankle even those closest to him. "You say, may God free me from money," Joseph Roth wrote Zweig in 1933. "Not so, dear friend! May God *give me* money, a shed load of money! Because in today's world money is no curse any more, and poverty no blessing. To put it bluntly, *that's* romantic . . . I need money! I write with money, I help six or seven people to get by with my money."

Nonetheless, Friderike's daughters had revealed themselves in Stefan's eyes to be petty bourgeoisie of the spirit—and this was the lowest class of all in his sociopsychological hierarchy. He never got over the fact that in the fifteen-plus years they lived together,

Suse and Alix didn't once ask to see his manuscript collection. The neglect seemed of a piece with the selfishness that had led them to prance down the Kapuzinerberg to shimmy in a Salzburg dance hall within hours of learning that their father had fallen gravely ill. Lingering bitterness about these failures of sympathy reflected Zweig's conviction that the girls were sports-and-dance-crazed harbingers of a greater cultural barbarism.

The gravity with which he reproved behaviors that might be viewed more sympathetically as typical symptoms of adolescence gets at the heart of Zweig's American problem. Long before he went into exile there, he'd fingered the United States as the source of all those cultural trends that were leading the public to pursue "amusement without exertion": global dance crazes, mass fashion, popular cinema, et cetera were leveling the cosmos of human expression "into a uniform cultural schema." It used to be the case, he wrote in one essay, that after a fashion caught on in Paris it would take years to spread into the countryside. "A certain boundary protected people and their customs from its tyrannical demands. Today its dictatorship becomes universal in a heartbeat. New York decrees short hair for women: within a month, as if cut by the same scythe, 50 or 100 million female manes fall to the floor. No emperor, no khan in the history of the world ever experienced a similar power, no spiritual commandment a similar speed." America, Zweig declared back in 1925, had undergone "an atrophy of nerves in favor of muscles." Devotion to the easiest and most comfortable way of living for the lowest common denominator ultimately meant nothing less than the annihilation of individuality, he argued. "Faces become increasingly similar through the influence of the same passions, bodies more similar to each other through the practice of the same sports, minds more similar for sharing the same interests . . . And since everything is geared to the shortest units of time, consumption increases: thus does genuine education—the patient accumulation of meaning over the course of a lifetime—become a quite rare phenomenon in our time." The United States had inaugurated a "rush into servitude" of the masses, clearing the way psychologically for dictatorships of every variety to seize power. If the Great War marked the first phase of Europe's destruction, he concluded, "Americanization is the second."

By the time Zweig got to Ossining and began working on his autobiography, he'd taken these ideas yet further, suggesting that even those people who'd managed to hold on to their individual character thus far were now doomed to lose their humanity in the wake of the instantaneous global dissemination of news. Thanks to the omnipresence of wireless radio transmissions—"our new methods of spreading news as soon as it happens"—no one could avoid being constantly sucked into the events of the hour. "When bombers smashed buildings in Shanghai, we knew it in our sitting rooms in Europe even before the injured were carried out," Zweig noted in his memoir's preface. "Incidents thousands of miles away overseas came vividly before our eyes. There was no shelter, no safety from constant awareness and involvement. There was no country to which you could escape, no way you could buy peace and quiet." While it might have been possible for the super-educated few to escape the lure of mass entertainment, the twenty-four-seven news cycle, with its constant feed of worldwide disasters, would overwhelm the sensibilities of anyone still able to feel.

Zweig's grudge against America worsened after he came to live there. "You cannot imagine how we are disgusted by the impoliteness, the rudeness, the arrogant way of the American children," he wrote to Lotte's sister-in-law from New York. Many émigré parents expressed similar concerns. Sociologists in the 1940s noted that conflicts regularly arose in exile families over issues such as "comics, listening to certain radio programs, going to 'wild west' movies." Research indicated that "the battle of comics was raging in many refugee homes with the parents usually doing a retreat, for they discovered that many schools use them as teaching devices and comics are so prevalent that it is a superhuman task to keep a child away from them." Sometimes the task could also trigger forms of defiance with sinister overtones. One refugee father recounted an incident when he forbade his son from listening to the broadcast of a boxing match. The child refused to go sleep and spent the hours of the match chanting loudly from his bedroom, "Down with foreigners! Foreigners are un-American."

Zweig became obsessively concerned with correcting Eva's etiquette in consequence of these invasive cultural influences. Indeed, one of the most surprising motifs of his correspondence with Lotte's family throughout their American sojourn is the way that—in the midst of laments about the millions of exiles, mass murder, and the end of Europe—he continuously reverts to his dismay at Eva's failure to write home more often. The carping begins to make sense when we realize the universe of cultural values that lay behind this insistence on good letter-writing habits.

When Lotte descended from Ramapo Road to visit the Main Street shops, she would have passed the Washington School, an oatmeal-colored Beaux Arts building that sat at the juncture of Croton and Dale. Carved across its façade, on three stone lozenges set between tall window panes, were the words "SCIENCE,"

"LANGUAGES," "HISTORY." The tall capital letters projecting above the bright grass were reminders of those principles of *Bildung* that had been so central to the Zweigs' lives in Europe and seemed to have such a small role in their new existence.

Part of what made it so difficult to convey the philosophy behind this word was that Americans had their own distinct but equally avid culture of knowledge and self-improvement. As Ise Gropius, the wife of Walter Gropius, one of the German émigré founders of the Bauhaus movement, wrote in an account of her first impressions of America, "One thing we have puzzled about in this country is the emphasis put on the knowledge of facts. The amassing of a stupendous amount of information, as is, for instance, demonstrated in the various quiz programs has baffled us like everybody else. We feel it may mislead people into believing that the aim of education is to acquire a vast collection of uncorrelated facts instead of learning a method to coordinate and correlate the things that come our way."

Gropius's reference to quiz programs also evokes a common perception among the refugees that Americans treated everything—the acquisition of knowledge and the earning of money alike—as part of the quest for a good time. The insistence on making everything fun seemed to bespeak a greater cultural immaturity. "On Europeans a group of adult Americans often has the effect of a group of playful children," one exile wrote. Many refugees were astonished to hear old married couples refer to each other as boys and girls. America's affinity for childhood was contrasted with French proclivity for old age and the German idealization of men in their prime. Auden said that Americans looked like "elderly babies." The American valuation of youth did not translate into an inability to feel life's vicissitudes, Auden suggested, but a resistance to letting one's face show the imprint of one's personal history. "To have a face in the European sense of the word, it would seem that one must not only enjoy and suffer but also desire to preserve the memory of even the most humiliating and unpleasant experiences of the past," he wrote.

The refugees were especially sensitive on this point, since the most radical change to family structure wrought by exile was that between the old and young generations. Through their experiences in school and elsewhere outside the house, children almost always became fluent in English and in American culture more quickly than did their mothers and fathers. "Foreign born parents discover a 'Trojan horse' within the home, manned by their children," wrote one researcher into the "Americanization" process. Social scientists of the era observed cases where parents became so disillusioned by the effort to assimilate that they abandoned the struggle altogether and became as helpless as infants, living completely in the past and leaving their offspring to do everything for them. In less extreme instances, parents encouraged their children to educate *them* on how to adapt. One Austrian refugee physician wrote of how, after his son spent two years at George Washington High School, the boy got his mother to begin cooking American dishes. "He tells us to which movies and theaters we should go. Our English has improved tremendously since he began going to school. He also made me give up my beloved felt hat and wear a straw hat in the summer. My patients are amazed at my knowledge of baseball and football. My wife and I seriously contemplate nominating our son as general information and publicity manager of the Kern family with a fixed salary for outstanding service!"

Beyond language or specific mannerisms, the ability of refugee youth to absorb the deeper message of the cataclysm gave them the edge in the New World. Writing of his own child, Martin Gumpert confessed, "While we cling, in doubt and dismay, to the lesson of experience, that of all possibilities the least favorable invariably will materialize, the daughter says, 'I am quite certain that Roosevelt will be elected for a third term, because in my life only things happen that have never happened before.'" Adult exiles were confused by the Second World War, Gumpert stated. "We live through it in an atmosphere of *déjà vu*. But our children are far more familiar with the function of the 'miracle.' To them it means something similar to what our own 'security' meant to us. They confidently expect the unexpected."

Ceding the mantle of educational authority in this manner was simply inconceivable for Zweig. Letter after letter to the Altmanns from both him and Lotte testifies to the dedication with which the couple sought out the most enlightened and demanding education America could offer Eva, as well as the kind of home environment that would best nurture her character development. Eventually Lotte traveled to Croton-on-Hudson to visit Amity Hall, an untraditional children's home run by Olga and Albrecht Schaeffer—themselves distinguished German refugees. Albrecht had been a friend of Freud's, who called Schaeffer "my poet" and wrote his final letter to this writer. Amity Hall was situated in a large green space encompassing a vegetable garden, an orchard, and a poultry farm. The dozen or so children living at the house at any given time all helped care for the garden and animals. They also had to make their own beds, clean their shoes, and help serve at the table. At different hours of the day, the children were supposed to speak French or German, rather than English. (When Eva had lived with the Zweigs in Bath, Stefan had been a martinet about insisting that all mealtime conversation be conducted in French to develop her fluency in that language.) There were only a few basic rules, Lotte reported, but these were strictly enforced: punctuality, writing home once a week, clean hands and good table manners, no "funnies," no radio except for special programs, movies only if there was something outstanding, and no chewing gum. Though Olga and Albrecht were Christian, there was no religious atmosphere beyond "a general 'Christian spirit,'" she added. Stefan could not have been more positive about the prospects of the new situation. Albrecht was "from a very good Protestant family and an excellent writer—all his books have been published by the Insel," he noted, as if it were a self-evident qualification for raising Eva to have been published by Zweig's old press. As another endorsement, Stefan recorded that of late Albrecht had become increasingly devoted to "philosophic and abstract work." He was, indeed, not just upright but "a completely immaterialistic man," while his wife was "very intelligent, active and motherly." They could rely on her, Stefan promised; "she is not greedy or business-like." He seconded Lotte's support for the idea that Eva would study in "a quiet atmosphere of English, American and also some, but only some Jewish children." This would enable her to become accustomed to a way of life that was at once simple and intelligent, while remaining in a Continental atmosphere instead of an American one. He was happy at the thought that Eva would be in a milieu closer to their own European conceptions, which combined "strictness and order with intelligence and culture." All this became especially important in light of what they saw all the time in New York—the thoughtlessness of all the people, "the stupidity of the refugees and the lack of real compassion."

Zweig never specified what he thought was lacking in American education, but I suspect the analysis made by Henry Pachter, a German exile who found work as a university professor after his own flight from Europe, would have resonated with him. In his memoir, Pachter recalled his distress at the way American students appeared "poorly informed, provincial, grade-conscious and difficult to interest in problems of universal significance." But it wasn't until his own daughter went to school that he began to really grasp "why American education fails to stimulate and slake the thirst for knowledge." The problem with college in the United States, he opined, was what failed to take place at the level of American high school and elementary school. Whereas his own concept of education was "based on the European model of elite culture to which, one hopes, the masses can be lifted up," Pachter wrote, "American education seems to strive for an optimum which neither develops the highest cultural potential for the elite nor the maximum useful and relevant knowledge for the masses." A more sympathetic observer distinguished the systems by noting that while in Europe education was directed toward scholarship, in America its primary aim was citizenship. This translated, in the opinion of one émigré professor, into the promotion of "a democratic social attitude and political behavior." Another refugee enjoined his fellow exiles to recognize that Americans "are not uncultivated or uneducated because they do not know Figaro's Hochzeit by heart. Think of it that this is a country where people *want to be good*. They are often quite clumsy in showing it, but they are sincere despite hypocritical detours in that they want to be good, square, decent. You have not seen such people anywhere in Europe . . . but art is not part of their lives. That is your contribution, for that their grandchildren will be eternally thankful to your grandchildren."

M y aim would be one day to become not a great critic or a literary celebrity but a moral authority," Zweig wrote to Rolland in January 1918. The ambition may sound perplexing, but Zweig was entirely serious, and the effort to establish himself as a kind of itinerant wisdom-teacher of pacifism, high cultural ideals, and other tenets of pan-Europeanism links his disparate activities from the end of the First World War right up to 1933. The impulse manifested itself not only through his writing, but also in the countless salon-like gatherings he organized, and in an increasingly ambitious series of lectures, which he delivered across Europe. Zweig tried to practice what he preached on a personal level as well. When he and Friderike moved into their new home in Salzburg in 1919, they had to negotiate with a family of squatters: a gardener's widow and her two children, who'd been living in the house since they were born. The nineteen-year-old Toni, "fatherless son of a superstitious, illiterate mother," in Friderike's phrase, was known as one of the roughest young men in Salzburg. Having gone off to fight for the emperor two years earlier and been caught in an explosion, Toni "had not been quite right in the head ever since."

With the new state institutions tinged by Communism and the whole notion of private property fragile, confronting the young man carried risks. Convicted several years earlier of involvement in the theft of a bicycle, Toni was now threatened with jail. He presented her and Stefan with "an interesting pedagogic problem," Friderike wrote. Stefan ultimately hired a lawyer for Toni who succeeded in clearing the charges against him. The mother, along with her goat, agreed to move into a room in town. The Zweigs briefly took on Toni's sister as a maid, but she soon succumbed to tuberculosis. So only Toni remained.

The Zweigs gave him permission to live on in the garden house, provided he did not bring with him the rowdies who'd formed part of his retinue at the main building. Before long, however, uproarious parties were being held there, accompanied by "savory odors," indicating that Toni had become part of a gang of poachers operating in the nearby mountains. Once again the couple chose not to intervene, and Toni developed an attachment to them, which proved not a bad thing, since he later rose to become a leader of the rebellious unemployed. The Zweigs found it only natural that the hardships of the times had led Toni to seek a new form of justice in the embrace of Communism. But they worried about his generation's eagerness for a new fight to rectify their socioeconomic conditions. "Stefan and I helped as much as we could to redirect and pacify excited minds," Friderike later wrote.

In this case, Zweig's impulse was aligned with that of Salzburg's new Socialist government. Instead of garden allotments, the administration sought to keep the unemployed off the streets by encouraging the pursuit of culture through open-enrollment "County Educational Courses." Schoolrooms were set up offering free adult classes, and Salzburg's intellectual elite was asked to volunteer in these new institutions. Both Zweig and Hermann Bahr taught courses on literature. The post gratified Zweig's belief that by helping workers grasp that the European literary-cultural canon was also their patrimony, he was both defusing the impulse to violent radicalism and activating the spiritual potential of the masses. Friderike, for her part, taught beginning French to seventy-odd pupils of diverse ages and backgrounds. Alas, while seeking to establish a common denominator among the students, she organized a recital in which her class sang "I had a comrade" in French loudly enough that the chorus reverberated along the Salzach quay, where some of Salzburg's unemployed language teachers happened to overhear them. The instructors turned to the program's administrators, demanding to be taken on as paid teachers and insisting that the pupils be charged tuition. The students couldn't pay; the original cohort of teachers refused a salary. Under pressure from the professional language instructors, the project fell apart.

It's unclear what happened to Toni after the Zweigs left Salzburg, but his story haunts the denouement of Zweig's own tale. Toni seems, indeed, to epitomize the Austrian problem of the interwar era that formed a counterpart to the Jewish "question." Unable to find regular work, Toni drifted into a life of petty crime and political radicalism—initially self-serving and then addressing a broader social context. Did his labors on behalf of the unemployed lead to Toni's joining the Socialist uprising against the Catholic, Fascist government of Chancellor Dollfuss in the mid-1930s—an uprising whose failure effectively destroyed Austria's activist left, removing the principal obstacle to Hitler's agenda for Austria? Did he end up in prison or exile? Was he among the considerable numbers of Austrian Socialists who switched over to the Nazi side as Hitler's popularity among the working class grew in the German-speaking world? Zweig's friend Alfred Polgar liked to cite a dialogue from

Lessing in which a ghost is asked, "What is the fastest thing on earth?" The ghost replies, "The transition from good to evil." Where did Toni end up? In what grave, in what land, after what manner of life and what kind of death?

Zweig continued promulgating his pan-European message to larger and larger audiences. But he never quite lost his aura of removal from the common lot, which worked against any real embrace of his social program, even when it earned polite applause. As the German author Irmgard Keun noted, Zweig always came off as "one of those noble Jewish types who, thin-skinned and open to harm, lives in an immaculate glass world of the spirit and lacks the capacity themselves to do harm." A less respectful observer of Zweig's legacy referred to his memoir as the "Glass-Enclosed Record of a Mind," accusing him of having inhabited such a "rarefied atmosphere" that he was oblivious to the fact that the masses about whom he made such "fine generalizations" had needs more basic than the intellectuals' "Utopian dreams." Along with the affection he could inspire, Zweig also incited resentment among a number of his contemporaries—and even some of his intimates.

Hermann Kesten recounted an incident from 1936 when he, Zweig, Joseph Roth, and Irmgard Keun were taking refuge from world events in the Belgian seaside town of Ostend. All day, they would hole up in their hotels and work. At night, they went out to opulent restaurants and bars on Zweig's tab. Roth had only one ragged pair of pants to wear on these excursions into the domain of privilege. Zweig became aware of this and took it upon himself to escort Roth to a tailor so that he could be measured for a new set of trousers. This proved a costly undertaking, since Roth insisted they be cut to the distinctive pattern of the old Austrian cavalry uniform he venerated. The tailor at first refused to make the special trim below the knees. Zweig's money smoothed over the resistance, and when Roth showed up that evening in his new fancy pants, Zweig felt gratified.

The next day Kesten chanced upon Roth and Keun at a bar in the marketplace. The waiter appeared, placing three glasses of a brightly colored liqueur before Roth. Roth proceeded to methodically dump the contents of each glass over his jacket while Keun clapped and cheered. "What are you doing?" Kesten asked. "*Punishing Stefan Zweig!*" Roth proclaimed. He told Kesten that he would wear the soiled jacket on their evening outing to embarrass Zweig. "Millionaires are like that! They take us to the tailor, and buy us a new pair of pants, but they forget to buy us a jacket to go with them." Roth was one of many who—even while sometimes benefiting directly from Zweig's largesse—saw Zweig as finally just too rich to "get it"—his sensitivity to the human condition muffled by the very fineness of his silk wrappings.

The single most devastating indictment of Zweig's existence was written by Hannah Arendt in 1943 for *Aufbau*, the German-Jewish periodical founded in the thirties in New York. By the time Arendt wrote her review of Zweig's memoir, she'd already devoted considerable thought to the question not only of what was being done to the Jews in Europe, but also of what the Jews had done to themselves. Her review of *The World of Yesterday* positions Zweig and his peers as paradigmatic instances of European Jewry's failure to provide for the future.

In her most biting passage Arendt protests, "Naturally, the world Zweig depicts was anything *but* the world of yesterday; naturally, the author of this book did not actually live in the world, only on its rim. The gilded trellises of this peculiar sanctuary were very thick, depriving the inmates of every view and every insight that could disturb their enjoyment. Not once does Zweig mention the most ominous manifestation of the years after the First World War, which struck his native Austria more violently than any other European country: unemployment." Had he and the other top-heavy humanists descended from their delightful Olympus to look at what was happening in the streets in consequence of mass un-employment, Arendt contends, they might have witnessed brutal scenes that would have spurred them to political activism. Her critique echoes Roth's prank, suggesting that Zweig was guilty of a culpable lack of curiosity regarding those less fortunate.

Zweig set himself up for such attacks by virtue of having been, undeniably, an awfully wealthy man who preferred the company of established great artists and ardent young male poets to just about anyone. Yet it's difficult to make the charge of obliviousness stick. In point of fact, unemployment is cited in *The World of Yester-day* as one of the reasons for Hitler's appeal. And long before the National Socialists' ascendancy, Zweig wrote Rolland about mak-ing what he called a pilgrimage through a working-class Viennese neighborhood, which filled him with rage. "I clenched my fists at the sight of the immense misery," Zweig wrote. "Children with skinny little faces were running around in rags. And while I looked into their miserable hovels, I heard the honking of luxury cars traveling with lightning speed through this hell." The sight of war profiteers roaring out from the Hotel Sacher inspired him with a thirst for justice such as he had never before experienced. "I believe this crew signs its own death warrant," he decided. Still, clenching one's fists and using them to punch are two different things.

It wasn't that Zweig didn't see the unemployment caused by the war—or even that he utterly failed to grasp the power relations behind that catastrophe. His posthumously published novella *The Post-Office Girl* confronts some of those issues head-on. But Zweig essentially flipped the slogan "Grub before ethics!" promoted by more Marxist-oriented writers such as Brecht on its head into something verging on "Education before bread!" The former obviously sounds far more realistic than Zweig's call to disseminate lessons in high culture to the lower classes. But Hitler too grasped that, in truth, social welfare programs always come packaged with some ethical message. "Bread *and* freedom!" chanted his early followers. The Nazis passed out food and taught the recipients why they hadn't had food before: namely, economic exploitation by Jews and the architects of Versailles. Instead of the proverbial page of the Talmud dipped in honey to sweeten the appetite of students for knowledge, Hitler steeped the bread he distributed in bile to stimulate people's bloodlust. If, by pushing education in high cultural ideals and tolerance as the best path to avoid social collapse, Zweig staked the wrong horse, it's not clear that the more traditionally doctrinal left wing did any better at fending off the rising fascination of National Socialism. As Friderike remarked, it was a pity more people hadn't followed the example they tried to set with their mentorship of Toni and active role in the Salzburg County Education Courses. When it came to the workers, most middle-class people insisted just on "showing those Bolsheviks a thing or two" about who was really in charge, she said.

Zweig had a way of throwing around the terms "pacifism" and "humanism" that can make them sound naggingly abstract. But by the end of the 1920s, he'd established an agenda for social change. It was the Italians who gave him the opportunity to articulate the program he developed, first in Florence, at the Palazzo Vecchio, in May

1932, where he surveyed historical trends contributing to the prolif-
eration of nationalism, and then at the prestigious Volta conference
in Rome that fall, for which he composed an address titled "The
Moral Decontamination of Europe." The latter was Zweig's most
important opportunity for making his case before an international
forum. His old friend the working-class poet Walter Bauer was one
of many young followers of Zweig who continued to feel inspired by
the latter address for years afterward. "The new education must have
as its starting point a new conception of history," Zweig's speech
announced. "It must be built on the thought of all that is common
to the peoples of Europe rather than of that wherein they differ."
The talk went on to expound on the obligation of writers, artists,
and musicians, "all of us who belong to a community of the spirit,"
to help lead youth by showing how every great achievement of every
country worked toward a common ideal. "We who are older must
show that admiration of others does not exhaust man's spiritual
strength but rather replenishes it." Only someone who has learned
to feed the flame of his enthusiasm through passionate support for
others can hope to renew his own youth, Zweig argued.

Zweig diagnosed the illness of the times as a form of repeti-
tion compulsion. All the political tensions and mass hatred that
remained latent in his generation from the Great War had simply been displaced from external foes onto internal demographics.
Propaganda and economic depression had exacerbated the situation. But a slow draining of the poison could still be undertaken
through education, Zweig counseled. School curricula might be
turned away from their focus on political and military history,
toward a program of cultural enlightenment that would eluci-
date the shared efforts of European peoples to create "a great and

wonderful spiritual edifice." He called for the founding of an international university, with branches in multiple European capitals.

Against the efforts to sway mass psychology through partici-
patory spectacle that Austrian politicians from Victor Adler, the
great leader of the country's Socialist Party, to Theodor Herzl
and Adolf Hitler had all adapted from Wagner's aesthetics, Zweig
made the case to step back and study. Having finally abandoned
his own ethics of fervor, he offered a plea for *appreciation* rather than
immersion. Zweig's program for mutual tolerance consisted in a
call for everyone to be educated as cosmopolitan connoisseurs.

Remembering the talk after the war, Bauer wistfully yearned
for Zweig "to stand up now before the bewildered young men
and women of our day" and repeat the remarks he did then. But
Bauer almost certainly knew that Zweig had not actually stood
up even before the audience in Rome. Having been warned that
the audience at the conference would include prominent National
Socialists—Goebbels and Alfred Rosenberg among them—Zweig
pleaded other engagements and arranged for his lecture to be delivered by a proxy. Not long after the conference, Bauer himself
began six years of service as a Nazi soldier. It's moving to think
of Zweig's most important speech on cross-cultural appreciation
echoing through the august hall in Fascist Rome in 1932, but it's
equally poignant that the address had to be made in another man's
voice, as though Zweig were already a ghost.

One of the saddest moments in all Zweig's correspondence
comes when he tries to explain to Lotte's family the reasons
he believes the pragmatic educational program in which they've

finally enrolled Eva is the right one. "In the coming world," Zweig argues, it will "be necessary to be effective, reliable and independent, it will not be a world for dreamers and the earlier she learns that one has to think for oneself, the better for her . . . More and more I see that one has to do all oneself." American popular culture seemed to smear Zweig's face in the failure of his grand educational program to lift up the masses—even as it reminded him of the threat against which he'd first concocted his plan. While Arendt lambasted Zweig for never leaving his gilded trellis, he did try to bring others less fortunate inside that homage to the School of Athens he created on his terrace in Salzburg. But in the end there just wasn't enough room. And what he was left with when that haven had crumbled, though Zweig could never acknowledge it as such, sounds a lot like classic American self-reliance.

Two years after the Zweigs left Ossining, as *The World of Yesterday* was appearing in American bookstores, the town showed evidence of having absorbed a different kind of lesson from Europe than the aesthetic one Zweig had striven to impart. A local journalist described a steady stream of uniformed men on foot passing by the Ossining high school. A "new order" had taken hold at the school, this writer reported. Courses on essential war subjects had been opened to the students. Marching had become part of the gym curriculum. A commando course had been set up on the athletic field at the back of the school. And as for Main Street, the writer reported, "Gone are the days of the laden push carts in the 'super' markets. Now, with point rationing of meats and canned goods and just plain rationing of coffee, sugar, hats and shoes, there is no more lavish and unreasonable buying. We have been accepting this as the democratic way of winning a war."

Chapter Nine

THE OTHER SIDE

Inside the cramped bungalow with its triple gables like a trio of witch's hats, Stefan Zweig paced back and forth, the past streaming through him. "I have nothing to report except that it is extremely quiet here and I am working hard and nearly without interruption," he wrote Huebsch. Neighbors returned from vacation. Children went off to camp, and young men came home on furloughs from forts deep in the south. Summer storms swept through the town, cutting phones and electricity; sailing boats tipped over in the river. In the middle of July, Stefan wondered whether he should continue his memoir past his fiftieth birthday. "You are quite right," he told Huebsch, "the third part is what the Jews call a 'Gegeifer,' a constant complaining and accusing and I ask myself if I should not do better to conclude the book with an epilogue." The British were beaten on the Syrian front and suffered terrible losses in Italy. The bombing of Moscow intensified. The

254 THE IMPOSSIBLE EXILE

warden of Sing Sing, retiring after twenty-one years, sent his last two killers to the electric chair. A line of young women in a local country club show made the goose step a sexual dance number. "The war seems more and more to become a regular form of life," Stefan informed his publisher.

All day and far into the night, the furious *rat-a-tat-tat* of the Remington's keys came through the walls, puncturing the haze of droning insects. Eva was sometimes enlisted to help order manuscript pages. One of Friderike's daughters was called on as well. *Four hundred pages in a few weeks.* The end of the first draft of his autobiography was upon them, and Stefan began toying with the book's working title: "My Three Lives." To his Spanish translator he proposed "These Days Are Gone" and "The Irretrievable Years." In letters to Huebsch, he bounced off other possibilities: "Our Generation" and the mawkishly despairing "Europe Was My Life." He was "extremely depressed," he confessed. The past seven years had been "a continuous harassing," and he'd been working like "seven devils without a single walk and mostly without to leave the house." Seven years of haunted nomadism; seven devils driving him on at number 7 Ramapo Road in the seventh month of 1941. He had no interest in publishing the book anytime soon, but was glad to discover that he could still work without ceasing, in a kind of trance. "I wanted to have finished it before I take a decision when I shall leave and so I have done the impossible," he announced.

The book's streaks of incandescence reflect the manner of its composition—a desperate appeal to a generation that has not yet inherited the earth. "Whoever went through this period or, rather, was hunted and driven through it—we knew but few breathing spells—experienced more history than any of his ancestors," Stefan wrote of the time within which he was still living. "But if we with our evidence can transmit out of the decaying structure only one grain of truth to the next generation, we shall not have labored entirely in vain."

The book is a message to the future. The key to its structure—the topography of scenes; its inventions and omissions—lies in Zweig's determination to pass on a document the builders of the future could actually *use*, a kind of elegiac instruction manual on what to do and what not to do in shaping a new society out of the ruins. *The World of Yesterday*, in truth, marks the final gesture of Zweig's educational mission. Critics have taken it to task for sentimentalizing the intellectual community Zweig helped constellate at his home in Salzburg. I think we must rather approach the scenes as if they were—not prescriptive, exactly, but at least glass-lantern slides of alternative paths. Here, Zweig says: this kind of conversation between this sort of cross section of artists, intellectuals, and philanthropists in this type of liminal setting on the border of nations might be something to crib from. Other scenes are diagnostic of wrong turnings. Look at the way propaganda feeds racism and war fever, he suggests. Zweig has no interest in exposing his own personal foibles à la Rousseau, but rather in rehearsing what he and his peers were trying to create in opposition to the maelstrom. Illusions are not to be eliminated but encouraged, since only the powers of imagination can summon a vision of a more humane future.

Friderike often sat on the porch at Ramapo Road with Stefan that summer, reviewing the life they'd shared, while Stefan made notes. She'd begun stopping round as soon as they moved in.

For, as fate would have it, she'd ended up moving to Ossining as well, though the town was by no means a refugee hub. Even after the bitterness of their divorce, they'd never broken off contact for any length of time. As soon as Friderike made it to America in January 1941, she and Stefan bumped into each other by chance at the British Consulate in New York. They saw each other periodically thereafter, both at larger gatherings of exiles and at more intimate dinners.

Stefan liked having Friderike close to check his memories against her recollection. And she enjoyed correcting her former husband on big points and small. She relished the thought that it was now *she* who boasted a public persona, through her work on various refugee committees and friendships with influential women such as Erika Mann and Alma Werfel. It was she who'd been living the life of an independent Bohemian in the flat she rented in the artistic quarter of Greenwich Village. Stefan paid her a call there as soon as she moved in. "Evidently feeling at home in a place where the domestic apparatus was reduced to a minimum, he remained for a long time," Friderike wrote. "Now the shoe was on the other foot: it was I who, even though involuntarily, lived in the 'student's freedom' for which he had hankered."

But if Friderike could help Stefan rekindle the past, she was welcome, Lotte felt. It was strange, she acknowledged to her family, yet so far as she was concerned relations between them were fine now. "Mrs. Zweig No. 1," as Lotte jokingly referred to her, seemed genuinely concerned with Eva's well-being. Her brother and sister-in-law had warned her about "the relationship of first and second wives and husbands, but it all seems perfectly natural and normal." Perhaps the great difference in their ages had something to do with it, she mused.

However, as July wore on, Friderike for her part was frankly appalled by what she saw happening at Ramapo Road. Stefan and Lotte were goading each other on to wild "exaggerations of diligence," she wrote. The only break from the typewriter the poor girl ever got was the exhausting train journey to and from Manhattan, where she was still receiving the injections the doctor told her would immunize her from asthma, though she only ever grew sicker. Friderike told Stefan that he could not keep up this pace of work; that it was too much for him and for Lotte too. But to all her remonstrations Stefan responded only that absorption in work was the most effective defense against Lotte's asthmatic attacks, implying that the resolve these labors called for held illness at bay as well.

Friderike watched Lotte straining every nerve to match Stefan's brutal tempo. "Like so many invalids, she was especially bent on persuading herself and others of her vigor," Friderike wrote. They were destroying each other's mental and physical powers of resistance. "A man near sixty and a frail woman believed they could escape the problems of the times by retiring behind a rampart of immoderate labor," she declared. In the most intense heat of summer the two of them shut themselves away, slaving over the story of his life, eight to nine hours a day.

But Lotte's work with Stefan was always a considered position of solidarity, rather than feeble acquiescence. She knew perfectly well how serious things were becoming. "Once in a while I must write a letter which Stefan does not 'censor' before I send it," Lotte informed her family the third week in July. "I am a little worried about him at present, he is depressed," she acknowledged.

An abyss opens beneath the words. The unsettled existence, the perpetual indecision, "the facts of the war, which is now becoming a real mass murder, and its seeming endlessness weigh upon his mind," she wrote. For a few lines, she gives a glimpse of what it is to be bound to a person writhing in anguish. "I hope this mood will pass soon and I wish I had something of those people who can talk others into cheerfulness and somehow inspire courage and hope," she continued. "My qualities are rather that I can stand any kind of life without complaining and feeling sorry for myself, but I cannot talk him out of his present mood, and can only wait until he gets over it himself—as he usually did in previous cases." What she offers Stefan is certainty that whatever he does, he will not be alone in doing it. And for all her self-deprecation, Lotte knows that this promise of fidelity is no reflection of weakness, but commitment. Wither he went, she would go.

Despite her own claims of surrender to the dictates of his mental state, she went on to beg her family to contact Stefan's British publishers and persuade them to send the manuscript of Balzac, which Stefan began while they were living in England. "Stefan says he does not want it but I am convinced that he will be quite happy when he gets it or knows Viking Press has it at his disposition whenever he will have finished his present work," she wrote.

Lotte's efforts to get the Balzac into Stefan's hands took on ever greater urgency in the ensuing months. She understood that Stefan would hurl himself into work regardless of what anyone did. But it mattered which book he buried himself in, because he took on the emotional color of what he wrote about. Balzac, for all the hardship of his existence, was a titanic life force. Becoming that author in his imagination might make Stefan believe again in his own creative potency. The same impulse may have helped motivate

Lotte's second request, that her family send the bibliography of Stefan's complete works. Perhaps she wanted to make palpable before her husband the Balzac-scale literary factory of his own production. The problem wasn't that Stefan ever really slowed down, but that he ceased to believe his works were part of any larger edifice. Lotte sought to persuade him that his words themselves formed a superstructure above the dark pyre of the times.

During their final weeks in Ossining, Lotte's efforts to imbue Eva with more and more knowledge mirror Stefan's intensifying work on his memoir. One more page of the book. One more lesson for the girl. If he is composing *The World of Yesterday*, Eva embodies in microcosm the world of tomorrow. On the last day of July Lotte reported to her family that she could write only a few lines, "being busy with supervising Eva's writing, knitting, typing and the maid's first try to make potato salad (still a special treat for your child)." She makes it sound as if 7 Ramapo Road has transformed into a one-room schoolhouse. On that same day, Stefan wrote Hanna and Manfred Altmann as well, noting that he hoped to cajole Eva into writing a few lines to them, but then he interrupts this allusion to his old bête noire: "No, she really likes now to write and is a big and intelligent girl," he concedes, hinting that their work with Eva is done. Soon they will finalize their traveling plans, he announces. They may not go away at all, given the uncertainties of the time, he maintains. "We would do our best of course to come back here after some time—what I want, badly want is some rest and New York is not the place for it. I have worked hard and want a little *dolce far niente*."

And then—as though for months they'd been rising up in a rickety car of the Cyclone roller coaster—up and up the cruel rails to the highest peak of the shuddering track—all at once they were over the top; all at once Lotte and Stefan were tumbling, shattering down the other side. You can almost hear the shrieking in her mind as their hands wave above them and they plunge down through space. Not a week had gone by after Lotte wrote her family to report that she was busily teaching Eva all sorts of things and working hard on Stefan's manuscript when they abruptly cut short their lease on Ramapo Road and were back in Manhattan.

The words that passed between Lotte and Stefan during the first days of August must have been harrowing. The pacing and sleeplessness, their numb, anguished repetitions upon repetitions of attempts to reason through their fate and envision a future—the rise and fall of exhausted voices in that tiny house as they tried and tried to conceive a way out—running through the ten thousand impossible possibilities for what to do next, again and again, is terrible to contemplate. And all their desperate weighing of alternatives diverted them not a hairsbreadth from the course they were locked upon. The moment they were wrenched out of the spell of day-and-night labor on his memoir, their American retreat was done.

On the sixth of August, Lotte wrote her mother to say that they were back at the Wyndham and had not yet decided what to do and whether they would really return to Brazil. On the same day, she told her brother and sister-in-law, "Our mind is nearly made up, and if nothing unforeseen happens, we shall leave for Rio on the 15th. Well—you will already know by cable, when you get this letter, what finally happened." The thought of all that had to be done to prepare for the journey loomed before her like a mountain—everything that had to be organized, all the documents, so many things. Before they left, they'd seen Eva. "She regrets that we are leaving, of course, but she is so much at home at Amity Hall that she will not really miss us," Lotte promised. While they were in Ossining they'd been able to spend more time with her at the Schaeffers', and Lotte had the chance to see that Mrs. Schaeffer really loved her, she said, and did not consider Eva only a boarder. And that Eva loved Mrs. Schaeffer they knew already, Lotte reminded them. Lotte's letter breaks down, interrupting itself—fragmenting—dissolving into ellipses. "It was a pity of course to have to leave Ossining so quickly and early, but there is not much time—fortunately—to look back and reflect how nice it would have been if . . . Many things would have been nice if not . . ." Stefan penned a note on the same page. "We have so much to do and all is so difficult. We do not know if we can leave because what can happen still!! . . . We have seen Eva, she is grown up and in excellent mood, she is now there already an important person and loved by all in the house even Mr. Schaeffer has a special liking for her." Grown-up Eva was eleven years old.

On the eleventh of August, Lotte told her mother they had their tickets and almost all the necessary papers. They would probably leave in a few days. About Eva she was not to worry. "I probably shall miss her more than she will miss us, in spite of all her liking of us." They had seen her frequently in the last days and would see her again before they left. It was a pity to leave almost on her birthday, but Lotte would try to leave some nice present, and she would have a party at Amity Hall. A pity to leave when they had finally adjusted. A pity to leave so quickly. A pity to leave the day before Eva turned twelve. Pity upon pity descended over them.

All through the final week they received callers day and night at
the Wyndham, a stream of fugitives and émigrés come to offer their
farewells. Among them was the German writer Joachim Maass, one
of the pack of young authors Zweig had buoyed along in his early
career. Maass had broad features, thick lips, long, narrow eyes,
and a swollen ovular brow, like a portrait frame filled with rising
dough. Wearing his trademark big bow tie, he could resemble an
underworld impresario, but he was a cheerful, kind character who
venerated Zweig and had become friendly with Lotte in London.
Zweig had telegrammed him at Mount Holyoke College, asking
him to travel down to the city to say goodbye.

When Maass arrived, Zweig was just showing Berthold Viertel
to the door. Lotte was typing in the next room. After the door
closed behind Viertel, Zweig seemed utterly distracted, Maass recalled, rubbing his hands together, struggling to elevate his spirits
to his old good cheer, then plunging back into anxious preoccupation. When Lotte appeared, he burst out, "Well children, what are
we going to do now? Let's go and have something to eat!"

They made their way to a Viennese restaurant not far from
the hotel. But the food gave Zweig no pleasure. The strong golden
wine, so cold the crystal clouded, brought no delight. After a few
sips, he shoved the glass away from him. Then he pushed the plate
away and lashed out in an uncharacteristic rage—cursing the bureaucracy of travel he was forced to navigate, the idiotic passport
authorities, the dull-witted customs agents.

"But, Stefan," Maass said, adopting the most carefree tone possible, "Even God, if he went traveling today, would have to deal
with these things."

"But why?" Zweig burst out. "What for? Why all this bollocks—this loathsomeness!"

Lotte tried to smile. She put her hand on his arm. He flew off again. *"None of it's worth it!"* And then, shaking his head, stroking his forehead with his left hand, he suddenly shoved his chair completely back from the table, away from everyone, so that he was sitting all on his own while Lotte and Maass continued eating.

The image seared itself into Maass's memory: Stefan Zweig, that paragon of epicurean courtesy, perched on a lonely chair in the middle of an Austrian restaurant in Manhattan, legs crossed, nodding incessantly to himself, tapping his foot and pounding his hands together—those beautiful, elegant, immaculate hands—while his malcontent stare roved the room.

Maass tried to change the mood by asking Zweig about his progress on *The World of Yesterday*.

"It's finished. Done," he said. "And believe me it makes me sick."

Lotte murmured to Maass, "Stefan's burned himself out. He worked too much."

"I can see that," Maass responded.

Stefan glared at them from his isolated chair. "Are you finished eating? Then we can go now."

As they walked back through the dark, sticky summer street, Zweig kept constantly a half step in front of Lotte and Maass, as though he weren't even with them. In the foyer of the Wyndham, he announced, "I have to take a nap. Go have a drink at the bar. But come say goodbye before you leave." Then he nodded and disappeared into the elevator.

Lotte and Maass sat down at a small table in the dimmest corner of the bar. She was overcome.

"I don't know what it is," she said. "I really don't know. His condition isn't good."

"No," Maass agreed. "It's not."

"I'm scared," Lotte said.

The rest of the conversation, Maass remembered, betrayed an anguished hopelessness. As he rode up in the elevator with Lotte, Maass could only think to say, "I'm glad you're with him. It helps."

"A lot of help I am," she said. "What can I do for him? The only thing I can do is make him drag me with him."

When they went into the bedroom, Zweig was lolling on the bed, wearing a set of gleaming white pajamas, reading a book. He lay the book aside as Maass approached, seating himself on the edge of the mattress—and Zweig seemed utterly transformed, speaking with Maass as he would have done in the old days, asking about the younger man's writing projects and teasing him about his conquests of beautiful young women. And then suddenly Zweig began talking with great emotion about the hospitality and beauty of Brazil, which almost made him feel at home.

At last, Maass had to take his leave. Perhaps the blackness of a few hours earlier had been only a passing cloud, he thought. Just as Maass was about to open the door, Zweig suddenly exclaimed, "Listen, my friend. You can have my typewriter. I don't need it anymore."

Maass was floored. "You don't need it anymore?"

"I want to buy a new one for Lotte," Stefan explained. "We don't want to drag this one with us."

It struck Maass as a breach of some deep writerly superstition: you don't leave behind a machine that produced such a wealth of manuscripts, an instrument that helped gain an author so much success and fame.

Maass protested.

"Just take it," Zweig said. "It's still working pretty well. Take it as a present for visiting me."

Filled with foreboding, Maass took the Remington that had typed *The World of Yesterday* from Zweig's hands.

O n the fourteenth, the day before their departure, they drove to Croton with René Fülöp-Miller to visit Eva. They tortured her, Lotte joked, by bringing a great mound of parcels to Mrs. Schaeffer's—birthday gifts and birthday letters and books from the family in England. Then, after so embarrassing her, though it was already well past bedtime, they whisked her off on a nighttime jaunt to Ossining "to say goodbye to Mrs. Zweig No. 1," and on from there to one of the popular drugstores—perhaps Kipp's, the most classical-looking of all the buildings on Main Street, with its white Ionic columns rising from the second story, or Ankerson's with its long soda fountain. "A coca-cola and ice cream at 9:30 p.m.! So I hope she will always remember that there is something nice in our leaving and not mind too much," Lotte wrote wishfully.

"We regretted so much to leave her behind," Stefan added after they got back to the city. But to force her to start again in a new language in Brazil would have been too much—"especially as we have the impression that she feels perfectly right and is very happy there. Mr. Schaeffer is absolutely reliable and the new house is just a dream." All he wanted for himself, he declared, was "to forget everything I had and everything I was formerly and to try again to write new books for the old and forgotten ones."

The fifteenth of August, the day their ship was embarking, dawned rainy and windy. "Our hearts are not light at all, we do not know when we will return," Stefan wrote in a letter. "Perhaps Brazil will help us with her beauty—but I doubt more and more if I ever shall see Bath again." At times they had thought to go back to England, he repeated, but he felt he would never again have a real house. If they had immigrated to America like the others, they might have begun a new life, "but I was bound by my nationality which has and will give us still many problems." His only wish, he declared once more, was that Manfred and Hanna should see their daughter, "grown up and more sympathetic than ever . . . I know there are millions and millions like us, but everyone feels his own life."

He observed that Lotte was at least better physically, and perhaps in Brazil they would have a calmer life—just to be through with their nomadic existence! "I would like to live in a Negro hut in Brazil if I should know I could stay there," he declared. At least, he repeated, "the younger generation will still have the reward for these enormous efforts—for me it is too late and I could no more enjoy the victory. But you and your child will see a better world!"

Lotte overflowed with non sequiturs in the last letter she wrote before leaving their hotel, asking for news of all the people who'd once composed her family's world, reporting that Mrs. Schaeffer was still deciding how best to celebrate Eva's birthday, offering opinions on *Fantasia*, which they'd recently seen. "Well, this is all for today and the last letter from USA, at least for a while," she added carefully. "It was a difficult decision to take and I had to think so hard as never in my life. I never missed you as much—though I always miss you—than in these weeks."

Mrs. Schaeffer took Eva down on the train from Croton late at night to the boat to see them off. The couple held her. And then they were gone. New York City slipped behind them. Night swallowed that long, glittering black island, like a pebble streaked with mica flung back without thinking, and the sea spread wide. On the boat, Lotte wrote her family that it had been "a thrilling way" for Eva to begin the day; Stefan repeated his conviction that, hard though it had been to leave her behind, Eva "is better there with her 'auntie' than with us who do not know where to we go."

Eva turned back to Mrs. Schaeffer, who loved her and whom she loved, Lotte had promised her parents, and to the dream house in which Mr. Schaeffer, the absolutely reliable philosophical poet, who had a special liking for Eva, also resided. Eva turned back, and the train shuddered back up the rails, alongside the black Hudson. When the train rolled into Croton Station, it was long after midnight. Two in the morning by the time they returned to Amity Hall. August sixteenth, Eva's birthday.

Chapter Ten

GARDENS IN WARTIME

At the end of one summer, I had my own moment of anagnorisis, that uncanny recognition Stefan Zweig experienced when he discovered the real Paris after knowing the
city only through books. For me, it happened in an English garden
behind a Georgian house set on a hill above Hampstead Heath,
when I found myself seated next to Eva Altmann, the niece of
Lotte Zweig—now an eighty-three-year-old woman, but with the
same bobbed hair, pursed lips, and thoughtful expression I'd come
to know from photographs in books.

The gnawing problem of Eva preoccupied Stefan, and especially Lotte, in the years of their exile. What could be done
to secure a girl's future by two people who loved her deeply but
who had no security themselves, and no sense of their own future? Changing plans for Eva recur throughout their letters at this
period—expressing the hope that this question, at least, might be

resolved, even if no others could be. And now here she was, the girl whose habits and tastes I had learned about—her fondness for big Alsatian dogs, her love of reading and of potato salad—sitting beside me, giving her account of the good homes and the rigorous education the Zweigs had striven so hard to arrange for her. "Albrecht Schaeffer? Oh, he was as cold as cold can be," she remarked. "He made me read Goethe. It meant nothing to me."

Eva and I sat on an extraordinary expanse of sweeping lawn, bordered with careful plantings of bright flowers and shrubs. Now, sipping tea as the late-summer English afternoon mellowed toward dusk, it was all rather like a scene from Henry James—perhaps the start of *Portrait of a Lady*, when the Touchetts and Lord Warburton sit together, talking fatefully in the garden before the arrival of their own young transplant from the other side of the ocean. Only whereas at the property James described, "privacy reigned supreme," Eva's home has always been divided with another European refugee family. "We called it 'the capitalist kibbutz,'" she said. Her own half is shared now with students from all over the world, this summer a gifted young musician from eastern Europe, whom we could hear practicing faintly in the background as we spoke.

The rooms of the house, I discovered when she showed me around them, are stark and momentous, sparsely decorated with treasures from Zweig's collection, such as a letter by Goethe, framed with the white quill Goethe used to compose it. Later I saw the large study that contains Eva's library of Zweig's books, stored in Zweig's own tall, deep shelves of caramel-colored wood. Row after row of volumes in language after language, along with special editions, such as a copy of his treatise on Handel's *Resurrection*, printed entirely on silk in the year of the Anschluss. And this was not even including his thousands of letters, boxes of which were stored elsewhere in the house. Gazing at the stupendous physical scale of his oeuvre, I thought of Viertel's description of Zweig's literary output—both his own books and translations—as a "tremendous gardening activity . . . dedicated to the park we call Europe." His labors may have been so intense, Viertel hypothesized, because Zweig was driven by "a presentiment, a more or less conscious purpose to conserve, to garner, to save the essentials . . . from perishing in the abyss."

Eva and I came to the subject of Amity Hall after I pressed her for recollections of the Zweigs' time in America. Five years earlier, when I was embarking on my study of Stefan Zweig, we'd had a brief correspondence, in which Eva offered a few tantalizing glimpses of Stefan and Lotte from the year she lived with them in Bath, as well as later in New York and Ossining. Eva described Lotte's temperament as being very like that of her own father, Lotte's brother: calm and quiet, but "with a very dry and active sense of humor." Tall and quietly elegant in Eva's recollection, Lotte was "always courteous, but quite determined and very efficient, totally loyal and loving . . . It's probably true that, again like my father, she avoided conflict wherever possible, but she was certainly able to assert herself, albeit unobtrusively." Eva also made clear that characterizations of Lotte as an invalid distorted her nature. "I don't remember her ever spending a day in bed, or otherwise behaving as though she was ill, even in America when she was clearly having problems with the medication she was on," Eva said. "Lotte was a strong person with a sickness, and occasionally the sickness flared up but most of the time it wasn't perceptible."

As for Stefan, Eva observed that his views on bringing up children were fairly conservative, and that he'd sent her "many critical letters chiding me of my failure to write home to them regularly." When she and a cousin had lived with the Zweigs, they'd been expected to devote themselves to their studies and keep extremely quiet whenever Stefan was working. But he had also enjoyed spoiling them, Eva wrote. She would never forget the night he brought her to a "glorious opera event," a gala production of *Don Giovanni* at Covent Garden—evening dresses and sparkling tiaras—when she was ten. And he regularly took her to have chocolate drinks in the best café in Bath after sundown, a practice frowned upon there for children. In New York also, Eva remembered visits with Stefan and Lotte to delightful restaurants and other places. "For me he was a very lovable, if demanding, person," Eva concluded.

Now that we were actually together, I wanted to form a clearer picture of what life had been like inside number 7 Ramapo Road, where Eva had spent many hours. Perhaps this interior, as well, had been imbued with some of that gracious aura the couple seemed to carry with them everywhere even so late in the story—at least in the eyes of a young girl who adored them.

I asked Eva what she remembered of that last home where she'd known them.

Eva's gaze drifted away to the garden. "It was grim."

"And so there was—" I stumbled. "In terms of details, something that redeemed the space—that . . ."

She shook her head. "No. There was nothing attractive about it. It wasn't nice."

"And Manhattan?"

"He hated New York. But in Ossining, he did have friends around."

I knew that his closest friends in the area had been René Fülöp-Miller and Erika Renon, a striking couple who'd rented a little house in the woods near Croton-on-Hudson. Fülöp-Miller was one of those young writers whom Zweig had helped with his youthful poetic production decades earlier in Vienna's old Café Pucher. But during that summer of 1941, Fülöp-Miller was working, in his words, "on a comprehensive treatise about death." Fülöp-Miller described how he and Stefan spent many nights together while the latter was in Ossining, "in eager discussion about all the questions connected with the 'last things.'" Later, Fülöp-Miller recalled how persistently Zweig would torque their conversation back to the topic of "maximum dosages of lethal drugs and to the psychology of the 'last hour.'"

Even such friends as Zweig did have in Ossining seem to have been confounded by his morbidity. Friderike's endless criticisms certainly didn't help Stefan's mood. Perhaps it was the urge to find some bright spot in this interlude that made me turn the conversation to Amity Hall. At least the Zweigs had the comfort—as innumerable letters testify—of knowing that in the distinguished man of German letters Albrecht and his loving, responsible wife, Olga, they'd found the ideal refuge for the Altmanns' daughter.

I was thus completely taken aback to hear Eva characterize him as so unsympathetic. And while Olga was not this icy, Eva said, the woman had yet never been able to make her feel at home. I asked Eva whether she knew what had become of the pair. She shook her head. "Some time not long after I left, Mrs. Schaeffer broke her arm," Eva said. "And there were complications. Children started leaving. Things started falling apart."

If things had not panned out with the Schaeffers, I didn't hold out much hope that Eva harbored fond memories of her first experience in the United States, living with the Salmons, the affluent Westchester couple who'd come into the role of foster parents through their relations with Zweig's brother and his wife.

Within a few days of Eva's arrival in America in September 1940, while Stefan and Lotte were on their first Brazilian expedition, Mr. Salmon wrote the Zweigs to report that he and Eva were "already very great friends." Lotte traveled out to New Rochelle to visit as soon as she got back to New York in January, and painted her brother and sister-in-law a detailed portrait of Eva's spacious new home in a pastoral corner of New Rochelle. Tastefully furnished, Eva's room, with its writing table and terrace, was everything one could wish for. The house itself was set in a woods full of children who were eager to play with Eva, Lotte wrote, and overlooked a little lake on which she would soon begin learning to ice skate. The first reports from New Rochelle make it sound as if Eva has been translated from Blitz-torn London into a Currier & Ives print.

How hard it must have been for Lotte, only days after reporting that Eva was so idyllically settled, to have to write to Hanna and Manfred again to explain that she'd had a long talk with Mrs. Salmon and they'd agreed it would be better for everyone if Lotte and Stefan found another home for Eva. "It's just that they are not suited to each other," Lotte confessed. Mr. Salmon "apparently tried very hard in the beginning to gain her confidence, did not succeed, and when he later tried teasing, apparently this did not turn out too well, either." It was not a matter of there having been "incidents" or "quarrels," but "only the difference of milieu—he likes football and fun—which makes them not absolutely suited to each other," Lotte added in a note of superlative understatement. Mrs. Salmon herself was more succinct. In words that capture the dismay experienced by many Americans who sought to embrace the refugees, she declared, "We thought of taking in a child, but she is just a guest."

"I cannot become an American by pressing the switch of gratitude, even though I be sincerely grateful," Hans Natonek wrote of the pressures he experienced as a new émigré. "A Collie dog may express a very ecstasy of thankfulness for the bone left over from my soup, but he cannot change himself into a Spitz by force of simple gratitude." Assimilation, Natonek observed, "is not self-eradication."

"And—the Salmons?" I finally asked. "Oh, they were *clueless!*"
Eva said, with a trace of a smile. "But I was difficult. I was impossible. It was an impossible situation. They tried. They got me very
nice gifts. I've thought back, and I've felt badly. I wasn't going to be
happy with anyone."

That of course made sense. The separation from family was
traumatic for most evacuated British children, even inside England.
To be across the ocean, knowing the danger to which her parents
were exposed, must have been unbearable. Yet as we continued to
speak, it also emerged that not long after the Zweigs left for Brazil,
Eva left the Schaeffers and moved in with a couple at Columbia
University who'd been friends of her parents. "And then I was fine,"
she shrugged. "It was almost like being at home . . . I've talked to
other people who came over then, some of whose experiences were
very mild, and some of whose, like mine, were miserable."

As Eva reminisced it became clear that the right kind of help
from people able not just to be kind but to empathize with what
the refugees were going through—to try to understand who they
were now in relation to the identity they'd possessed before going
into exile—could transform the experience. The fate of the exiles
was not only a matter of their own personal temperament or material fortune. When Eva was still living with the Salmons, Lotte
had written to Manfred and Hanna reassuring them about not
having received much communication from Eva's foster parents.
"If they don't write often, it does not mean anything," Lotte wrote.
"They are very American, kind, gay and without any imagination
beyond their own scope."

————

Our conversation on the lawn continued for some time. We spoke of Stefan's surprising last-minute donation of a large part of his library to the Hebrew University in Jerusalem. And we talked about Bath, where I'd been staying before coming to London, and from which Stefan at last departed Europe for good for a jumble of reasons that never quite hold together. But as we spoke I found that the questions I'd come with—about physical details of different scenes, about specific moments in her interactions with the Zweigs—seemed awkward, or somehow beside the point.

The point, I later realized, was Eva's presence: here, at this place, and this time, in the work that she did. For the profession and life Eva chose to cultivate have made substantial contributions to this world. She was among the first women admitted to the London Hospital Medical College. She became a professor of epidemiology and did important research into Down syndrome and birthrate trends, while also performing active public health work in underprivileged neighborhoods of London. One of her sons is a violinist with the London Symphony Orchestra. Her second son works with Amnesty International. The home she has created emanates gravitas of purpose—a rigorous engagement with culture and public service. Eva's life, indeed, seems to realize Stefan and Lotte's vision of *Bildung*. However much the values and knowledge the couple imparted to her during the years of their shared exile directly contributed to that process, it came to fruition. The Zweigs were a part of Eva's "higher education" and would have seen its fulfillment in her destiny.

At a certain point in our conversation, Eva asked about the genesis of my interest in Stefan, Lotte, and the larger subject of exile. I spoke a little of my own family's flight from Austria to Switzerland and on to Italy, and of my father's first experiences in the United States. "There are so many stories," Eva said. "But what gets me is there are so many exiles *now*. You see, I worked in the East End of London for a long time. And the way that neighborhood has just seen wave after wave . . . First the Huguenots. Then the Irish. Then the Jews. And now the Bangladeshi."

I mumbled something about the interesting aspect of the tide of exiles to which Zweig belonged being in part the incredible preponderance of intellectuals. "There was something unique—"

Eva cut me off. "What about the Huguenots?" She shrugged. "They were quite intellectual, weren't they?"

Again Eva resisted—indeed refused—the imputation of singularity to her own experience, or to that of Stefan and Lotte. It had all happened again and again. And it is happening right now, she insisted. The present broke to the surface of our conversation. And wouldn't stay under, like a body that keeps bobbing back up above the dark waves.

Before I visited Eva Altmann I had walked through another English garden, in the elegant city of Bath—smaller, yet no less peaceful. It was terraced, as the garden had been in Salzburg, opening onto hilly views in which fine steeples and chimneys projected from folds of trees. It was no less beautiful, if not so mythic—more string quartet, less operatic—than the vistas of Alpine crags visible from the Kapuzinerberg.

The garden was lovely and the Liddells, the couple who now lived in Rosemount, the house to which it was attached, enthused over its different levels, with their varied distribution of sun and shade, making for different horticultural worlds. It was evident how much time the family spent in that garden, working and thinking about the little pastoral scene it composed. Nicola Liddell explained that there would have been many fewer buildings surrounding it in Zweig's time. Many of the trees, also, wouldn't have yet grown around the property. "None of those awful houses would have been there," she said. The views would have been far more expansive. Though one could walk to the center of Bath in twenty minutes, Rosemount in the 1930s would have felt "very rural, very agricultural."

Zweig spent many hours in this garden as well. There he formed an attachment to its caretaker, Edward Leopold Miller, an elderly man and an institution of sorts—perhaps the last of Bath's old-fashioned, vocational gardeners in the fullest sense of the term. He'd been head gardener at nearby Lyncombe Hall for fifty years before going to work at Rosemount, having begun to train on the former land as a boy. His philosophical approach to horticulture had earned him a reputation as a sage by the time he came to Rosemount. Zweig found his presence soothing, and the two men would sit on the garden bench while Miller alternated between puffing silently on his pipe and delivering his ruminations on the state of the world. Miller's devotion to his labor—the fact that the gardener still rose before dawn each day in summer to begin his long toil weeding the rows of his plantings—took on an exemplary character for Zweig. He told others that the fruits of Miller's work, his peaches and apples, his flowers and vegetables, were nonpareil—a testament to the man's purity of character, touched by some elusive higher grace.

For a time, under Miller's tutelage, Zweig seriously applied himself to learning the art of gardening. And these labors at

Rosemount, combined with his long meditation on English character, culminated in a kind of hymn to horticulture, which he
wrote at the end of his time in Bath. In *Gardens in Wartime*, Zweig
wrote of how fascinated he'd been by the British reaction to the
start of war. He recalled how in Vienna in 1914, the declaration
of war had unleashed a kind of ecstasy. "Vast hordes streamed
from houses and businesses into the streets to form enthusiastic
columns; suddenly flags appeared, no one knew where from; there
was music, people sang in chorus, cheered and shouted with joy,

no one knew why," he wrote. People felt the need to speak of what created a communal excitement, he said. They "simply telephoned each other incessantly house by house, to ease their inner tension through words; the restaurants and Viennese coffeehouses were packed for weeks on end late into the night with people bent on discussion, exultant, nervous types who chattered on and on, each one a strategist, an economist, a prophet."

But when, living in England, Zweig learned that war had been declared again, he stepped outside the office where he'd heard the news, only to discover everything so calm that at first he didn't think anyone else knew yet what had happened. "All was peaceful, the people were not walking at a quickened pace or in an excited manner." Then came "the flickering white of the newspapers, blowing about . . . People bought them, read them and continued on their way," Zweig marveled. "No high-spirited groups, even in the shops, no anxious gatherings. And so it was week after week, each fulfilling his function placidly, without agitation, silently and replete with calm resolve." How did the English manage to sustain their equanimity day after day? Zweig became obsessed with solving the riddle.

Throughout his adult life, Zweig idealized environments that inspired people to cast aside prejudices of race and class to mingle uninhibitedly with their fellow human beings. Thus he rhapsodized over the eroticized social freedom of Paris in the early twentieth century—and the eroticized political freedom he discerned in Brazil in the 1930s. In Great Britain, as well, he discovered a version of his democratic idyll. "Millions of English people, the allegedly so unromantic English, are, at weekends or after work, found labouring in their garden or allotment: evenings or mornings, the worker, the clerk, the minister, the businessman, the priest reach for their tools, put spade to earth, prune the shrubs or take care of their flowers," he wrote. "In this *gardening*, this daily activity that is not sport, nor work, nor a game, but where all those activities gradually coalesce, the English earn their solidarity, social differences disappear, the distance between rich and poor is abolished." This practice, Zweig opined, by "detaching people from all outside events," was the source of the "marvellous calm the English people enjoy." The rewards of this sublimated passion were evident in the country's resilience. In place of the pleasures supplied by less restrained forms of leisure, the modest gardens of the English offered their caretakers a palliative insulation "from nervous excitement, from uncertainty and the drone of chatter." And the stoicism the country's gardeners thereby acquired taught the world "the grand spectacle of moral constancy, a spectacle almost as great as that of nature itself."

How hard Zweig strove to take this lesson to heart! Zweig wanted to love England. He felt so strongly that after all he'd experienced in febrile Central Europe he *should* love England. He knew that the sober calm and relative immunity from political fanaticism he'd sought for so long existed there. There were moments, certainly, when he *did* love the country. It's not by chance that his autobiography ends with his sojourn in England. The possibility England presented of being, as the British said, "*of* Europe, but not *in* Europe," cast itself through the web of his exile. I spoke with Eva about the relief Zweig found in England's sobriety and rationalism, just as Freud had done. "Yes," she laughed. "England. *Boring and safe.*" And in saying this she also indicated another feature of the place that might have resonated with him: British humor—the way that nothing was taken too seriously, even when it was serious. "In Berlin, things are serious, but not desperate. In Vienna, things are desperate, but not serious," people used to say.

In his memoir Zweig wrote of how he chose to live in Bath "because that city, where much of England's glorious literature, above all the works of Fielding, was written, soothes the eye more reliably than any other city in England, giving the illusion of reflecting another and more peaceful age, the eighteenth century." Bath allowed Zweig to dream that he'd traveled back in time to a moment when civilization and nature struck a rare balance.

His vision of the dissolution of class boundaries occurring around the cultivation of British soil was, of course, romanticized. Nicola Liddell, who grew up in Bath, observed that the kind of intimacy Zweig formed with his gardener would have been viewed as peculiar and inappropriate by the upper crust of Bath society. But Zweig himself, she noted, would not have been able to penetrate that realm. Indeed, she speculated that Zweig might have left Bath on account of its "parochial, cliquey" side. Bath, she said, is full of people who couldn't quite move at the highest levels of London society, and who came to Bath, where they could afford to live on the town's famous crescents, in order "to be somebody." Zweig might have come to Bath expecting to find his niche as a highly regarded author in a small, cultured city only to fall victim to its snobbery—what Cyril Connolly called "the true *maladie anglaise*."

When I mentioned these observations to Eva, she recalled the moment when Stefan and Lotte were making inquiries among some of Bath's better class of citizens about which school they ought to send her to. "'Well, the best school in Bath is such and such,' they said. 'You, of course, will send Eva to the other school.'

But they didn't," Eva smiled. "They enrolled me in the best one." However, the story seemed more a source of amusement than of rancor. And Eva went on to say, "Zweig used to laugh about 'the Bathonians.'" I suspect that Zweig couldn't take the pretentions of Bath society seriously enough to be much bothered by them. For all that he might have gone weak-kneed before the artistic luminaries of the age, he never expressed any interest in society as such.

Besides, away from the crescents, in the less fashionable vicinity of Lyncombe Hill, where Rosemount was located, Zweig's arrival was generally greeted with friendly curiosity. Even in the late 1960s, there were still a number of people in the area who recalled the arrival of the Zweigs—"two rather oddly assorted individuals," about whom people whispered, "Very famous you know . . . the Austrian author—a refugee—probably Jewish . . . Wonder why he's come to live here . . . And the girl. Very quiet. Looks ill." After which, in the words of a biographer who interviewed locals at this time, "with typical British summing up of a barely guessed-at situation: 'Ah well . . . they seem a very nice couple. Hope they'll be happy here.'"

Zweig liked nothing better than walking through the English countryside, for which he adopted the distinctive outfit of a brown jacket, plus fours, and a beret. Through these rambles, he became a familiar figure along Greenway Lane, the old Somerset & Dorset railway line, and Entry Hill. He always wore a preoccupied expression, neighbors recalled, but when they met and fell into conversation with Zweig, he struck locals as sympathetic: "An unusually kind and understanding man," said one; "remarkably patient and so interested in everything around," recalled another.

So what, finally, drove Zweig away from the serene house he'd bought in this architecturally exquisite town in a democratic, gardening nation where he'd consecrated his second marriage to a woman he loved and whose loving family was settled there? It's true he'd been thrown into a paroxysm of bitterness on being designated an enemy alien in September 1939, but though the Home Office had been insultingly slow to annul this classification, in March 1940 he'd actually been granted his certificate of naturalization. Zweig was now a British citizen—and less than six months later he cast himself back into the whirlwind.

After we'd wandered through the garden, the Liddells showed me the interior of the house, which might have been custom-built to accommodate Zweig's habit of restless pacing. Rosemount's intricate plan of circulation includes two doors in every room, so that you can circle all through the house without once doubling back on your steps. They also showed me the cool stone cellar, arranged to facilitate storage in ways that made the Liddells wonder whether Zweig had kept his wine there. I mentioned my trip down to the cellar at Rosemount to Eva, asking her about this hypothesis—bottled memories of the good life, perhaps.

"Well, I don't know about wine, but there was soap," she chuckled. "There were tins and tins of food and legs of lamb and—I just remember all the soap! You see, Zweig was a pessimist. Essentially. And he was absolutely right about this."

Eva's family actually lived off Zweig's stockpiled provisions as the war dragged on and rationing grew more acute. The household help at Rosemount recalled the way that over time Zweig's study became more and more filled with books and other literary material, while underground, in a process that paralleled the multiplication of manuscripts above, the cellar was crammed with more and more food—the entire house becoming simultaneously "a museum and storehouse for canned goods." Some of the laborers whose work took them downstairs said that Zweig himself had given two explanations for this hoarding. Either, Zweig said, it would enable him to withstand a lengthy siege when the Nazis landed on British soil, or, he sometimes remarked, the stock could be used for a last-ditch attempt to barter his way to freedom.

In that haunting image of a cellar becoming more and more packed with tins of food and dry goods, while the upper floor piled higher and higher with pages of imaginative writing, perhaps we come closer to the solution of the mystery as to why Zweig could not remain in England.

The Bathonians who met Zweig on his walks through the rolling hills and recalled his quiet, genial manner remembered something else about his presence as well. Whenever the conversation turned to the events in the news, Zweig would invariably ask, "Do you honestly believe that the Nazis will not come here?" To which the locals would inevitably respond, with classic British sangfroid, that a Nazi invasion of England was impossible. Whereupon Zweig would shrug and stare at his interlocutor with an expression of compassion. "Nothing can stop them now," he would say. "Nothing . . . *I know.*"

Edward Miller's son, Frederick, also worked in the garden at Rosemount and had his own poignant memories of Zweig's time in the house. Occasionally, Frederick recalled, Zweig became very depressed, and when this happened he would call over both father and son, asking them to sit down, one on either side of him on the garden bench, looking out over the green lawn toward the fields beyond.

"Do you think they'll ever get here?" Zweig would ask the two Millers of the prospects for a Nazi landing.

"They will never get here as long as you live," Edward Miller would answer. "You're all right here, you stick here."

"Oh, I must go," he said. "I must go. I must get out of here."

It's an image that conjures a tearful child trying to be soothed after a nightmare, unable to believe that what he sees in his mind's eye is only a dream.

Zweig's feared Nazi invasion did not materialize, and yet in April 1942, in reprisal for the RAF bombing of Lübeck, hundreds of high-explosive bombs and incendiary devices were dropped over Bath. Some 900 buildings were completely leveled and another 12,500 were damaged, while more than 400 people, many of them women and children, lost their lives.

Of all the deliberate shadings to the actual course of his life Zweig gives the story told in *The World of Yesterday*, none is more striking than the moment near the book's final page when he cites the line from Shakespeare that forms the book's epigraph. The scene is the summer of 1939—immediately before the declaration of war everyone knows is imminent. As the month of July 1914 had been in Austria, the weather is impossibly glorious. "Once again the soft, silken blue sky was like God's blessing over us, once again warm sunlight shone on the woods and meadows, which were full of a wonderful wealth of flowers." Nature anticipates history's haunting tendency to repeat. By every reasonable calculation,

Zweig writes, he ought to have been packing up his books and manuscripts as rapidly as possible to depart. For England would soon be at war, whereupon, he knew, his freedom would be dramatically circumscribed. But something inside him resisted the voice of reason that would enable him to save himself. "It was half defiance—I was not going to take to flight again and again, since Fate looked like following me everywhere—and half just weariness. 'We'll meet the time as it meets us,' I said to myself, quoting Shakespeare." In this line from *Cymbeline*, the king of Britain is expecting the imminent invasion of the Romans. Defiant, he resolves to stay put come what may. Though Zweig found this sentiment so powerful that he set it at the head of his autobiography, it expresses the precise opposite of Zweig's actual life course, which, ever more through his exile, might be better encapsulated as "Whatever else, let's not meet the time as it meets us." Zweig kept leaving and leaving before the time, until he'd left time behind.

In the diary he kept during the summer of 1939, in which he contrasts the unruffled scenes in Bath after Hitler invaded Poland with the Austrian mood in 1914, Zweig recalls the sight of young men volunteering to fight in Vienna twenty-five years earlier: "With flowers like the thoughtless victims in the antic [antique] temples they went along," Zweig writes. But in his journal, unlike in his autobiography, Zweig acknowledges that he himself was among those intoxicated Viennese marching off to the slaughter, so eager to enlist that he could not "support the idea, to be behind for one day." And in these private notes, along with registering the astounding British calm, Zweig also expresses uncertainty as to whether this feature of their character is quite so admirable as he later makes it out to be for the purpose of his essay on gardens.

Zweig's diary bluntly asks—and leaves unanswered—the question of whether English determination is a matter of "moral training," or simply "lack of imagination."

After war is declared, Zweig at first seems just selfishly impressed by the way he is able to osmotically absorb the prevailing British equanimity—amazing himself by his own ability to sit still and "listen at the radio so concentrated and quiet." But once this initial tranquilizer effect of the general atmosphere begins to wear off, uncertainty about how the English manage to preserve their composure increasingly disturbs him. Indeed, even after Hitler had unleashed the full power of Germany's army, Zweig's profound opposition to war under any circumstances left him full of ambivalence about England's decision to honor its treaty obligations and enter the battle. Haunted by a tangle of memories and visions of the future, he states in his memoir that he actually began to hallucinate. Watching people go about their business in Bath's well-stocked, tidy shops, Zweig experienced an uncanny stutter in time. He abruptly saw through the shops in front of him to a scene from 1918, "stores cleared-out and empty, seemingly staring at one with wide-open eyes. As in a waking dream I saw the long queues of careworn women before the food shops, the mothers in mourning, the wounded, the cripples, the whole nightmare of another day returned spectrally in the shining noonday light."

It's telling that of all English characters, the one Zweig felt most captivated by was Shakespeare's unstable, wildly overreaching King John, as depicted by William Blake. Zweig venerated Blake himself as "one of those magic natures who, without planning their own way in advance, are borne on angel's wings by visions through all the wilderness of fantasy." This is hardly the classic English temperament

he'd once praised for its humble pleasures of "cats, football and whiskey." Zweig purchased Blake's portrait of King John early in his career as a collector and kept it with him as jealously as Freud clutched to the little statuette of Athena that he brought with him into exile in London. "From the ruins of my library and my pictures, this one leaf has accompanied me for more than thirty years; and how often the magic flashing glance of this mad king has looked down from the wall at me," Zweig wrote in his autobiography. "The genius of England, which I tried in vain to recognize in streets and cities, was suddenly revealed to me in Blake's truly astral figure."

If Zweig discovered the genius of England only in Blake's drawing of a deranged character from Shakespeare, this suggests just
how remote his sensibility was from the behavior he actually encountered in the country. The English nation's placid acceptance
of the call to war seemed the very opposite of "astral"—just as
Zweig's own extreme pacifism revealed his febrile, visionary overi-
dentification with disaster. "People talk so lightly about bombard-
ments, but when I read about houses collapsing, I myself collapse
with them," Zweig announced to Franz Werfel in one of his final
letters. As Thomas Mann would later remark to Friderike, Zweig
"was a man of radical, unconditional pacifist disposition and convictions. In this war . . . a war which is being waged against the
most infernal and unpacific powers that have ever attempted to
shape human nature in their own image—in this war he never saw
anything but just another war, a blood-stained misfortune and the
negation of his whole nature." He'd even praised France for choos-
ing not to fight and so "saving Paris," Mann bitterly charged. Was
this attitude further evidence of Zweig's moral weakness, or did it
indicate a clairvoyant lucidity, born of his profound pessimism,
which recognized that France stood no chance against Hitler's
armies and would simply be annihilated if it attempted open resistance? France—the realm of Zweig's most free-spirited, erotically
sublime European experiences!

There's no question but that memories of the euphoria he'd
once known on the continent grew more vivid as the real, torpid
nature of his exile in England sank in. And Zweig's resolve to stay
put in the spirit of Cymbeline finally broke down not just out
of fear of Nazi invasion but also from angst over the prospect
of being buried alive in the British countryside. The devotion to

gardening might have been relaxing, as Zweig wrote, but where amid these gentle pastures filled with English people on their knees putting "spade to earth" could a Viennese Jew grab some stimulation? He griped to Rolland that all the English cared about was "sport and society news," disclosing his desire to leave the country even the previous summer, in 1938. The only thing that kept him there, Zweig said, was that he couldn't figure out where to go, "and so I stay with a feeling of ingratitude, because I feel more isolated here than anywhere else in the world." As Jules Romains observed, Zweig found the country's insularity oppressive and could not adjust to the way that English cities "lacked all outward appearance of happiness." Just two days after the British declaration of war, Zweig noted in his diary, "The evenings are terribly sad now. The streets dark and empty, one must carefully avoid the slightest light-opening in a window and we are still in the beginning of September, where darkness starts but at 8 o'clock. How will this become if darkness starts at five o'clock, at four o'clock! And no theatres, no cinemas, nothing, nothing, nothing." Suddenly Zweig plunges into nostalgia for the very same Viennese spirit of delusional revelry he'd cast in such a negative light relative to British sobriety less than a week before. "If one remembers Vienna in 1914, even 1918 with the Opera, with balls and pleasures, with the security of life and sleep," Zweig exclaims.

The security of life and sleep! Much as he sometimes pretended otherwise, *life*—a vibrant, art-rich, sensual being—was ultimately as crucial to Zweig's sense of security as any degree of calm. So powerful was this strain in him that he invokes the dreariness of present-day English existence as proof that the war cannot long continue. "The life without joy, without diversity will become too awful to stand through," he asserts. "Darkness for month and month and month—I cannot imagine such an ordeal."

As the conflict persisted, despite his predictions, Zweig felt he had the answer to the question he'd asked on the first of September about what lay behind English composure. British social snootiness was one thing—ultimately risible in light of the cosmopolitan intellectual society Zweig had been at home in. The phlegmatic national spirit was another matter. In mid-October, he expressed horror at people's failure to understand how little time it would take for the power of destruction to impoverish the whole world: "Always the same default in mankind," he burst out, "a thorough lack of imagination!"

Two years later, recalling in his autobiography that morning when Britain declared war on Germany, he wrote of how he and Lotte "stood in silence in the room, which was suddenly deathly quiet, and avoided looking at each other. Carefree birdsong came in from outside . . . and the trees swayed in the golden light . . . Our ancient Mother Nature, as usual, knew nothing of her children's troubles."

As much as Zweig struggled to make the case that regular contact with nature replenished the nation's spirit—as much as he wanted to learn from the English ritual of gardening—it's clear that he also found something terrifying in Mother Nature's obliviousness to human anguish. Mother Nature too, he suggests, can display a criminally vast lack of imagination. For his trust in nature to be restored, Zweig would have to move beyond the humanly cultivated garden into the wilderness.

Chapter Eleven

THE ARCADIAN EXILE

After dark, Stefan and Lotte descended the fifty stairs that led from their house to the street, brushing the rain-swollen clusters of hydrangea blossoms that grew rampant over the property, and turned their steps toward the trees. Their voices were low, when they spoke at all. There was often nothing to say, nothing better to do than appreciate together the beauty enfolding them more completely the farther they walked. They always discovered new paths to follow. Cutting off from the principal roads of Petrópolis, they'd find an old trail that plunged them into the forest. Giant serrated fronds and mud-spattered leaves splayed before them. Vines hung everywhere, twisting and coiling. They'd walk and they'd walk, held by the quiet. Flowers lit tiny fires through the leaves. All at once, they'd cross a little stream. They'd come upon a little hut. Out of nowhere, they'd step from the trees onto a hillside that overlooked a storm of dark mountains. Everywhere they went, they moved "under myriads of stars," Stefan wrote. "It is Paradise," he repeated again and again. "*It is Canaan*," he said. And Lotte felt as one with him. There was no end to the delight of their night-walk discoveries—the way that in just a few minutes wandering from their home they could pass into the most picturesque tropical wilderness.

"We live together like turtle-doves," Stefan wrote her family in November, three months after arriving in Brazil, "and try to forget the world and I wish the whole world would forget us." Now at last the garden had swallowed them.

Stefan was grateful for Lotte's contentment with their retired life. Others would find their existence tedious and monotonous, but they loved their quiet walks and reading, he reported to everyone he still knew. What a joy it was to think that they would not see any trunks or suitcases for the next six or eight months, and instead just this wonderful landscape! "You cannot imagine how varied and full of stimulation life is here, and how just the primitive things of life here teach us how much of our usual claims to life is in reality superfluous," he wrote to Ben Huebsch. "I remember that Tolstoi said, that a man of sixty should retire into the wilderness and our solitude is a very beautiful one—I never have been in a more beautiful scenery than here in Brazil," Stefan informed Lotte's family.

Sometimes the pair would prolong their enchanted walks deep into the night. They paid no real heed to the direction of their steps. For however far they wandered through what Stefan called Brazil's "virginal atmosphere," into however distant a valley, they knew that eventually they would come upon some modest settlement served by buses that would carry them back to the center of

Petrópolis. Besides, they hardly cared. They both felt lighter than they had in ages. Lotte was "ready to climb all the mountains," she announced. Stefan felt "indifferent against all possible annoyances and worries," he declared. They could keep going and going.

The threads drawing them back grew fewer and fainter. "In such times," Stefan wrote in his notes on Montaigne, "the problems of life for man merge into a single problem: how can I remain free? How can I break loose from the snare. How free myself from fear." Perhaps they would keep walking through the woods, through the night, through this life, into freedom.

T*his* is what I wanted to show you." My companion, Maria Wolfring, a tall, elegant woman in a flowing suit of beige and gold, pulled to the edge of the road and stopped the car. We stepped outside, and Maria breathed in deeply. "*This* is the Petrópolis I remember from the 1940s."

Long emerald blades fringed the lane's broken cobblestones; fine weeds thrust through the cracks; voluminous canopies of leaves above us waved in a breeze. Birds sang everywhere. The air was fragrant. There were views off the side of the road into ragged hollows and toward higher mountains farther away. A few red-tiled roofs and white walls peeked through the dense foliage surrounding us. Everything felt overgrown, tranquil, and surrendered to nature's luxuriance.

Maria is in her seventies. She told me that when she'd recently remarked to a friend something about being a senior, he'd replied, "No, no—you're in *the dessert phase of life*." "Isn't that lovely?" She smiled. "The dessert phase of life!"

In Maria's case, the phrase seems apt. She'd driven me from Rio to Petrópolis, zipping up into the striking, lush mountains at a dauntless clip. ("Good—no traffic. Just the way I like it—*fast*," she remarked as we whirled up the corkscrew highway.) And for the past several hours we'd meandered through the town while she showed me the Petrópolis she remembered from her childhood.

The scale of Petrópolis is deceptive, since the hills dancing around its center each nestle their own small valleys cradling little clusters of development, remains of land grants Emperor Pedro II made to German farmers in the mid-nineteenth century in a push to encourage European immigration. Describing the entry into this town that the imperial family chose for their own summer residence, Zweig wrote of how, after turning and twisting higher and higher for about ninety minutes up from Rio, while the air became progressively cooler and fresher, one reached a plateau "with pleasant-looking houses flanking the street, and a canal passing through it, one drives into a small watering-place, a summer resort giving rather an old-fashioned impression with its red bridges and rather antiquated villas . . . one is reminded of a German provincial town." Arriving at the center of Petrópolis today, one receives much the same impression. Even in Zweig's time, the graceful layout of the town had been compromised by new development, and he wrote of how "the people and the houses seem a little cramped; the streets originally built for slow and heavy carriages are now alive with automobiles." And yet, he added, "the charm of the place will never be seriously endangered, because the landscape itself is lovely. The mountains have no sharp contours, but leave the town in gradual, undulating hills, while flowers blaze everywhere in this town of the gardens." And this, also, remains true. We drove by Petrópolis's somber gray cathedral and around the main canal past the emperor's unaffectedly handsome cinnamon-hued summer palace. From there we passed into a long, rather shabby commercial strip, then drifted off again to glide by a few impressive houses and several well-regarded old schools. But it was after we'd veered farther from the center, curving along a narrow, quiet road that climbed a steep hill, that Maria's eyes sparkled.

Maria and her family moved to Petrópolis from Rio not long after the Zweigs. There were deeper parallels also that made her story resonate. Her parents were from Germany, with a complex Jewish ancestry that turned her father from a citizen of the Reich working for the Brazilian branch of a German firm into a job-less exile over the course of the 1930s. The Rio Maria knew as a child—the same Zweig first encountered—was very undeveloped. "There were no ACs," she told me. "Summers were very smelly and very hot. Mosquitoes were everywhere—all sorts of swamp-type diseases. Meat and fish and whatever you needed were sold by men carrying bamboo poles with baskets on either end. You can imagine—wandering around all day in forty-degree heat, what that meat was like—all the flies!"

Eventually, to escape the heat and disease of the city, and be-cause it seemed there might be more opportunity in the mountains, where soft, good water nurtured a thriving textile industry, which had long been a major source of livelihood for Jewish immigrants to Brazil, the family moved up to Petrópolis. I asked Maria what came to mind first when she thought of the town in her youth, when its environment would have been essentially the same one Stefan and Lotte encountered.

"Foggy! Very damp! Very cold! Doors didn't really close. Win-dows didn't really shut. The houses were unheated. You'd go to bed and the beds would be damp. I *hated it!*" She smiled. "But I didn't know that at the time, because it was all I knew, and we children had such a good time."

Stefan Zweig's name never came up in the course of my American education. I discovered his work only years after I'd graduated, when I embarked on a writing project centered in Brazil. To orient myself, I yanked all the books on the country off the library's shelves. Among these volumes, one stood out for being engagingly conversational, fast-moving; jazzy, even, in the way it riffed between genres: from travelogue, to history, to philosophical meditation on the relationship between nature and civilization. The book was Zweig's *Brazil: Land of the Future*, published there just weeks after his arrival in August 1941.

The book is easy to criticize for its exoticisms and omissions. But it's filled also with such exuberant passion for the people and the country that the criticisms often seem to miss more than they reveal. Coming to *Brazil: Land of the Future* with no prior knowledge of Zweig, it would never have occurred to me to question Zweig's own view of the book as his "love-song" to the country. Whatever its errors, there is a poignancy to the generosity with which Zweig celebrates Brazil's success at realizing the humanist values his native Europe had so wretchedly betrayed. "One who has just escaped the crazy destructiveness of Europe first greets the total absence of any hatred in public and private life as something unbelievable, and then welcomes it with infinite relief," he wrote of Brazil. "The fearful tension that for a decade has been ruining our nerves hardly exists here . . . Instinctively one breathes more freely, feeling grateful for having escaped from the stuffy air of race and class hatred to this calmer and more humane atmosphere."

In the opening pages of the book, Zweig writes of how, on receiving his first invitation to Brazil in 1936, he didn't expect much from the visit. He held the typical "arrogant European" notion of the country. All South American republics were more or less identical, he'd thought: "They all had a hot and unhealthy climate, political unrest, and desperate financial conditions; they were badly governed, and semi-civilized and then only near the coastal cities." They had beautiful scenery and unexplored possibilities, "in short, a land for desperate immigrants and settlers, but never one from which to expect intellectual stimulation. Being neither a professional geographer, collector of butterflies, sportsman, nor businessman, I presumed that a visit of ten days would suffice. A week, ten days, then back again, I thought." When he at last arrived in Rio, Zweig wrote, "I received one of the most powerful impressions of my whole life. I was fascinated, and at the same time deeply moved. For what lay before me here was not merely one of the most magnificent landscapes in the world—a unique combination of sea and mountain, city and tropical scenery—but quite a new kind of civilization."

The appealing humility of this introduction, coupled with a spirit of wide-eyed discovery, carries through the book, which includes material from his first trip to Brazil in 1936 but was mostly written during and just after the visit he and Lotte made in 1940. When I began to understand how famous Zweig still was at the time, his self-censure before the spectacle of the young South American republic seemed more impressive.

The house on Rua Gonçalves Dias, Petrópolis, where Zweig
lived has only recently opened up as a small museum com-
memorating stories of exiles who made their way to Brazil between
1933 and 1945. Multimedia displays blare and flash in the tiny space,
which is otherwise stripped and sanitized, save for a couple of
small display cases. It couldn't be less evocative of what the bungalow was when Zweig and Lotte called it home. My immediate
reaction on going inside was frankly one of horror. Couldn't they
have left *anything* as it might once have been? I walked out onto the
home's large balcony. At the base of the house a giant black-and-
white mosaic chessboard has been installed—a kitschy testimony,
it seems, to Zweig's final novella, *The Royal Game*, which centers
on a chess contest. At least one could stare off above the plumes
of palm fronds and brown-red roofs into the dips and swoops of
deep green hills, with higher mountain ranges on the horizon. I
prolonged my stay on the balcony, concentrating on the verdant
panorama, listening to the wind and birds.

But when I went back inside, Maria was taking photographs
of the long roster of names of exiles inscribed on the back wall of
the house. She later told me how powerful it had been for her to
find the names of several relatives who'd had to begin life anew as
refugees, among them an uncle who'd been a distinguished higher
court judge in Germany and who in old age had to start over in
Brazil selling tins of insecticide door to door. Moreover, a question she asked an attendant revealed that the giant chess mosaic
out front would soon begin to be used to teach young people from

the local public schools how to play chess. Zweig wrote fondly of the beautiful children in Petrópolis. He might well have been touched by the thought that his house would become a place where they could study the game that meant so much to him. Certainly the idea of freezing his last residence as a shrine-like mausoleum would have appalled him, much as I might have liked to see and hear something of what he'd experienced there. I came, on reflection, to feel that my judgment had been over-hasty. There wasn't space in the little house for a time machine.

Zweig's discovery of Brazil brings to mind the classic dream in which a person suddenly finds that their home contains an extra room they never knew about. Even as he first sailed into Rio's harbor, in 1936, this nocturnal fantasy seemed to be coming true. In his diary, Zweig described the experience of gliding into the harbor in morning mists, with the city draped about splendid bays, "forever beginning afresh, repeatedly interrupted by the foothills, which reach down like the fingers of a hand to hold it all together. It's the most beautiful sight imaginable." Perfumed breezes blew from the land, interlacing with ocean smells. All in all a truly "warm southern welcome, whereas New York greets you no less grandly with its stone icebergs and its triumphant clamour. New York calls out, Rio awaits; one is masculine, the other feminine, and there is something about these undulating lines that puts you in mind of a woman rising up from the waves, Venus Anadyomene."

By 1936, Zweig believed Europe's cultural and natural resources were tapped out. Letters he received from Jewish friends still inside Germany made clear how rapidly and dramatically life was unraveling there. Elsewhere across the Continent, he saw people infected with an eerie indifference to their own impending destruction. "Europe is congestionnée," he wrote in a foreword to his friend Joseph Leftwich's book *What Will Happen to the Jews?* Pronouncing the entire continent to be "overful of blood, and therefore irritable, provoked, hyperdynamic," he concluded that "if the barbaric method of warlike bloodletting is to be avoided, the surplus people of this overcrowded 'little peninsula of Asia' as Nietzsche called it, should be diverted and canalized into the sparsely populated parts of other continents."

Then, suddenly, in August of that year he found himself inside a country that was, he wrote, "still as much *terra incognita* in the cultural sense as it was to the first seafarers in the geographical sense."

A place, moreover, of such vastness that it should really not even be called a country, "but rather a continent, a world with space for three hundred, four hundred, five hundred million people, where beneath the luxuriant and undisturbed earth there is incalculable wealth of which hardly a thousandth part has been utilized . . . a land whose importance for coming generations cannot be estimated even with the boldest reasoning. And with astonishing speed the extremely superfluous baggage of European arrogance that I had taken along on this trip melted away. I knew I had gazed into the future of our world."

Another factor played into his response, as well, which he did not write about in his book: from the moment he stepped off the boat, Zweig was anointed a superstar. At a time when he'd just lost the most important market for his books and his larger European stature was undergoing violent contraction, he found himself a celebrity in Brazil on a level exceeding anything he'd *ever* known on the Continent. His arrival in Rio in 1936 marked the start of a "fantastic and exhausting fairy tale," he told Friderike. Four high officials from the Ministry of Foreign Affairs, along with the Austrian chargé d'affaires, met him at the harbor, and he was swept off to a four-room suite at the Copacabana Palace. A "grand auto and a chauffeur to drive it are always at my beck and call; a charming Attaché from the Ministry is in attendance all day long." The foreign minister hosted a huge dinner for him at the Jockey Club. He went on to meet President Getúlio Vargas himself at a reception to which "all the notables" showed up: "the Naval Commander and the Ministers, one after the other, to get a picture of me or my autograph—and you must consider that this isn't a village, but a city of a million and a half and a country with a population of forty million." However large Zweig's audience might have been among general readers in Austria and Germany, there was a clean split between such popularity as an artist and the sphere of political action. To find himself feted this way by government authorities simply dazzled Zweig. On the verge of becoming stateless, he was given a reception befitting a head of state.

His standing among the Brazilian public proved no less exalted. Ernst Feder, a German refugee journalist who emigrated to Brazil in 1941 and became close to Zweig, later averred that he had never gone into a Brazilian house "without finding several of his books, whether the family library consisted of a dozen or a thousand volumes." The minute Zweig first stepped into his rooms at the Copacabana, he found a mountain of visiting cards awaiting him; his daily itinerary had been printed in all the newspapers. "If I should want to deliver a series of public lectures here, I could fill Albert Hall four times over," he reported, without exaggeration.

Fresh pictures of him appeared in all the newspapers every morning. When he did lecture, at the Academy of Letters, two thousand seats were sold out in a snap and the queue to get into the hall stretched for two blocks. When he gave a more intimate, unadvertised reading in a smaller auditorium, 1,200 people forced their way into the space, even though half of them had to stand through the event. The mob scenes on the streets of Rio may have exceeded those sparked by any author before him in that city, native or foreign, and when he visited São Paulo, the reception was the same. There he toured a large prison, and while the official prison photographer—himself a triple murderer—photographed Zweig at least forty times, the prison band marched into the courtyard. Zweig was escorted out to review them, whereupon the

inmate musicians broke into the Austrian national anthem: "The first time in my life that it has been played in my honor," he noted. In Rio he was writing five hundred autographs a day and had developed crippling writer's cramp. For the past week, Zweig wrote, "I have been Marlene Dietrich."

It was while in Marlene mode that Zweig began articulating what became the signal refrain of his Brazilian rhapsody. Not only were the people of the country utterly charming, but also, he asserted, "this is the only place where there isn't any race question. Negroes and whites and Indians, three-quarters, one-eighth, the wonderful Mulatto and Creole women, Jews and Christians, all dwell together in a peace that passes describing." Zweig convinced himself that he'd landed in a transracial paradise. Of course, things were considerably more complicated, but relative to anything he'd experienced in Europe it's not surprising that he responded as he did to a country where, on the surface anyway, a vibrant inter-mingling of peoples did take place. Zweig embraced the popular Brazilian adage that, by contrast with the Spanish, the Portuguese had "conquered through the bed, rather than through bloodshed." The Vargas government's alleged efforts to encourage interracial marriage as a means of promoting Brazilian unity seemed a further advance on this approach: desegregated erotics as the gateway to a greater egalitarianism. Zweig discerned the happy results of these policies in the sight of mixed-race individuals filling "the schools, in the public offices, in the churches, in the professions and the military, at the universities, in the professorships."

Indeed, Zweig never stopped marveling at the physical beauty of the people that resulted from the absence of ethnic barriers to intimate relationships, and he was convinced that the children of every skin color he saw walking arm in arm wherever he went con-duced not just to national solidarity but also to the prospect of a new societal model for people everywhere. Brazil, he wrote, had "created a thoroughly individual type, lacking in all the 'degener-ate' characteristics against which race fanatics try to warn us." In contrast to Europe's overstrained nervousness and North American business-obsessed dynamism, Brazil's unrestrained melding of races had shaped a temperament Zweig could never stop praising: "intel-ligence coupled with quiet modesty and politeness." For Zweig, the rich assortment of races composing Brazilian ethnicity was a kind of genetic expression of his own great projects of collection: the com-munity he tried to gather on his terrace at Salzburg; the manuscripts he collected in an effort to bring together the moments of creative epiphany of humankind's greatest artists; the panoply of countries he obsessively traveled through, gathering impressions. The Brazilian acquired something of this profound convocation of spirits and places in the blood, as a natural birthright.

Rio captured Zweig's heart because it struck him as a distillation of this sublime heterogeneity, a quality he identified in Rio's mastery of "the art of contrasts." An exclusively modern city soon became boring, he wrote. A backward one eventually grew uncomfortable. Luxurious cities were dull. Proletarian towns were depressing. Rio enfolded all these urban identities within a single fabric; spread out far and wide, they yet "fuse again into a peculiar harmony" and became thereby magical. Every type of house and garden and street and building coexisted in Rio, in consequence of which the city offered inhabitants "free play for all forms of existence." One could eat ice cream in an air-conditioned patisserie with prices like those found on Manhattan's Park Avenue, while around the corner one could get precisely the same treat for half a cent. "In a white linen suit one can ride in a luxurious car, or in a tram together with the workmen. Nothing is hostile, and wherever one goes, to whomever one talks, be he a bootblack or an aristocrat, one encounters the same courtesy," he wrote. "What an art to be able to ease the tensions without destroying them, to preserve this variety without trying to organize it by force! May this city continue in this way forever!"

He expressed his fervent hope that the city would never surrender to the "geometrical mania" of the street grid, "which sacrifices to unity and monotony of form whatever character the town may possess—the surprises, the caprices, the quaint little corners, and above all the contrasts—these contrasts of old and new, of city and Nature, of rich and poor, of work and ease, which one can enjoy here in such harmonious abandon." Just as the insomniac dreams of the room where sleep will prove irresistible, the insatiable wanderer fantasizes about the harbor that contains enough reminders of every place on earth to anchor him. In Rio, Zweig sensed the convergence of so many peoples, histories, topographies, architectural styles, and mysteries that whatever one's origins or predilections, the sense of exile was impossible there. As a crowning touch he noted that the beach boulevards reminded one of "the white margin round the printed text of a book; and it is as though each page of this book were opened by the hand of God, a book whose pages one never tires of turning, for each one reveals yet another beauty." In Rio, Zweig imagined himself actually stepping inside the divine book of creation.

B razil: *Land of the Future*; *The World of Yesterday*—even in their titles, Zweig's last two full-length works mirror each other. Within a few months of completing his study of Brazil, he'd plunged full-force into the autobiography, completing the final draft of the latter work almost exactly nine months after finishing the book on Brazil. The two volumes were written on a continuum, in the throes of one accelerating emotional freefall. Although the Brazil book was written first, on the level of ideas the memoir can be understood as a kind of prequel to that work. While obviously not an undertaking of the same scale or depth as the autobiography, looked at as a blueprint for a new world, *Brazil: Land of the Future* is nonetheless also ambitious. As Zweig sat in New York City and New Haven poring over his Brazil notes, he began to question the whole set of life values he'd espoused hitherto.

In this process, the meditations on nature he'd begun trying to articulate in England passed through the looking glass of his New World experience. Zweig asked himself anew what it meant to live naturally, and became only ever more convinced that the Brazilians had discovered a way of life that nurtured the sense of true freedom.

The word "freedom" may be the most repeated noun in the whole of *The World of Yesterday*. The pursuit of freedom—and the tale of the gradual loss of freedom once attained—constitutes, indeed, the book's overarching theme. As young men, Zweig and his classmates fought for freedom from the deadweight of the schools—freedom from the bourgeois tenets of their homes—freedom from all hidebound authority—and pursued liberation through variant forms of artistic freedom. When he received his doctorate at the age of twenty-three, Zweig recounts, he was then "*outwardly* free and all the years up to the present have been devoted to one struggle—a struggle which in our times grows constantly more difficult—to remain equally free *inwardly*."

Most of his European contemporaries had lost even the memory of "how much freedom and joy the soulless, voracious bogy of the 'State' has sucked from the very marrow of their soul," he declared. "All peoples feel only that a strange shadow hangs broad and heavy over their lives. But we, who once knew a world of individual freedom, know and can give testimony that Europe once, without a care, enjoyed its kaleidoscopic play of color. And we shudder when we think how overcast, overshadowed, enslaved and enchained our world has become because of its suicidal fury."

It was true, he conceded, that Brazilians evinced a greater tendency to indolence than Europeans did under the relaxing influence of their climate. Yes, one found "less vehemence, less strong a vitality—in short less of just those qualities which nowadays are tragically overestimated and praised as the moral values of a nation." In a moving passage, Zweig announced that "recent years have considerably changed our opinions concerning the meaning of the words 'civilization' and 'culture.' We are no longer ready to parallel them with the words 'organization' and 'comfort.'" Judging by the "materialistic science" of statistics, "the most cultivated and most civilized peoples would seem to be those who have the strongest impetus to production, the maximum consumption, and the greatest sum in individual wealth," he wrote. Yet it had now become clear "that the highest form of organization has not prevented nations from using just this power solely in the interest of bestiality." Calculations regarding efficiency and scale of production leave out the most important element: the art of cultivating peaceful thinking and humane attitudes, which remained "the truest criterion for the measurement of culture and civilization." On this score, Brazil struck Zweig as "one of the most worthy of emulation, and therefore one of the most lovable countries of our world." In consequence of the country's profound *tolerance*, Brazil now knew more individual freedom and contentment than almost any place on earth, he concluded.

Through Brazil, Zweig came to see the attainment of personal freedom and the realization of a genuinely civilized state as linked endeavors. Both relied on reverence for individuality in all its endless variants, a reverence for what Zweig, citing Goethe, called this "open secret" that paradoxically necessitated acceptance of our common grounding in Nature.

While living in Brazil, Zweig added one completely new section to his memoir, a chapter entitled *"Eros Matutinus."* It's a kind of
secret afterthought inserted into the folds of the book, which only
Brazil could tease out of him. Indeed, these ruminations on sexual
awakening in the Vienna of his youth can be read as the hidden
lynchpin of the whole story.

In the past, Zweig wrote, the authorities had an easier, more
honest way of keeping the passions in check than the system prevailing in the modern era: they devoutly attributed sensual urges
to the devil and sin. Lacking "so drastic an anathema" as that
which was available to religious authorities in the past, the powers in Zweig's time had viewed sexuality merely as disgracefully
anarchic. Desire had no place in decent society, so Eros was exiled.
What resulted was a "sticky, perfumed, sultry, unhealthy atmosphere." A dishonest "morality of secrecy" hung over his youth
"like a nightmare."

Zweig details the ways that fashion embodied the spirit of repression: the high, rigid collars of men—"the choker," which made
movement of any kind almost impossible—the stiff whalebone
corsets of women, which blew them out like a bell below the waist
while all above was buttoned and strapped to the brink of paralysis. But all the ways that, in its sexual angst, society sought to
conceal the distinguishing features of the genders served only to
spotlight them in the imagination. People lived in a constant state
of overexcitation, which found release through the rear door, as
it were, of the metropolis. Zweig asserted that there was hardly
a fence or privy wall in the whole of Vienna not covered with
obscene graffiti; every bathing pool had its peephole, every back-
street its pornographic theater and cabaret. Restaurants had their

chambres séparées where one could dine in lewd seclusion with the right kind of shopgirl. In every one of the city's coffeehouses there were men peddling nude photographs to half-grown boys under the tables. The taxonomy Zweig provides of fin de siècle Vienna's erotic underworld is the most historically original section of his book, and probably its most carefully detailed as well. He had his heart in this portrait.

Zweig describes "a gigantic army of prostitution"—the streets of Vienna so thick with women for sale at every hour at every price that it was more difficult to avoid them than to find them. On top of the street action, prostitutes filled the so-called closed houses— the nightclubs, dance halls, bars, cabarets, and brothels—some of which boasted rooms with one-way mirrors and rooms filled with nuns' habits.

In *Brazil: Land of the Future* Zweig also wrote of Rio's sex trade. But his depiction of that city's "great market of love" was intended to reflect the city's openness and freedom, where countless women "of all races and colour, of every age and origin" awaited customers in doorways lit with multicolored lamps. "Large Senegalese Negresses, next to French women who can barely paint out the wrinkles of age; delicate Indians and fat Croats," all together. Describing the prostitutes' clients, he wrote of how "without shame, and with the honest frankness of the southerner, these young people wander past these doors, and sometimes, with a flash of light on their white suits, they disappear into one." He might have added that the white suits flashed not only into rooms harboring women, but also into others holding men. Rumors persist about Zweig's own forays into the realm of Rio's inviting young male seducers. "Even this remote spot," Zweig concluded, "which in other cities is hidden away in the ugliest and most dilapidated quarters as though shamefully aware of its profession, still retains in Rio a certain beauty."

Zweig's account of prostitution in Rio is tinged with exoticism, but the point he strives to convey about how the relationship between erotic desire and the social order can take less clandestine, torturous forms than they had in Vienna is an important one. He uses the notion of the denial of nature that imprisoned his youthful sexual identity to introduce a larger indictment of European civilization. Observing that he sometimes has to explain to younger comrades that his own youth was not especially favored compared with their lot, Zweig acknowledges that his generation had more political freedom than the current one. Moreover, he writes, "We were able to devote ourselves to our art and to our intellectual inclinations . . . No one questioned us as to our beliefs, as to our origins, race, or religion." But the problem of sexuality hung so heavily over the times that it nearly outweighed all their other advantages. "If morality gives man freedom, then the State confines him. If the State permits him freedom, then morality attempts to enslave him," Zweig explained. "We lived better and tasted more of the world, but the youth of today lives and experiences its own youth more consciously." Once again, Zweig elevates the positive value of liberated youthful desire—which he missed so terribly in his own upbringing—into an absolute. Young people in 1941, Zweig wrote, "no longer dream of all the suppression, intimidation, and tension that was forced upon us, no longer know anything of the bypaths and secretiveness with which we had to secure the forbidden, which they correctly conceive to be their right." Astonishingly, given his lifelong devotion to *Bildung*, Zweig now declares that while the new sexual freedom might come at the price of a diminished "respect for intellectual things," along with the loss of a precious aspect of love itself—"a secret reticence of modesty and shame, some kindliness and gentleness"—still, the ability to be fearlessly candid about one's urges makes the trade-off worthwhile. "I cannot recall a single comrade of my youth who did not come to me with pale and troubled mien, one because he was ill or feared illness, another because he was being blackmailed because of an abortion," and so on, Zweig writes. He implies that Europe got sick of constraining the hunger for ecstasy—and got Hitler as a result. The overwrought nerves of the previous era had been simply too much to sustain. Civilization in a European sense was caught on a hopeless binary circuit between the brutal suppression of nature and a bestial unleashing. Both prewar European society and the Nazi regime were guilty of trampling the ideal of true individual freedom in the interest of maximizing industrious social conformity. Throttling amorous desire and letting out bloodlust were two ways of channeling strong energies into the service of national interests. If the old Europe had been less afraid of sexuality's power to disrupt productivity, the temptation to mass rapture presented by Fascism would never have borne fruit. Where Freud claimed that anatomy was destiny, Zweig tried to show that the drive to autonomy was something greater than destiny. The *sensation* of perfect autonomy was, indeed, what it meant to be young—in Zweig's schema, in other words, what it meant to feel truly alive.

No wonder Zweig made a point in his Brazil book of casting doubt on the whole notion of technical progress toward national wealth, which in the end only enfranchised "greed and lust for power," he wrote. No wonder Zweig wanted to believe that in Brazil he'd discovered an entirely new form of civilization, free of Europe's pathological hatreds and material ambitions, in which "the harmonious disposition of nature had become part of the attitude of the whole nation."

I thought of Zweig's profound investment in the idea of freedom while visiting the Imperial Museum, now housed in the old summer palace of Petrópolis, which preserves the extraordinary feather-shaped pen, made from solid gold, with which Queen Isabella signed the proclamation emancipating Brazil's slaves. And I thought of it again when Maria Wolfring made the last stop on our tour of the town. At the summit of that quiet, curving street where we stopped to feel the air, we reached a hillcrest on which a shrine to a Catholic saint now stands, from where it's possible to gaze out over a large swath of Petrópolis. We left the car behind again and stepped to the vantage point. At the base of the drop-off, a jumble of mausoleums and tombs cluttered a hollow between clumps of trees, spilling across another road that descended deeper into the valley. Over the other side of the road, the first green hills buckled up, dotted with white houses under adobe tile roofs. Everywhere around us the whirring and piping of birds sounded like some music box mechanism beautifully broken.

"We had the run of these hills when we were children," Maria suddenly said. "It was wonderful." She shook her head with a sad smile. "We'd walk for hours and hours. And everywhere you walked you'd eventually come upon a little hut. You'd ask for a glass of water—you could always get a glass of water. And you'd ask for a banana. You could almost always have that. They grew everywhere. Sometimes the people who lived there would give you an egg and a banana. And you'd suck the raw egg and eat the banana, and then you were well fed and you could go on."

My eyes had turned back out to a chain of higher green hills beyond, sketched on the horizon like waves frozen while peaking.

"I remember one time walking through the hills not so far from here, and we came upon a little hut high up above a small road," Maria continued. "There was a very elderly black man sitting in front of his little house. And he was old enough to remember the time when the slaves were freed. The man described how there were days when he'd see scores of former slaves walking by on the road beneath him gently singing, stumbling with fatigue. They were leaving their owners. Without water. Without food. Great lines of people walking and walking through these hills." After I'd left Petrópolis, the image stayed with me of this long river of people moving onward, to who knew what destination, softly singing, sometimes falling in their steps as they passed through the dark green sea of the hills.

Chapter Twelve

REFUGE

The trip from New York to Rio in August 1941 took twelve days through calm waters. Stefan and Lotte kept almost entirely to themselves. Lotte refused point-blank to do any work at all. Stefan kept his own incessant fiddling with manuscripts to a minimum. He read methodically through the best sellers of the past four or five years, and found the experience instructive. Last time they'd made this voyage, they'd been so "frightfully tired" from days overcrowded with work and worries they "fell down like Homeric heroes on the battlefield." This time they collapsed with no sense of glory.

They lay still, and they slept. Halfway through the journey Zweig began to feel he was waking from a trance. Only now did he realize how exhausted he'd been. Paging through his memoir on the tranquil deck of the *Uruguay*, he realized that the book was not done after all. He confronted the fact that he'd churned out too

much in the last weeks. Now he'd begun "slowly correcting and altering and enlarging the autobiography and as soon as we have settled somewhere I will make out of it a real manuscript," he told his publisher. He was on the mend now, he informed Friderike, and also felt "spiritually freer." Only later did he understand that he'd suffered an actual breakdown in Ossining, he confessed to

Lotte's family, "with black thoughts what all may happen, (and some of it may happen)," he added. "Lotte was only bones and coughs for weeks."

But on the ship all that time began falling behind him. He and Lotte were studying Portuguese. It was right that he'd left for Brazil; that much was certain. He thought with pleasure of the telegram he'd received while still in New York from a Brazilian minister who'd seen the manuscript of *Brazil: Land of the Future* and sent his warmest congratulations on the book's impending publication. He still had no faith he would ever see Rosemount again. He wanted Lotte's family to take it over completely. They were to make use of everything left there: "clothes, shoes, furniture and so on," he kept saying. "I have written it all up the chimney," he declared—invoking an Austrian phrase meaning he'd detached himself from everything. Where they were going, they needed nothing at all.

On the pier in Rio, a party of dignitaries awaited the ship's arrival—just as had been the case for his previous two visits. There was his good friend Claudio de Souza, a prolific, well-to-do writer with close governmental ties. And there among the cluster of government officials was no less a figure than Osvaldo Aranha, the tall, imposingly handsome foreign minister. Zweig had made such a point to his dear Brazilian publisher, Abrahão Koogan, that this time there was to be no mad rush of receptions and invitations— they had to rest, for goodness' sake! Still, the gesture was heartwarming. Lotte and Stefan descended the gangway, bracing themselves for the barrage of flashbulbs and handshakes. Aranha led the entourage from the Foreign Affairs Ministry in greeting the Zweigs—then immediately turned away and moved off to welcome the Japanese diplomat whom they'd actually come to meet.

Stefan had expressed his wishes—and still it was unsettling. There was no chauffeured car waiting to whirl them off to the Copacabana. No friendly official to serve as their factotum. This time around, they were on their own in Brazil.

But once they'd settled back into the Hotel Central, the Zweigs realized with relief that nothing fundamental had changed. Rio's sensory kaleidoscope was just as divine as before; the hotel just as delightfully simple. They'd been booked in the very room they'd occupied last time around, with its large terrace offering sweeping views of the bay. The food was the same; so were the sea and the kindness of the people. After weeks upon weeks in which it had seemed everything was over, Stefan began to feel fired up again to work.

The city would get hot soon, however. It seemed best to figure out at once where they would reside for the Brazilian summer, before the throngs started migrating up to the mountains. Two days after arriving, the Zweigs drove to Petrópolis and began house hunting; it was "*the* summer resort for all who want to remain near Rio, even more so than Brighton and Eastbourne were for London," Lotte explained to her family. In less than a week, they'd found a six-month rental that suited: a small, tolerably furnished bungalow, thirty minutes' walk from the center of town, perched on an elevation—as the houses in Ossining, Bath, and Salzburg had been. The setting was quiet and the air from the large veranda, with its beautiful mountain vistas, smelled of springtime in Europe.

Now that they'd settled the problem of where to base themselves, they could take advantage of being in Rio for the present to handle other business. They submitted their passports to the police to register for the relocation to Petrópolis, and what should have taken a minute or two ended up requiring weeks. The curse of bureaucracy struck here as well with a fury. Stefan had his last remaining teeth removed under the care of an excellent Viennese dentist, who crafted a set of dentures, with which he was immensely pleased. He wished Lotte would take advantage of this time to get rid of her asthma, which seemed to be worsening again, for then they would have all they needed to begin living and working quietly after so many months of unspeakable strain.

When they weren't dealing with teeth or bureaucracy, they wandered the city, rediscovering Rio's charms. How he loved the city's mysterious, narrow streets! They recalled a time when everything one needed was close at hand; when automobiles didn't rumble by every moment, and you could stare into ground-floor shops where old-fashioned handicrafts made a series of Dutch genre scenes: shoemakers with apprentices nailing boots; women washing clothes in courtyards; basketmakers mending chairs. How he delighted in the sight of the old *bondes*, the open trolley cars. At night their overcrowded interiors were flooded with light. White-suited men clutched to the running boards; a wave of multicolored faces swept by, making it seem as though a handful of blossoms were being flung past one's eyes. And again and again, the countless cafés—one on every corner, doors swinging all day and all night. What an abundance of color and life!

B*razil: Land of the Future* was published almost in tandem with the Zweigs' arrival in Rio—and for three days in a row, Brazil's most important newspaper, *Correio da Manhã*, published withering critiques of the book. In the midst of a smattering of decent reviews, other critics as well took Zweig harshly to task for historical errors and gaps. Many intellectuals—especially on the left—refused to even touch it.

Zweig's circle in Brazil had never included the country's activist intellectuals, nor the country's more radical artists. He'd operated for the most part in Brazilian high society. With a few exceptions, such as the respected German refugee journalist Ernst Feder, the writer comrades he did find were viewed with distaste by the country's artistic vanguard. Claudio de Souza was perceived as a lackey of the Vargas dictatorship. Guilherme de Almeida, scion of a prominent monarchist family, was viewed as an anachronism. Other figures in Zweig's circle included an assortment of Catholic aristocrats, international notables, and governmental ministers. After the book's publication, even some of those Zweig counted as "dear friends" in Brazil seemed to grow aloof from him.

Playing down his distress, Zweig wrote Friderike to observe that she would probably be "surprised" to learn that his book on Brazil "was not considered enthusiastic enough by the local people—they don't like the very features of the country we like, and are much prouder of their factories and cinemas than of the marvelous colorfulness and simple, natural way of life."

This interpretation of his rejection was and wasn't true. It's indeed the case that Zweig was pilloried for failing to give proper due to the country's enterprising dynamism—favoring the picturesque over Brazil's manifold technical achievements and substantial investment in modernist architecture. And there's no question that the book's disengagement from contemporary literature did not endear him to the great Brazilian authors of the era. (His

account of Brazilian writers stops with the nineteenth-century authors Machado de Assis and Euclides da Cunha.) For the most
part, Zweig frames Brazilian culture as a legacy *in potentia*. This potential was, however, unimaginably great, Zweig argued. He wrote
lovingly of the exploding national interest in intellectual production—bookshop after bookshop opening up everywhere and the
Brazilian publishing industry now surpassing the Portuguese one.
"More than in Europe, where in a disastrous way sports and politics are diverting the attention of youth, artistic and intellectual
achievement is the center of interest for a whole nation," Zweig
asserted. One rarely met "a workman or a trolley-car conductor
in his free moments without a paper, or a young student without a book." Europe, Zweig concluded, "has infinitely more tradition and less future; Brazil less past, and more future. Everything
achieved here is a part of what is still to be achieved." It's as if the
two hemispheres hang on a scale: more here, less there.

But neglect of Brazil's present-day cultural and industrial
achievements was only part of the problem. Still more unfortunate for Zweig's standing among the intellectuals was the celebration of Brazilian dynamism he did render as homage to Vargas's
Estado Novo, the dictator's New State. Thanks "to the accelerated power of the machine and the even more wonderful organism
of the human mind," one year under the rule of Getúlio Vargas,
Zweig wrote, could "achieve more than ten years under Dom Pedro
II . . . or a century under a King João . . . In recent years a new
strength has been added to the forces of yet unknown and un-
exploited Brazil: national consciousness." Vargas, Zweig declared,
"this present and very effective ruler," had risen to power with
as little upheaval as had marked all the previous transitions in

Brazilian history. Indeed, in both domestic and foreign politics the country had always shown the same personality, only strengthened now under Vargas—absolute commitment to "peaceful settlement of all conflicts by mutual tolerance."

The Vargas legacy is hugely complex. His decision to place the power of the state squarely behind the Brazilian worker had lasting positive consequences. But the models for his Estado Novo were the Portuguese and Italian Fascist dictatorships. Members of the intellectual left were being actively persecuted while Zweig was writing his book, as well as at the time of its publication. Moreover, the nationalist and nativist policies of the Vargas administration were influenced by the many advocates of European race theories in his cabinet—including defenders of the most virulent strains of Nazi-inspired anti-Semitism. Legislation had been enacted in the 1930s to severely curtail Jewish immigration for the same kinds of reasons Jews were deemed undesirables in the Old World. In 1937, the year the Estado Novo was formally decreed with the support of the military, Brazil's Ministry of Foreign Relations issued a secret circular prohibiting the granting of visas to all persons of "Semitic origin"—though an attached memo clarified that exceptions could be made for "well-known Jewish cultural, political, or social figures." The instigator of this circular—which immediately slashed Jewish immigration to a quarter of what it had been—was none other than the man at the pier when Zweig's boat docked: Osvaldo Aranha.

To a number of intellectuals, the novelist Jorge Amado and the poet Carlos Drummond de Andrade among them, Zweig's book appeared such a naked apology for the Vargas regime they assumed he'd been paid off by the government to write it. The accusation mortified Zweig, and was false—up to a point. He refused an offer of lump-sum financing made by the government, but did accept "operational support" to help with his travel around the country while conducting research. When reports of Zweig's having been "bought" by Vargas continued to circulate weeks after the book's publication, Zweig finally spoke out in an important Brazilian newspaper, declaring that he'd written the book independently, "giving it all of the enthusiasm that I had within me when I observed and understood the present and future of this admirable country." This, also, is correct. But, as scholars have pointed out, Zweig's stature made what he said and did not say in *Brazil: Land of the Future* especially resonant. Whether intended as an endorsement or—more probably, given Zweig's character—a somewhat overheated gesture of gratitude, the book certainly did nothing to detract from Vargas's legitimacy at a moment when the left would have welcomed a boost for their antiauthoritarian positions from a figure of Zweig's renown.

Zweig was a very good guest. Whatever he grasped of the more troubling sociopolitical nuances of the moment, part of him had to be thinking that, having decided Brazil might be his own future, he could not afford to alienate the government, which had shown itself willing to host him. It's possible there was another calculation at work as well. Zweig's correspondence indicates his awareness of the expanding Brazilian nationalism and drive for influence on the world stage. He must have realized that these burgeoning ambitions would carry weight in the choice Vargas made between casting Brazil's lot on the side of the Axis or the Allies—a decision Vargas held off on until January 1942, when he did, indeed, align Brazil against the Nazis. Zweig no doubt worried that any kind of validation of the intellectuals opposing Vargas coming from an international, stateless Jewish writer—if it had any effect at all—would be most likely to incite a hostile backlash against the cause he espoused.

However much Zweig finally knew or didn't know of the political and cultural complexities of Brazil that go unmentioned in his book, his shock at the criticisms suggests that he was out of his depth. Despite Zweig's life of deft diplomatic maneuvering in different cultural capitals and among different intellectual cross-currents, he balked at the prospect of even attempting to find his way through this New World labyrinth. "I am more of a European than I thought," he confessed to Romains in September 1941. It's an alarming remark. How on earth could Stefan Zweig—who'd done nothing but declare himself to be fully, fatally, and forever a European for decades—discover himself to be even *more* European than he'd realized hitherto? If Brazil drove this home to him, the land of his own future was barren.

And yet, along with the cold shoulders and barbs, in the ensuing weeks it became clear that Zweig's book was proving enormously popular among the general public. Ernst Feder recalled conversations with numerous Brazilians in the wake of the book's publication who spoke of the deep emotions stirred by their experience of reading the book. They were moved not just by the work's literal content, but also by a profound sense of kinship between the author's emotional disposition and their own attitudes toward life. Feder speculated that this feeling of a shared sensibility lay behind the overwhelming success of Zweig's larger body of work in Brazil. Zweig's combination of wistful romanticism with intermittent yearnings to become lost altogether in a joyous crowd is certainly suggestive of the paradoxical Brazilian mix of *saudade* (lonely brooding melancholy) with the spirit of Carnival. So powerful was the Brazilian identification with Zweig that Feder went so far as to claim, "It is no exaggeration to say that no other writer, native or foreign, has been so much and so generally read as he has." Zweig surely had an inkling of this. And the recognition that his stature among the general public was not just intact but had ballooned still higher in consequence of his Brazil book's publication took the sting from his repudiation by the intellectuals. It also, no doubt, further confirmed his sense that Brazil's greatest achievement lay outside the realm of modernity—in the kindness of the people en masse, and a beauty derived from the preservation of natural, colorful ways of life from the past.

Stefan and Lotte moved to 34 Rua Gonçalves Dias in Petrópolis on the seventeenth of September. For the first time in more than a year, they emptied their suitcases and stored them away. The town was still "beautifully deserted, like Ischl in October," they found. And Stefan couldn't believe how inexpensive it was: five dollars a month for two maids and a gardener who ran errands; two cents for a cup of divine coffee. He didn't want to seem cheap, he told people, but really it was an enormous relief to realize they could live for next to nothing without being dependent on newspaper work or literary agents. He loved the Brazilian devotion to the rituals of the café—tossing back a cup in one gulp, like a liqueur, at a temperature so hot that, as the locals said, a dog would run howling if it got splashed by a drop. And the taste—delightful, strong—a black fire honing the senses, making thought crystalline. It was apparent that life in Petrópolis would be paradisiacally comfortable, Zweig announced.

"If I can succeed in forgetting Europe here, regard all my possessions, house, books as lost, be indifferent to 'fame' and success and thankful only to be permitted to live in such a divine countryside while Europe is desolated by hunger and misery, I will be content," Stefan told Friderike. His goals had narrowed and purified: all he wanted was to achieve a state of inner spiritual detachment. And to edit and put more intensity into the autobiography. And to plan out a new novella. And to write several short stories.

It didn't take him a week to chart out his daily circuit in Petrópolis. He'd scoped out his cafés and his barber. He'd arranged his writing table on the covered veranda. He'd assembled a tiny but sufficient library of old classics and a book of the most famous chess matches. He'd begun reworking his autobiography. Lotte devoted herself to building up a working knowledge of Portuguese and relearning how to cook by showing the maid what to do—no easy task, between the smoky kitchen stove (reminding her of toy stoves from her youth) and the fact that the young woman had never prepared anything but manioc and black beans. The servants' limited frame of reference amazed the Zweigs. Potatoes and rice were already a luxury, Stefan claimed, and fish an unknown creature. Their maid took home the Zweigs' empty tins as a treasure, and used them for glasses.

Zweig was disturbed only by Lotte's continued asthmatic hacking. She was losing weight again. The air was so still and clear it transmitted sound a great distance. Whenever she began to cough, a dog in a house far away began to bark also. Every night, he told her family, one or two duets took off between them. He kept insisting to her that she had to get some further treatment. Yet what, exactly, was she supposed to do?

Although it was the beginning of spring, the weather deteriorated. It rained almost all day, almost every day, and it was cold. This only encouraged Stefan to work harder on revisions of his autobiography, and Lotte also, in consequence, though when the downpours really set in, she found it hard not to sleep later and later.

"At my age one has to learn the 'via contemplativa' and to leave all fame and wealth to the others," Zweig declared a few weeks shy of his sixtieth birthday. "We are not quite sure if we should not have a dog—only we fear to get attached if one day we should have to move or to leave again." In the latter part of October and the first weeks of November, as he came to the end of his rewrite of *The World of Yesterday*, a spell of happiness ensued. It wasn't that any of the larger questions were resolved. When he thought about the fact that he would never again have a house, a home, or a publisher, and could no longer help his friends left behind in Europe, his sense of the whole having come to an end was complete. But for surprising stretches of time, in the midst of this beautiful, uneventful life, he did not think about these things. He was grateful that the radio broadcast only Brazilian news. And he made a practice of trying to read every newspaper that came his way as though it had been written a hundred years ago. "Montaigne speaks with infinite sorrow of people who live the sorrows of others in imagination, and advises them to withdraw and isolate themselves," Stefan observed. "A small share of egotism and lack of imagination would have helped me a lot in life." Sometimes he dreamed about beginning a major Austrian novel, but for this, he would need to comb through ten years of newspapers to get the right details. Such an undertaking would be possible only in New York, and he had no desire to go back there anytime soon. If only he weren't always so worried about producing—since he knew perfectly well that "creative production must gradually be extinguished like a light without oxygen, if there is no new influx."

But for now, so far as they could limit themselves to now, they were happy. He suggested to Huebsch that the little chess story he'd been inspired to begin by the hours he and Lotte spent playing through great games of the past might make a fine "edition de luxe" for aficionados, of which there were quite a number. It was a real pleasure to try to create a short story in this environment, which he described to Franz Werfel as "an orgy of color and gracefulness."

By the end of the first week in November, the autobiography was more or less finished. To Huebsch, he declared his hope that it was now an honest and vivid book. To his old friend the Austrian screenwriter Berthold Viertel, Zweig expressed his belief that it was a very human, very decent book, without exaggeration or boasting. "I think you will like it. It is actually a hard and realistic image of sexuality in our youth, and bitterly anti-romantic." The erotic revelations now dominated his vision of what he'd written. And just at this moment, to Lotte's great relief, Zweig's Balzac manuscript finally arrived from London, so that he could resume work on this book as well. Perhaps "work" was the wrong word, since he lacked the right documentation, he wrote Lotte's family;

but he could at least "play" with the text, and perhaps even shape a few sections into definitive form. Zweig's relationship with Lotte began to undergo its own transformation during his labors on Balzac. The book's editor, Richard Friedenthal, noted that for this work, which Zweig intended as his magnum opus, the manuscript pages made evident that Lotte's cooperation "was by no means confined to the mechanical labor of copying. Her queries and marginal comments were clear and very much to the point, and frequently they provided a salutary counterpoise to his flights of lyricism." When Zweig was tempted by his theme to "sing an aria," as he said, Lotte reined him in.

Even after the manuscript's arrival she kept writing to England, double-checking whether they'd really sent off the whole thing, and requesting the family to mail all Zweig's black quarto ring-books of notes. She pored over each page with him. The fate of this manuscript is poignant as well. Fragments of it were scattered in a kind of diaspora of their own—some ended up in London, some in Bath; sections were deposited at various banks. And when Friedenthal was at last able to regather a complete draft of Zweig's Balzac, on two separate occasions in two different London flats, the working copy of the manuscript was literally ripped from his hands and blown across the room by German bomb explosions. "The ceiling collapsed and buried the notes in rubble," Friedenthal wrote. "Fragments of glass splinters and grains of plaster are still embedded in the pages."

The downpours continued. Lotte spent hours with the maid re-learning how to cook the old European dishes on which she'd been raised, *Palatschinken*, *Schmarren*, and *Erdapfelnudeln*. In the shops you could buy everywhere *Streuselkuchen* and *Bolus*, and the old-fashioned biscuits they'd loved back in Frankfurt, she noted. When the gardener came to wax the floor, he and the maid took all the furniture and carpets outdoors and beat the carpets with sticks, the way Lotte remembered from her childhood. Laundry was painstakingly treated with *Waschblau*, an old-fashioned homemade bleach. Mayonnaise was made by hand, and chickens were bought live at the market and brought home to be killed. She expected any day to start making cream cheese and pickling her own meat. Memories of their old lemon creams were struggling to come back. The past kept rising up and overwhelming the present. "You would feel here like in your grandmother's household," she exclaimed to her aunt.

I see strictly *nobody* for weeks," Stefan wrote Lotte's family on the tenth of November. They now regularly socialized with a world-famous Chilean poetess, who'd also moved to Petrópolis, a prominent German refugee doctor, and a number of French-Brazilian intellectuals, Lotte wrote her family on the seventh of November. Stefan's notion of seeing nobody for weeks on end was not everyone's. They lived "a monkish life," he repeated over and over, yet a healthy one. "It was necessary to take this silent cure," he told Jules Romains. Lotte's asthma was finally improving. It troubled him no end that Rosemount gave Hanna and Manfred the problems it did. "Do not loose your time with my damned things," he pleaded. "Let things go easy . . . *ich hab mein Sach, auf nichts gestellt*," he added, citing the opening of Goethe's poem on the vanity of earthly things. *My trust in nothing now is placed.*

Stefan's dreaded sixtieth birthday on the twenty-eighth of November was almost upon them. He gave orders that there were to be no celebrations, no notices in the papers, no gifts, no visits. But just in case, he also made plans to spend the day in a mountain town four hours away with Lotte and his publisher.

When the day came, persistent rains made the high mountain roads impassable, but they got so far as Teresópolis, another hour above Petrópolis, and the fateful day passed as uneventfully as could be hoped. A few telegrams were the only acknowledgment

Zweig received from the world beyond Brazil. His publisher gave him a cute wirehaired fox terrier that lacked the intelligence and masterful character of the springer spaniel Zweig had owned in Salzburg, but boasted a mile-long pedigree, "which doesn't impress us descendants of Abraham as much as his nice manners." The dog gave their house a homey feel. Someone else presented him with Hungarian goose liver of such quality it might have originated in the 2nd District of Vienna. And Lotte—Lotte had somehow managed to find for him a complete edition of Balzac in French.

"I am very happy that Stefan is feeling better and got over the period when he thought everything useless on account of the war and postwar and even lost pleasure of his work," Lotte wrote after the birthday. "Thank God this seems to be definitely overcome." His writing interested him once again, and he'd even gone off to visit some people who he thought might be able to procure material he needed for his research. Spending the time they had in Ossining with the Fülöp-Millers and Albrecht Schaeffer, Lotte had seen that Stefan's depression was not an isolated incident, but something affecting the different European authors, one after another. This recognition had done nothing to lift Stefan's spirits, but helped Lotte understand "why writers, owing to their imagination and on account of the fact that they are free to indulge in pessimism instead of their work, are more liable to be affected by these depressions than others." Sometimes, she confessed, she wished that she knew some local women with whom she could just talk over mundane household affairs she was afraid of boring Stefan with. The few women she did know in Petrópolis were all "either enraged housewives or too little interested." Sometimes they talked of Eva, regretting having left her behind, but sure they'd been right to leave her with the Schaeffers.

Their life was small. Their life was poor, shabby, and undignified. Their life was nothing at all. But, then again, they were living through the greatest catastrophe in history, Stefan kept reminding himself. Everyone was "fixed like with nails" in one place and "cut off from the great stream of life," he wrote. "I am prepared for everything." His work was going extraordinarily well. He was almost done with the chess novella. The Balzac was bringing real happiness! And the Montaigne—the Montaigne spoke to another corner of his mind. "I read Montaigne like a discovery," he wrote Jules Romains. "Certain authors reveal themselves to us only at a certain age and in chosen moments." To Viertel, he described Montaigne as "the champion of inner freedom . . . suffering the same despair but remaining just and wise by this fanaticism of freedom (missing and despising all exterior timely success)."

Lotte asked the family in England to send a recipe for linzer torte; their old-fashioned stove should be able to handle that. Their new plan was to stay another half year where they were, Stefan decided. They spent hour after hour trying to find another house to rent for longer. But everything was so damn expensive. How he wished he'd bought something in Brazil five years ago! Prices were going through the roof! Life was so ridiculously cheap here! They should just forget about the garden at Rosemount, Stefan demanded of Manfred and Hanna. *Forget it.*

The Japanese bombed Pearl Harbor. Stefan and Lotte felt even more isolated from Europe. Oh, the terrible excitement that must be consuming the United States. How happy they were to be nowhere near that! He was in "complete despair," he wrote an exile friend in Rio who was working on a German translation of Valéry for the refugees. "Our world is destroyed." What "a curse it is to have to think, live, write in that very language," he cried. "What heroism on your part to translate *into* German!" Plucky, the fox terrier, was proving a delightful companion. But each night they locked him in the bathroom and he wept at being unable to sleep with them. Sometimes he trotted off to the Café Elegante all on his own. Oh, their peaceful, small life; their beautiful solitude! The constant rain made them incapable of concentrating on anything. "Believe me that I think quite clear and if I do not fulfil your wish which would give you Lotte back before Eva, it is because I see the possibilities of some complications which may arise," he told her family. Everyone had to have patience now. I wouldn't complain, he insisted, if life had to go on like this for months!

Fewer and fewer letters reached them from the outside world. "Getting older one feels perhaps more the value of every warming thought of others (as King David physically the body of Abigail)," he told Huebsch. Holding the girl close to his shivering bones as a source of heat when his own flesh could no longer warm itself.

Zweig asked a friend whether she thought the Nazis might invade South America. She reflected a moment, then said, "*Yes.*" She didn't glance at him before delivering her answer; when she did so she was shocked by the expression in his eyes. He looked stricken. It was a casual remark! She was hardly a competent judge on military questions! But she couldn't take back the effect of her answer. Zweig told a young friend in Brazil that the Japanese entry into the conflict made this the first true world war in history. People were not really fathoming what that meant, he explained. From the corpse of this war it was inevitable that a whole new order of pestilences, both of the flesh and of the soul, would begin breeding and permeating the globe.

On New Year's Day he wrote Viertel a long letter in which his thoughts career from wall to wall like a blindfolded driver through a tunnel. The only thing he looked forward to in life was to see Hitler crushed! He'd just read a forgotten play, *La Malquerida*, by the great Spanish dramatist Jacinto Benavente, and was stunned by its dramatic strengths. The impatience of a great work! Freudian before Freud! Viertel must try to get hold of a translation, because there was no question it would be a tremendous success. A real rediscovery! He himself was deeply immersed in his work on Montaigne. "Then I have written an actual long short story." His autobiography was about to be published in Sweden and the United States. But nothing he did had any "pep."

"The life of our generation is sealed, we have no power to influence the course of events and no right to give advice to the next generation, having failed ourselves," he wrote. "You remember surely our talks—all what happens now will perhaps be helpful to the next or overnext generation, but not more to ours and those of us who went away were perhaps the wisest; they had a round life while we hang over like shadows of ourselves." As for life in Petrópolis, it was as solitary, quiet, and anonymous as possible. He read a good deal, mostly classical works. He wished he could write poems. "But who could give his full measure while his thoughts are wandering from Singapore to Libya and Russia? My dear friend, remember I am not living like you with the nourishment of intelligent talk and friendly discussions, that letters mean still something in a Brazilian village and the appearance of the postman becomes 'the' event of the day."

And then Zweig broke into wonder; he was freefalling through time. "It is like in the first days of my youth and everything reminds me here of the times of fathers and grandfathers, the kitchen stove which is heated with wood and fanned by the black servant, the bath which has to be prepared with hot water, the kindness and naiveté of the people, the simplicity in all things—it is for me a strange adventure after having gone through all cities to return to such forms of life." He'd gone all the way back to the world of the day before yesterday.

Ernst Feder was with Zweig the evening of January 8, the day on which a letter arrived from Roger Martin du Gard in Nice. The best letter, Zweig announced, that he'd had from anyone in years. He was so excited that he insisted on reading it aloud to Feder as they sat on the veranda. Feder could never forget Zweig's radiant expression as he read. After the war, du Gard anticipated *"un Nouvel Ordre,"* utterly different from present-day reality. Men of our age, du Gard said, should content themselves with being only spectators at the great drama—or rather, tragedy. It was left to the young to play an active role. "Our part consists merely in remaining silent and making a dignified exit." He has expressed precisely what I feel! Zweig cried, as though he'd just been handed revelation from on high.

Zweig appeared genuinely startled when Feder objected that Zweig's creative powers showed no signs of flagging and listed the many projects he was involved in. He just shook his head, smiling. "It's true, in the past there was some kind of lustre in my writing."

Stefan and Lotte seized every break in the weather to take one of their long walks after dark. Occasionally Feder would join them. "We're turning you into a 'night owl,'" they teased him. They were night people, and the night had always been a time of being with others, and now, in place of concerts and theater, they watched nature's mystery play unfolding around them. Some nights the whole

forest glittered like a Christmas tree. "Do you understand my secret wish," he wrote Werfel, "to vegetate primitively for a couple of
months amidst beautiful vegetation?" He envisioned himself and
Lotte becoming one with the jungle.

In the middle of January, into the middle of their quiet, monotonous existence came a flurry of eventfulness. The gardener's wife
went into labor. Lotte became emotional. She could not contain herself. Stefan laughed at her. During "the great moment," Stefan noted
to her family, in a tiny room half the size of his study in Bath the
husband, the midwife, a sister, her child, a dog—all piled in together
around the woman. Lotte strained to see what was happening. Even
the smallest comfort, such as running water, was absent from this
cramped space, which still had the kitchen stove in it. Lotte was so
worked up! She came rushing to him afterward, needing to tell him
every detail of what she'd witnessed. No element of modern con-
venience or science was present, but "nevertheless a brown boy was
brought to the world, a very quiet child, which makes no noise till
now. Lotte was very excited about it, not so the husband who immediately after went quietly to the café," Stefan observed.

For Stefan, the event's significance lay all in its value as a didac-
tic homily. One was constantly amazed by the poverty of people
in Brazil; from that poverty one learned how many things in sup-
posedly civilized life were superfluous. When he thought back on
Ossining, where René and Erika also had a young baby—all the
sterilizing and protections! Here in Petrópolis "a black midwife does
(and not very cleanly) all the work and the children grow nonetheless here like strawberries." Their maid had five! Everything around
them happened the way it had happened two hundred years ago. A
short while later he wrote to Lotte's family again. "I believe we told

you that the workman who lives in a hut connected with our bunga-low got a baby, a tiny creature; so Lotte could have some 'Ersatz' by it and the dog, but she is not so interested in it as I supposed."

There are many moments in this story when Zweig's behavior is troubling. But this little domestic interlude is one instance where he seems repellant, especially when we think of Lotte's position in the scene as a young woman of thirty-three who's tied her fate absolutely to that of a man whom she knows she will not have children with, a man who has dragged her with him all over the world, now to a country nearly six thousand miles away from her family in England, to a tiny village where there seem to be no "regular people" she can befriend. And then, suddenly, there's this extraordinary occasion— the entrance into the world of a new life. Lotte sees a baby being born as the world goes up in flames, and she's overcome with feeling. And he laughs at her. Joking about her getting some "Ersatz."

It's true the laughter suggests the jeer of a man in terrible pain, confronting, in her flush of excitement, what he too is per-manently excluded from. The torture not just of being excluded, but of knowing oneself to be the agent of exclusion. "At a certain age one pays for the luxury not to have had children," he told Viertel at this time, adding, with a burst of misery, "and my other children—my books, where are they? Many have died before me, many are inaccessible and they speak other languages than I did."

Then it was February. Summertime had made the house more *vivid*, Stefan declared. "The wife of the workman who has a room next to us has got a baby, we have got a dog, the dog has got fleas, we are getting them from him mixed with bites of mosquitos, spiders, and other little animals." The tropical summer was tattooed across their skin. Especially Lotte's, he added, of whom all the animals were as fond as she was of their doggy: "All her suppressed mother-instincts are heaped upon him." Two snakes had appeared in the garden.

He wanted Lotte to get some liver injections so that she could start regaining some weight. More and more, her letters protest against Stefan's characterization of her as an invalid. She's been much better than she used to be; only one attack since getting to Petrópolis. They hoped very soon to get some news on whether or not they would be able to keep the house for the next term. They did not want to move. Reading was his best help. Reading only the good old "*proved* books, Balzac, Goethe, Tolstoi." How they missed the good talk with people who understood what was going on and what was coming. Every day the couple carefully watched the postman's rounds and, when he passed without entering their gate, just as carefully tried to explain to each other why the letter they'd been expecting might have gotten delayed. Sometimes they spent half the morning on the steps awaiting the mail.

The weather at last turned dry. Sunny and clear and the mountains beautiful and the flora gorgeous. Everything would be perfect, Stefan exclaimed, were it not for cloudy thoughts. Carnival was upon them and Stefan decided they would go down into Rio for the festival. Not the fashionable one, but the real people's Carnival in Praça Onze. Their feelings were rather mixed, needless to say, about going to see the fantastic explosions of joy when in nearly the whole of the world, explosions were killing people. "But it would be stupid not to assist such a unique spectacle (as we have been in no theatre, no concert and nearly no cinema since half a year and more)," Stefan wrote.

They drove down to Carnival on the sixteenth of February with Ernst Feder, Zweig chatting away engagingly the whole time about a work of Balzac's he was using for a *Reader's Digest* article. When they came upon the first parades of brilliantly costumed children, Zweig burst out with pleasure, "Now, isn't that pretty!" And when they reached Guanabara Bay, Zweig exclaimed, "How marvelous!" as though, Feder observed, he'd never seen it before. Throughout the day he seemed to revel in sharing the riotously colorful scenes with Lotte.

All his life, Zweig had venerated two things: the dream of human unity on earth and the capacity of art to induce a sense of earthly transcendence—all woes and petty factionalism sublimated in aesthetic rapture. And here, in the Carnival of Rio, he saw those two lifelong ideals playing out harmoniously around him. "How one would have enjoyed in the old days seeing a whole city dancing, walking, singing for four whole days without police, without papers, without business—a multitude made one by joy alone!" he rhapsodized to Jules Romains.

But he'd ceased by this time to believe in his own existence.

Friends who were with Zweig at breakfast on his second day at Carnival, when he saw the newspaper headlines about fresh Nazi advances in the Middle East and Asia, registered his horror. But by this stage anything could have toppled his spirits. Europe had committed suicide, he repeatedly wrote. He could not overcome the sense that he no longer belonged anywhere, and there was nowhere left to travel. In everything he did now there were overtones of the end of everything. The lure of nothingness. There was everything and nothing, and nothing any longer to choose between them.

What followed in the days after the Zweigs' return from Carnival was an extraordinary dispersion of belongings—along with the composition of farewell letter after farewell letter. It was an amazing work of *de*-collecting. Books went to friends, and to the Petrópolis library. Papers were sent to various archives. Clothes were given to the couple who'd served them and made their stay in the house on Rua Gonçalves Dias, as Stefan wrote its owner, "still more agreeable." Plucky, should the owner, Mrs. Banfield, want him, would go to her. "I know that he would have a good time with your boys," Zweig wrote. His letter to this woman, in English, is remarkable. "I am so awfully sorry, but we have taken another decision than to rent your nice house again," he explained.

On Friday, February 20, he built a bonfire in the back of the garden and began burning his papers. Did he think at all of the book burnings in Germany and Austria? On his trips to the cinema, had he seen any of the newsreels of those scenes with military music blaring and men marching stiffly by the pyres, chanting harsh nationalist anthems, hurling book after book into the writhing flames? If one looks closely at these images, one sees the way that, when the books are not immediately immolated, many rise up for an instant or two as they hit the updraft of the fire, their covers flapping like birds taking wing.

On Saturday the twenty-first, Stefan called Feder and invited him and his wife to drop by for a visit. The couples chatted, and the Zweigs were their usual "amiable, gracious, and empathic selves," Feder reported. Stefan said he'd been sleeping poorly of late but had gotten a lot of reading done. He'd finished a biography of Napoleon and gave that book to Feder to read, in addition to returning Feder's Montaigne, which he said he no longer needed. Lotte returned an

Austrian cookbook to Feder's wife. Feder challenged Stefan to a game of chess, as was their custom. It was no pleasure to be his opponent on the black-and-white board, Feder remembered. He himself was a poor player, but Stefan was so inept at the game that it was difficult wrangling even the occasional win for him.

Sunday, the Zweigs kept to themselves, taking walks and writing letters.

Monday, the couple hadn't emerged from their beds by lunchtime. The maid was surprised by their tardiness, but heard what she thought was a snore from the room and left them to their slumbers. Only at half past four did she and her husband look into the room. Stefan and Lotte lay absolutely still. Not answering. Not moving anymore.

The police were called. Detectives followed. Photographs were taken. A French architect friend happened by. Neighbors came. Journalists. The news traveled through Petrópolis like fire through paper. Claudio de Souza phoned Vargas and got permission to stage a state funeral. The next day, when the flower-bedecked coffins were carried through town amid great crowds of mourners from all parts of society, the shops of Petrópolis all closed their shutters in solidarity. A rabbi who'd been granted a special dispensation delivered the funeral benediction in the town's Catholic cemetery, in which the Zweigs were buried. The Zweigs' deaths filled Brazil's newspapers, with some of the major dailies printing a dozen tributes apiece. Everywhere Feder went in Petrópolis—in restaurants and offices, in the public library and town hall—he heard people murmuring about Stefan, trading stories, expressing grief and shock as if he'd been a personal friend.

Lotte is all but absent from most accounts of the event, as she is from Stefan's own public suicide letter, written a few hours before the end. His powers "have been exhausted by long years of homeless wandering," he writes. "I salute all my friends!" the letter concludes. "May it be granted them yet to see the dawn after the long night! I, all too impatient, go on before."

In private valedictory letters, Zweig seems no less heartened by his decision. To Friderike, he wrote, "When you get this letter I shall feel much better than before. You have seen me in Ossining and after a good and quiet time my depression became much more acute—I suffered so much that I could not concentrate any more . . . Love and friendship and cheer up, knowing me quiet and happy." To Hanna and Manfred, he explained, "We liked this country enormously but it was always a provisory life far from our home, our friends and for me with sixty years the idea to wait still for years of this terrible time became unbearable." He added that Lotte's continuing ill health, and the absence of Eva, had broken their will to continue. "We decided, bound in love, not to leave each other," he wrote. "I feel responsibility against you and Lotte's mother, but on the other hand you know how perfect we two have lived together these years and that there was not a moment of disagreement between us."

Stefan's letter to Eva is heartbreaking—alternately sweet and macabre—telling her one moment to be a good girl and work hard to make her parents happy, and then expressing perfect certainty that she will do exactly as she ought. Asking that she not forget them, but asking also that she not feel lonely and be grateful for all those who love her. She would see a better world, he assures her, where loved ones are not separated. It has been a hard decision, but he and Lotte have had such a bad time as she can't imagine, Stefan tells her. They would have so liked to be present for each stage of her maturation, he declares—to have seen her go to university and experience her first romance—to have followed each step in her growth with love and pride. But they can only tell her that they have done so many times, for so many hours, in their dreams. He concludes by telling her that she has been in his thoughts with feelings of love until the final moment.

Lotte's last letters are more clipped, worn, and grim than Stefan's, with none of his intermittent notes of exaltation. To her sister-in-law, she expresses regret that they could not do more for Eva personally by having her live with them, "but on the other hand it is my sincere conviction that it has been better for Eva to be with Mrs. Schaeffer whose understanding love and way of education is so much similar to your own. Having her with us, she would have felt our moods . . . Believe me it is best as we do it now." To Eva she wrote only a handful of lines, wishing that they could have had her live with them; they would have so loved to have her. But wishes have no currency now; the brutality of this war touches them all. Eva must just look for the time when the Nazis will be destroyed and she can go home again. It will not be too long now before she goes home, Lotte promises.

It's clear that Stefan Zweig's suicide had been all but inevitable for a long time. And to me, the truly harrowing aspect of the event is not his death, but the fact that he created a situation where his young wife, whom he did deeply love, felt no choice but to accompany him. Or perhaps, better put, made that decision to follow him. Lotte's death *is* shocking. And a residue of mystery lingers over her end. For the forensic evidence revealed that she did not die at the same time as Stefan. When the bodies were discovered, hers, unlike Stefan's, was still warm. She'd taken her poison after him.

The police photographs present untold stories. Stefan lies on his back, perfectly coiffed, in trousers, a buttoned-up shirt, and a carefully knotted tie. Lotte is in a kimono. Her underwear lay on the floor of the bathroom in a manner suggesting she'd undressed in a hurry. And though Lotte's pillow and sheets were crumpled, so that she'd clearly lain down on her own bed frame, she moved at some point before dying completely onto Stefan's mattress, turning over onto her right side, slipping beneath his dark blanket, resting her cheek on his shoulder, laying her left hand over both of Stefan's, which are folded together, curling her slender first and last fingers into him. He looks dead. She looks in love.

What happened in the interval between when Stefan took a fatal measure of Veronal and the time Lotte took the dose that killed her? A number of scenarios might have played out. She could have been in the bath when Stefan took his dose without her—an act, on his part, either of cruel impatience or, more charitably, of desperate hope that she, finding him already dead, might rethink the deed at the last instant. Perhaps he made a sound while she was in the bath that made her rush out, realize what was happening, and, instead of reconsidering as he'd dreamed she might, fly to join him. It's also possible that in the end, he rethought his own willingness to take her with him, and she persuaded him she would *not* follow—waiting until he'd taken his dose to begin her own poisoning. Or perhaps when Stefan began to kill himself, Lotte *did* think again. Spent a period of time rehearsing the decision and considering anew whether or not to go through with it.

Or, perhaps, nothing was ever in doubt or in haste. She may have been simply too distracted by the thought of being about to die to care about her strewn underthings. And perhaps she waited a little longer not because anything was ever reassessed—either at Stefan's promptings or under the pressure of her own ambivalence—but because she wanted a last moment of life *to herself*. Perhaps she wanted to step once more onto the terrace and look over the dark green undulations, down at the café, where life went on. Perhaps she wanted a moment more to remember her life, her loved ones, to see and hear the world, and then she was ready, and then she lay down and enfolded her beloved other half.

And quite possibly none of these imagined scenes transpired. Whatever took place between the moment Stefan took his poison and that in which Lotte took hers—whatever motions she made and thoughts she had—remain forever entirely hers. The last mystery of the end of Stefan Zweig's life is Lotte's alone, and she deepens before our eyes as she dies.

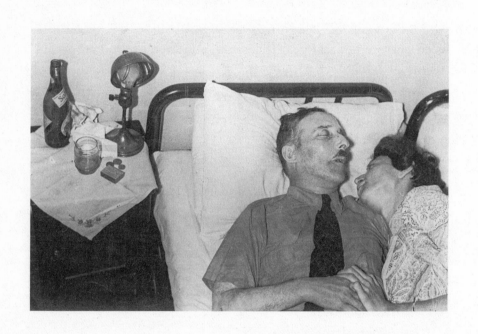

EPILOGUE

What kind of mark can any individual make on the world? How do we conduct our lives so that the space we leave behind proves fertile to the imagination of those who remain?

I thought of these questions as I traveled back to Vienna one fall and wound my way through the different neighborhoods where Zweig had lived and made his presence felt, from the opera and Burgtheater to the cafés, museums, and parks. All his life, Zweig struggled with the conundrum of how much realization in this world our dreams can sustain before they become hopelessly muddied. On the one hand, as Berthold Viertel remarked, through all his metamorphoses "as critic, translator and historian, Stefan Zweig had one objective: the creation, preservation and proclamation of the Europe that was already alive in him. He was its 'public agent' and distributor of its spiritual values. Indefatigably he drew together the scattered members of this much-tried continent." The undertaking relied on the fantasy that by means of his almost superhuman productivity he could single-handedly help unify and pacify Europe as a homeland for individual freedom.

Yet Zweig also harbored deep suspicions regarding what became of even the most inspiring visions once they left the imagination and walked the earth. Summing up the legacy of his hero Erasmus in 1934—acknowledging his failure to realize *any* of his humanistic prescriptions for society in the face of the Lutheran juggernaut—Zweig asserted that ideas which cannot be victorious in the concrete world retain "a dynamic force" in the mental realm and that "unfulfilled ideals often prove the most unconquerable." Indeed, he argued, precisely because the ideal of a figure such as Erasmus has not been embodied in action, it "is neither worn out nor compromised in any way," and so can continue "to work as a ferment in subsequent generations, urging them to the achievement of a higher morality."

But though the conceit flickers through his writing, Zweig never really believed in a realm of pure spirit. The gift he made the world depended on the sensual heat in his veins. It is "the body alone that can truly *experience*," Zweig once told a friend. Remaining human meant accepting that—like blotted handwriting on the manuscripts he collected with such meticulous attention—spirit and matter were always mixed, fed by a single current. As he wrote to Jules Romains at the end, he was certain that everything he'd given others came from "an interior élan. I could seize the imagination of others because I myself was seized, and that produced a communicative warmth. Without faith, without enthusiasm, reduced solely to the power of my brain, I walk as though on crutches."

Richard Friedenthal commented after Zweig's death that his work "originated in friendships . . . and it was lack of personal contact with his friends, homesickness for human companionship . . . that brought him to his end."

Questions of legacy did not haunt Zweig at the close of his life. He was concerned with the residue of his exit from the world only in the sense that he devoted enormous care to the distribution of his remaining possessions in the hope that everything of his that could be reused would find its rightful home. In the final months, he wrote of feeling "like Keats who had carved on his tomb, 'Written in Water.'" But the times demanded that everyone become used to such notions, he avowed—in truth the principle was one he'd long contemplated and even valorized. I remember being in the midst of conversation with Eva about Zweig's literary afterlife when she suddenly remarked that she thought his strongest reaction would have been one of surprise, surprise at everything—at the fact that he continued to be read at all. "I think he believed he would be completely forgotten," Eva said.

In the same way Zweig knew that his power as an author required the constant infusion of his carnal passion, he understood his popularity to derive from a confluence of factors, which made the spirit of the times stream through his words. And he accepted the price of this relation to the Zeitgeist. As he wrote in one essay, "Some great force, primarily devoted to the cause of oblivion, must counteract the forces of production in our world; otherwise there would be no room for the new things—the storerooms of the past would crowd out the workrooms of the present." What mystified him, Zweig declared, was not the transience of fame but the sheer physical disappearance of so many millions of books each year. They must, he concluded, lie buried on the shelves of unknown individuals. "Like the shades in Homer's underworld, they do not lose their human form and substance; these forgotten heroes and heroines of yesteryear still live in thousands of places, within the confines of their faded covers." As such, they retained an uncanny capacity for future resurrection—but only on condition of their being discovered, rewritten, revised, and transfused with the blood of a living author. Only another writer, a new name, could make the dead book speak again, he wrote. Still, it was one thing to muse over these ideas in an essay, and another to find himself going into oblivion even before he'd died. Zweig's sense of his name being written in water at the end seems another instance of that syndrome whereby exile forced him to live out an idea he'd once entertained as a philosophical tenet.

Be that as it may, rather than concern over the prospect of vanishing, it was the thought of imposing his ghost on this world that revolted Zweig. In truth, the overriding motive for his suicide was his sense that he was *already* doing so, against his will—leading, again in Keats's phrase, a posthumous existence. "My inner crisis consists in that I am not able to identify myself with the me of my passport, the self of exile," he informed Romains. Another way of framing Zweig's dilemma would be to say that the state of exile made Zweig feel trapped in someone else's narrative. And the falsity of this position was far worse than the prospect of complete erasure from the world.

Zweig, as we have seen, never really felt at home anywhere. But before Nazism, he'd been able to at least preserve the pretense of wandering out of an inner necessity. His craving to "unravel the secrets" of great individuals and movements turned him into a "Flying Dutchman," Rolland commented, echoing Zweig's own view of his motivation. The switch to a sense of having his movements dictated by external forces—to having his *own* secrets unraveled by others—proved intolerable. In his autobiography, he described the feeling of waiting in Bath to learn whether or not England would declare war. "I sat, like everyone else, in my own room, defenceless as a fly, powerless as a snail, while matters of life and death were at stake along with my own private person and my future, the ideas developing in my brain, my plans already made or yet to be made, my waking and sleeping, my will, my possessions, my entire being." Compounding this angst, Zweig also had a lifelong visceral terror of bureaucracy—*Bureauphobie*, as he called it in one essay, describing the panicky nausea and heart palpitations triggered by the mere idea of entering an office, let alone actually going into one. If Zweig was feeling this way in 1919, imagine his sensations after the start of war in 1939, when encounters with officialdom multiplied beyond measure and travel required proliferating identity cards, visas, tickets, invitations, fingerprint copies, and health certificates. The more proof of who he was he had to carry around with him, the less he felt like himself—or for that matter like anyone at all. The official externalization of identity meant the elimination of the interior self.

Over and over Zweig wrote his friends that the only thing left for him was to withdraw with dignity from the scene. And while many refugees expressed not only shock but also anger at Zweig's renunciation, because it seemed to confirm fears of there being nothing left to live for, his death also provoked a surge of life-affirming unity among the exiles. Carl Zuckmayer was moved to compose the only public message he issued during the war, a pamphlet titled "A Call to Life." Hans Natonek accused Zweig of a "final escapism," but concluded, "When I understood that he was dead I realized as well the miracle that I was still alive. I who belonged to the brotherhood of the weak. I accepted the miracle. I took the despair upon me. I swore to continue the struggle to its final end." Bruno Frank, writing in *Aufbau*, said, "Let us hold together, let us help one another materially and morally, that no more shall fall before we see the light." André Maurois declared, "Many men of feeling, throughout the world, must have meditated, the day when they learned of this double suicide, on a responsibility which belongs to us all and on the shame of a civilisation that can create a world in which a Stefan Zweig cannot live." A *New York Times* editorial observed that while Stefan Zweig had died a man without a country, his decision to commit suicide revealed that it was, in fact, the Nazis "who have exiled themselves, not only from the graciousness, the art, the learning, that were the best of the old Austria, but from civilization itself. They are the wanderers, branded with the mark of Cain." In closing, the writer expressed hope that Zweig's death would enable those who remained to "understand a little more personally the problems of the exile for conscience' sake. Such men are the salt of our earth."

Whether in resentment or mourning, Zweig's suicide provoked reflection among the exile community and beyond. His acknowledgment of defeat inspired many with determination to make the end come out differently for those left behind.

———

I spoke with Barbara Frischmuth, an Austrian novelist born in 1941, about her memories of growing up in the country after the war, and the first thing she remarked was, "We had no books." The only books left in the country, she explained, were the semi-Fascist writings of those who'd remained in the country and might not have actually killed anyone but were guilty of complicity with the Nazi regime. Books revealing what had been going on in the world all the years Austria was in darkness—books from which young people could take inspiration—weren't being printed in the country, and when a rare copy somehow became available, it was so expensive they couldn't afford it. What happened in consequence, she said, was that she and her friends bought books collectively and passed them from person to person. "We tried to read together," she said. "We felt we had to live up to the standards of Europe."

Most of what the children of the war hungered for was avant-garde literature. They wanted to know about surrealism, and Dadaism, and all the other radical movements. They didn't want to be weighed down by the past. They wanted something entirely new. But there was one book Barbara mentioned as our conversation drifted to the subject of exile literature that did not fit into this category. For all of Austria's belatedness in reckoning with its history during the Hitler years, Zweig's *The World of Yesterday*, she said, was actually taught to them in school. It managed to slip into the curriculum because it was taught in a literature class, rather than as a work of history, she added. Still, this book became part of their *real* education—the growth in understanding about what had happened in their country, regarding which so few adults in the country were willing to speak. Even those who had done something against the National Socialist regime were generally mute, she said.

Zweig's memoir was one work that did not collude in the silence. And what she and her friends came to, in the process of uncovering their country's unspoken history, was a wholesale rejection of Austria's self-image of victimhood as the first country to be occupied by Hitler. For many of her peers on the left, this translated into a recognition that it was impossible to countenance what their parents had done. A rift opened between the generations, she said, that culminated in the dramatic protest movements of the late 1960s.

With all its nostalgia, its flaws, and its willful illusions, *The World of Yesterday* perhaps helped then to plant a tough revolutionary seed. I think of Zweig's intense investment in the idea of his autobiography as a message to the future. "If we with our evidence can transmit out of the decaying structure only one grain of truth to the next generation, we shall not have labored entirely in vain," he declares in the book's introduction. At the close of his memoir he expresses his recognition that while "the past was done for, work achieved was in ruins," yet "something new, a new world began," albeit one that felt too far off for him to reach. In the final lines of his book, Zweig contemplates his own shadow, which fell before him, he writes, in exactly the way that the shadow of the last war lay behind the war they were in the midst of then. He speculates that this same shadow may have fallen across some pages of this book he is writing as well. "But, after all, shadows themselves are born of light," Zweig concludes.

The causal relationship between shadow and light haunted him—especially with respect to the writer's vocation. In another context Zweig once declared that between power and morality there was rarely a bond, but rather an unbridgeable gap, which it was the author's duty to expose, over and over again—rather than attempting the violence of worldly action. A reviewer of one of Zweig's short-story collections observed that Zweig's social conscience was "alive and awake and disturbing." But he had no interest in "economics, Fascism, Communism, the New Deal, the English holdfastness or the French watchful waiting." At heart he was "an equivocating Tolstoyan, a decadent early Christian." Potentiality was the only truth that could be passed forward through time, Zweig believed. "Let us seek our brotherliness on the other side of politics, let us think aside from geography and history—no, let us not think at all," he wrote near the end of the First World War. "The ground of our potential community of action can only be in feeling, in the feeling that never since sun and stars have stood over the muddled world has man been so desecrated." In an interview Zweig gave in New York on his 1938 trip to America, he declared that he'd never actually been especially interested in biography—only the tragic element of character. "I have always avoided writing of successful persons," he said. "I do not like the victors, the triumphant, but the defeated, and I believe that it is the task of the artist to picture those characters who resisted the trend of their time and who fell victim to their convictions." The alternative, he felt, was to glorify those who made millions of others the victims of their convictions.

When I wander the streets of Vienna today, the physical beauty of the city stuns me. I love the Jugendstil architecture, the stately parks, with their noble statues and, in autumn, the neatly raked fallen leaves at the base of the trees, like little mounds of golden coins. The art in Vienna's museums is breathtaking, and it is still possible to hear sublimely transporting music in the city. The people I speak with, as a tourist or researcher, are invariably nice and helpful to me. It's true that it took much longer in Austria than in Germany for the past to be grappled with. And I remember when I was growing up how my father's resentment over what he'd lost was almost never directed at the Germans, whose behavior seemed to simply baffle him for its "strange," mythic dimension, but against the Austrians, who'd been such "just plain mean bastards." However, in recent years my father has ceased to speak about the past with anger, and, outside of his family, the most important young people in his life today are the Austrians who've chosen to do their national service as interns at the Holocaust Museum in Washington. They visit him regularly. They ask him all sorts of questions about what happened to him. He loves taking them out to lunch and is constantly marveling at the superiority of their education relative to that of the American students he comes into contact with. "They're informed about everything," he says with admiration. "They know so much history!" After a lifetime spent defending the United States as the greatest country in the world, in part because America had the decency, as he puts it, to take his family in when no other nation would accept them as refugees, it's remarkable to hear him praising another country so fervently. Remarkable, also, that this country should be Austria.

He's not only made his peace with the place, but even thought for a time about retiring there in one of the facilities run by the state, where he'd be entitled to care as a Holocaust survivor, until he heard from friends that rather than one of the pristine mountain villages he remembers so fondly from family summer holidays, he would be likely to find himself assigned to a home in one of the dreary industrial cities of the plains. "Now if it was Hallstatt," he laughed, "or anywhere in the gorgeous country above Salzburg—that would be a different story!"

Now that I am grown and have had the chance to travel around the cities and countryside, I can see why my father gets a pull at the heartstrings when he speaks of the beauty of Austria. When Austria is beautiful it simply couldn't be prettier, or more majestic either. There've been moments writing this book when I've flirted with the idea of moving to Vienna myself. To have access to the sight of all that splendor day after day—manmade and natural. The woods surrounding the city . . . the vineyards . . . to have my child educated in schools where he would actually learn something. The German language, for starters. Why not, exactly? The past has been dealt with by this point, hasn't it? And whatever hasn't been engaged with surely in no way indicts the young people now. They are a bright, enterprising, socially responsible generation, from what I've seen. Perhaps it's time to think seriously about going back to Europe, to Austria, to Vienna.

With such thoughts revolving in my head, on my last Saturday in Vienna, after a day filled with great art and excellent coffee, I visited the Vienna Academy of Fine Arts, to which Hitler unsuccessfully applied, and which happens also to be the city's first official public art museum. The academy displays work by many great European artists, but its acknowledged masterpiece, at the end of a long series of rooms, is the glowing *Last Judgment* triptych by Hieronymus Bosch. In this terrifying painting, which breaks with the iconography of Bosch's time to present a panorama of sin and its consequences, the gates to celestial paradise have been replaced by imagery of unmitigated suffering. Everywhere, naked, emaciated bodies are being impaled by blades and spikes, mutilated, burned, subjected to unspeakable tortures at the hands of grotesque beasts in gray armor. Jesus, floating in the clouds above, moving his hands like scales, appears utterly detached, inaccessible to appeals for mercy.

In the background of these scenes of torment, ghostly fires blaze in a sinister landscape. The extraordinary feature of Bosch's painting is that with the exception of a tiny handful of souls, *everyone* is damned. Humanity in this last judgment is beyond redemption, and the realm of eternity will be defined only by infinite tortures.

Standing before this painting in Vienna, I found it impossible to escape thoughts of the concentration camps. I recalled also Carl Zuckmayer's account of being in Vienna the night following the Austrian chancellor's surrender to Hitler. The horrors unfolding around him on the streets appeared such a revocation of the grounds of civilization that Zuckmayer had the uncanny experience of finding himself without fear. "I felt nothing but rage, disgust, despair and a complete indifference toward my own survival," he wrote, adding that he'd seen his share of wild mob scenes before. But even the start of Nazi rule in Berlin gave no precedent for that night in 1938. "What was unleashed upon Vienna was a torrent of envy, jealousy, bitterness, blind, malignant craving for revenge," Zuckmayer declared. While revolution might always be horrible, that horror can be comprehended "when it has sprung from genuine need . . . But here only the torpid masses had been unchained. Their blind destructiveness and hatred was directed against everything that nature or intelligence had refined."

What had happened, he wrote, was quite simply that hell had broken loose. "The underworld opened its gates and vomited forth the lowest, filthiest, most horrible demons it contained." The air of Vienna filled with continual screeching and hysterical cries throughout the whole night. Seeking an image for what took place, Zuckmayer wrote, Vienna "was transformed into a nightmare painting by Hieronymus Bosch."

At last I could no longer bear to look at the images, and I returned to descend the broad stone switchback staircase that led out of the academy. As I did so, I thought of Hitler bringing Bosch's vision down to earth, literalizing the last judgment in response to the original sin of race. I imagined him descending the stairs of the Vienna Academy of Fine Arts for the last time, with his rage and resentment, his implacable decision to revenge his humiliation.

Forgiveness is a virtue. Vienna is not what it was then. The young Viennese do not bear a trace of the guilt of the past. I repeated these words to myself. I believe them. But some things that happened long ago are yet part of our physical beings, stronger than we are, stronger than the human as such.

It was raining, cold, and gray. I crossed the park before the academy, where, on the plinth below a statue of Schiller holding a book, staring defiantly out at Vienna, a large bronze medallion depicts a face wearing an expression of absolute terror, surrounded by stormy locks of hair with two blades crossing over the place where the throat should be. The head is decapitated, and a laughing satyr hides in its tangle of hair.

With no clear sense of purpose beyond the semi-biological, semi-theological drive to return to the point of origin, I walked

on toward the Belvedere and my father's old apartment house. The rain ceased as I made my way up Rennweg at last, to the street where my father's building stands. A dull yellow façade, now dirty. Number 13, on a nondescript street in a down-at-heel neighborhood. I slipped inside. Everything was gray and white at first; gray tiles beneath my feet, gray medallions in long white oblongs studding the foyer walls. The light seemed chalky. The sky out the windows shone pale between swirling dark metal grills; the winding stairs and dark metal cage of the elevator were overgrown with green, serpentine metal vines.

I began climbing the staircase.

For all Stefan Zweig's endless ambivalence about Vienna—his labeling it "an accursed city in horrible decay, rotting instead of

dying" after the Great War and calling it a supremely cultured place to live, full of merriment, "free of all confinement and prejudice," just months before his suicide—his sense of loss when the city became Hitler's had about it something final. "How timid, how petty, how lamentable my imagination, all human imagination, in the light of the inhumanity which discharged itself on March 13, 1938," he wrote afterward. "The mask was off." The weeks following the Anschluss were, he said, the most wretched of his entire life, and he characterized the decision by a writer friend to throw himself out a window as "the most philosophical" response to the end of Vienna.

I recalled my father describing the long bloodred banners that were hung down the façade of his building the day before Hitler drove into the city. All night long he heard those banners rippling, cracking like whips outside his window in a harsh wind that blew through to the dawn. And when Hitler rode into town, the roars of the cheering crowds were deafening. That's my father's final memory of being at home in Vienna.

At every landing, my steps echoed. Now and again came the clink of loose tiles. It was very quiet; faintly through some of the doorways I could hear the murmuring of voices, but it was almost entirely soundless, frighteningly still. The light was so gray, and everything seemed frozen and caked with dust. I kept going up and up the curving staircase; I had no idea why, but I just wanted to keep rising. I felt like a ghost, yet more ethereal: doubly impossible in this place. First, because my father had been exiled from this building seventy-four years earlier. Second, because if he had remained in Vienna I would never have been born. There is survivor's guilt, and then there's the guilt of the second generation who owe their existence to the displacements and relationships in new worlds entered through the door of catastrophe. I went up and up that gray stone space until I reached the top floor. What was I doing there? I felt like a thief, trying to steal the past from the present. And I thought of my grandparents, my father, and his brother, for whom I am named, and who died young in the New World, creeping away from this very building in the night with the handful of belongings that they could conceal on their persons, stealing away from their home like criminals, going into hiding full of fear and uncertainty. Where would they go next? How would they cross the border? What would happen to them? What had happened to the world?

I stepped at last to the window. The glass was frosted. You could see nothing through the pane. The white paint of the frame was chipped and flaking everywhere. But what focused my eyes were all the dead winged insects that lay on their backs along the sill beneath the dangling threads of an old torn spiderweb. All those winged bodies fallen still.

ACKNOWLEDGMENTS

My publisher and principal editor, Judith Gurewich, was extraordinarily generous with her time and passionate intellect in her work on this book. I'm deeply grateful for all the ways that she pushed me to take the ideas of the book further—and very aware of how rare the kind of concentrated attention she gave to the editing process has become. I feel fortunate to count her as a friend and ally. I'm thankful also to Marjorie DeWitt, whose fine editorial eye also made substantial contributions to many sections of the book. Tynan Kogane gave me extensive help and excellent suggestions in gathering the photographs and determining their optimal relationship to the text. Yvonne E. Cárdenas provided crucial help at many junctures in enabling the finished manuscript to become a book. I'm thankful, as well, for the help of my agent, Jin Auh.

Talks with friends and family members helped me work through my understanding of Zweig's story and larger issues of exile throughout the writing of this book. I'm grateful to Paul Holdengräber and Inigo Thomas, who played an important role early on in urging me to write about Zweig. Paul continued to point me to works that became critical sources for my book throughout its composition. His conversation as a child of book-loving Viennese exiles with a deep appreciation for Zweig was always enlightening. Adam Cvijanovic shared insights on many critical points in the argument of this book, especially in relation to the implication of the arts in larger, sometimes troubling socioeconomic trends. Natalie d'Souza's intimate understanding of what it means to live between cultures and fantasies of home was always a reminder of the contemporary resonance of Zweig's story, and she also translated for me some of Zweig's correspondence with Hermann Broch in which the two men discuss their complex vision of the future of democracy. Sandra Kogut's thoughtful ambivalences about Zweig's work helped shape my arguments about his fiction, particularly in relation to questions of melodrama in his writing. Klemens Renoldner, the director of the Stefan Zweig Centre in Salzburg, gave me a very helpful tour of this resource a number of years ago, and subsequently assisted me with my research. Oliver Matuschek's contributions to my research were invaluable and innumerable throughout the process of writing this book. The meticulous work of Stephan Matthias on the part of Stefan Zweig's library housed in Eva's home was inspiring to watch and helped me think about Zweig's own relationship to the physical object of the book. Sina Najafi, Wolfgang Schivelbusch, Arnon Grünberg, Michael Greenberg, James Livingston, Laura Kipnis, Tom Levin,

Lawrence Osborne, Jonathan Nossiter, Barbara Wansbrough, and Fred Kaufman spoke with me on different occasions about exile and issues related to Zweig, sharing perspectives that found their way into this book.

The experiences of exile and refuge undergone by my father, Martin Prochnik, made the writing of this book imperative for me. My gratitude to him and my mother, Marian Prochnik, is boundless. My siblings, Elisabeth, James, and Ethan, have always been thoughtful and generous supporters of my work; my fortune in their kindness is something I appreciate only more over time. My brother Ethan maintained a closer relationship with "Aunt Alice" than did any other family member—and I'm very grateful to him for sharing some of the dramatic anecdotes from her past. My children, Yona, Tzvi, Zach, and Rafael, are an inspiriting delight and both ground my thoughts and remind me of the brighter aspects of that reverence for imagination on which Zweig and his peers staked so much. I hope that they will find in this book some fertile link between the worlds of yesterday and their own tomorrows. The lucid intellect of my wife, Rebecca Mead, gave structure and clarity to my writing in this book on both the most detailed and panoramic levels. When thoughts of exile threatened to engulf me, her cheer and gentle confidence made me feel at home again.

NOTES

Zweig's *The World of Yesterday* was a constant reference point, inspiration, and foil for my own reflections on his story. The book's reserve on details of his private life has been much commented on, but the emotion in Zweig's tone is often so immediate and unguarded as to be revelatory about his character and mental state in ways that technical candor about personal scandal can sometimes obscure. I came to feel it was a more naked book than it has been generally taken to be—shot through with surprising admissions that are easy to overlook amid the fluid recitations of happy meetings with famous intellectuals, rewarding aesthetic pursuits, and sweeping, tumultuous scenes of social change. The enigma of certain statements Zweig makes about his personal experience, along with the larger milieu he moved in, becomes only more provocative on closer scrutiny. While most of this book was being written I relied on the serviceable English translation by Zweig's publisher, Benjamin W. Huebsch, with Helmut Ripperger. I was fortunate to read Anthea Bell's new translation (Pushkin Press, 2009) late in my work. Hers is often the livelier and more persuasively colloquial version. A small number of quotes from her translation are interspersed through the text, which otherwise cites the earlier version.

LETTERS

Zweig's voluminous correspondence also provided crucial source material for this book. Among the collections I consulted were Zweig's letters with Friderike, some of which have been published in English under the title *Stefan and Friderike Zweig: Their Correspondence 1912–1942*, translated and edited by Henry G. Alsberg with the assistance of Erna MacArthur (Hastings House, 1954). I drew as well on the more complete and accurately dated German collection *Stefan Zweig Friderike Zweig Briefwechsel 1912–1942*, edited by Jeffrey B. Berlin and Gert Kerschbaumer (S. Fischer Verlag, 2006). The meticulously edited *Stefan and Lotte Zweig's South American Letters: New York, Argentina & Brazil, 1940–1942*, edited by Darién J. Davis and Oliver Marshall (Continuum, 2010), was a frequent reference for me, with respect to both specific citations and background on the general atmosphere of the Zweigs' life in Brazil. This volume also contains a section on the couple's time in New York, with citations from many of the letters the Zweigs wrote in this period. All of the letters published in this collection were originally composed in English, as were a number of Zweig's letters to Friderike, Ben Huebsch, and other correspondents, especially after war between England and Germany broke out, when the advantages of writing in English to avoid issues with censors came to outweigh the problems of Stefan's English. (Lotte's English was better but still irregular.) I have kept their mistakes in grammar, syntax, and punctuation intact except in several instances when a misspelling or syntactical error seemed more befuddling than suggestive. For example, both Stefan and Lotte tended to write New York as one word: "Newyork." I've corrected this. I've also regularized the spelling of the name of Lotte's sister-in-law, which she always spells as "Hanna" and Stefan almost always spells "Hannah." Along with the letters between the Zweigs and Lotte's family published in Davis and Marshall, I was fortunate to make several visits to the Stefan Zweig archives at SUNY Fredonia, where I read both published and unpublished letters of the Zweigs, including their complete correspondence from the United States to Lotte's family in England. Gerda Morrissey, the principal archivist of this collection, assisted me on innumerable occasions in vital ways. Not only did she track down difficult to find sources, she gracefully accommodated my sometimes frantic pleas for last-minute scans of material and even assisted with the translation of letters. A writer couldn't hope for a more helpful archivist, and I am deeply thankful. Many of the most important letters in the correspondence between Ben Huebsch and Stefan Zweig have been published in two very insightful essays by Jeffrey B. Berlin. A number of their earlier letters appear in "Some Unpublished Stefan Zweig Letters, with an Unpublished Zweig Manifesto," published in *Turn-of-the-Century Vienna and Its Legacy: Essays in Honor of Donald G. Daviau*, edited by Jeffrey B. Berlin, Jorun B. Johns, and Richard H. Lawson (Edition Atelier, 1993). Key passages from the two men's later correspondence are quoted in "Stefan Zweig and His American Publisher: Notes on an Unpublished Correspondence, with Reference to *Schachnovelle* and *Die Welt von Gestern*," in *Deutsche Vierteljahrs Schrift für Literaturwissenschaft und Geistesgeschichte* (J. B. Metzler Verlag, 1982). I also drew on the unpublished correspondence between Benjamin Huebsch and Stefan Zweig archived in the Benjamin W. Huebsch papers at the Library of Congress. *Stefan Zweig: Briefe 1932–1942*, edited by Knut Beck and Jeffrey B. Berlin (S. Fischer Verlag, 2005), the final volume in a multi-book series of Zweig's selected letters, was vital to my research, and a number of citations in my book are drawn from this anthology. The correspondence between Zweig and Joseph Roth is vibrantly rendered in *Joseph Roth: A Life in Letters*, translated and edited by Michael Hofmann (W. W. Norton & Co., 2012).

ZWEIG'S PUBLICATIONS

Among Zweig's published works, the most important for this book were *Erasmus of Rotterdam*, translated by Eden and Cedar Paul (Viking Press, 1934); *Kaleidoscope: Thirteen Stories and Novelettes*, translated by Eden and Cedar Paul (Viking Press, 1934); *Jewish Legends*, translated by Eden and Cedar Paul (Markus Wiener Publishing, 1987); *Émile Verhaeren*, translated by Jethro Bithell (Constable and Company, 1914); *The Struggle with the Daemon: Hölderlin, Kleist, Nietzsche*, translated by Eden and Cedar Paul (Pushkin Press, 2012); *Mental Healers: Franz Anton Mesmer, Mary Baker Eddy, Sigmund Freud*, translated by Eden and Cedar Paul (Viking Press, 1932); *Joseph Fouché*, translated by Eden and Cedar Paul (Viking Press, 1930); *Beware of Pity*, translated by Phyllis and Trevor Blewitt (Pushkin Press, 2003); *Twenty-four Hours in the Life of a Woman* and *The Royal Game*, translated by Anthea Bell (Pushkin Press, 2003); *The Invisible Collection* and *Buchmendel*, translated by Eden and Cedar Paul (Pushkin Press, 1998). The version of *Letter from an Unknown Woman* I quote is the Jill Sutcliffe translation, anthologized in Stefan Zweig, *The Burning Secret and Other Stories* (E. P. Dutton, 1989). My quotations from Zweig's *Marie Antoinette: Portrait of an Average Woman* are from the translation by Cedar Paul and Eden Paul (Viking Press, 1933). I used both the 1943 Viking Press edition of *Brazil: Land of the Future* and the recent translation by Lowell A. Bangerter published by Ariadne Press in 2007.

MEMOIRS, BIOGRAPHIES, AND REMINISCENCES

Despite its omissions and distortions, Friderike Zweig's memoir-biography of her husband, *Stefan Zweig* (Thomas Y. Crowell Company, 1946), remains an important and often engaging work. Read in tandem with more scrupulous accounts, it provides a trove of insights into Zweig's character. I also made extensive use of reminiscences written by others who knew Zweig, in particular the essays contained in *Stefan Zweig: A Tribute to His Life and Work*, translated by Christobel Fowler, edited by Hanns Arens (W. H. Allen, 1951). *Der große Europäer: Stefan Zweig*, edited by Hanns Arens (Kindler Verlag, 1956), is a larger commemorative anthology and was my source for the enlightening essays on Zweig by Joachim Maass, Klaus Mann, Thomas Mann, and Irmgard Keun.

I am indebted to the work of many scholars and biographers whose pioneering archival work and thoughtful insights color my narrative and helped to shape my own perspective throughout this book. Donald Prater's excellent *European of Yesterday:*

A Biography of Stefan Zweig (Oxford University Press, 1972) was an invaluable resource, especially for the tremendous number of letters he excerpts in the course of his narrative. Any reader interested in understanding the full trajectory of Zweig's story should seek out this lamentably rare book. Oliver Matuschek's *Three Lives: A Biography of Stefan Zweig*, translated by Allan Blunden (Pushkin Press, 2011), appeared while I was writing this book and provides a wealth of new biographical material and critical understanding of Zweig's story. Prater both profited from and was limited by his conversations and relationship with Friderike Zweig. Oliver Matuschek's book is free from this bias and offers a portrait of Zweig's life that is exemplary in its objectivity and scope. But long before the book appeared I had benefited from Oliver's unstinting collegial support. He directed me toward many sources I would otherwise not have had access to, and my gratitude for his knowledge and generosity is immense.

I am thankful to Eva Alberman for having shared reminiscences and insights that deepened my understanding of Stefan and Lotte Zweig's story.

CHAPTER REFERENCES

The citations below are not intended to be comprehensive. I've striven instead both to make clear how much this book owes to the work of others by indicating the most important sources behind my quotations and arguments, and to provide interested readers with guideposts for tracking down key sources.

Introduction

In the opening of the introduction, I drew on Davis and Marshall's *Stefan and Lotte Zweig's South American Letters* for quotations and general atmosphere. Zweig uses the term "primitive" in letters to describe not only lunches at home in Petrópolis, but many other elements of their Brazilian existence as well. The note on Montaigne from Zweig's journal is cited in Prater, as is the remark Zweig made to André Maurois about the process of exile. Zweig writes about the translation of Austria into a tropical language in a letter to Franz and Alma Werfel in Beck and Berlin's *Stefan Zweig: Briefe 1932–1942*. Joseph Roth's Austrian patriotism is described in Friderike's biography of Zweig. Jules Romains's remark on Zweig's Ossining domicile is from his essay "Derniers Mois et Dernières Lettres de Stefan Zweig," which appeared in *La Revue de Paris*, 62e anné, 2 (Feb. 1955), and was an important source for my book. Klaus Mann's report on his encounter with Stefan Zweig on the streets of New York in his autobiographical work is mentioned in Mann's autobiography, *The Turning Point* (L. B. Fischer, 1942), and described more fully in his essay "Er war ein Verzweifelter," in Arens, *Der große Europäer: Stefan Zweig*. *The Turning Point* is also my source for the story about Zweig's response to the 1930 Reichstag vote. Carl Zuckmayer's account of his Vermont life and dinner with Zweig are taken from both his memoir, *A Part of Myself: Portrait of an Epoch*, translated by Richard and Clara Winston (Harcourt Brace

Jovanovich, 1970), and Zuckmayer's essay "Did You Know Stefan Zweig?" in Arens. The Bruno Walter quotes are from Bruno Walter, *Theme and Variations: An Autobiography*, translated by James A. Galston (Alfred A. Knopf, 1946). The quotation from Heinrich Mann is taken from Wolfgang Schivelbusch's excellent *The Culture of Defeat: On National Trauma, Mourning, and Recovery*, translated by Jefferson S. Chase (Picador, 2004), which was helpful to me at different junctures in the writing of this book. I received information on Zweig's house and the larger environs of Ossining from the archives and helpful curators at the Ossining Historical Society. The line about "the typical U.S.A. rapture" is from Maurice R. Davie, *Refugees in America: Report of the Committee for the Study of Recent Immigration from Europe* (Yale University Press, 1947). Max Brod's comments about Zweig's bachelor flat, taken from his essay "Erinnerungen au Stefan Zweig" in Arens, *Der große Europäer*, were cited in Matuschek's biography. The atmosphere in Zweig's Hallam Street flat and the "in-between life" were described by Hilde Spiel in her eloquent memoir *The Dark and the Bright*, translated by Christine Shuttleworth (Ariadne Press, 2007). Richard Friedenthal writes of Zweig taking comfort from the spirit of other famous exiles of the past in his lecture "Stefan Zweig and Humanism," in Arens. Zweig's determination to find in Piccadilly Circus the world axis is recounted in Jules Romains's valedictory 1939 Paris lecture on Zweig, *Stefan Zweig: Great European*, translated by James Whitall (Viking Press, 1941). Gershom Scholem's comment on German-Jewish writers is from his lecture "Jews and Germans," anthologized in *On Jews and Judaism in Crisis*, edited by Werner J. Dannhauser (Paul Dry Books, 2012). I am indebted to Christian Witt-Dörring's deep knowledge of Vienna for his help deciphering the significance of the medallion on the Schiller statue—a process facilitated by the ever helpful and insightful Michael Huey.

Chapter One

In my descriptions of the cocktail party, I drew on the Zweigs' letters to Lotte's family, an unpublished journal of Lotte's, which Oliver Matuschek shared with me, and Zweig's essay "The Spirit of New York," which I discovered in a Swedish translation from the *Stockholms Dagblad*, December 20, 1936. The article was translated for me by Monica Löfgren. Klaus Mann also describes Zweig's demeanor at the party in "Er war ein Verzweifelter" in Arens, *Der große Europäer: Stefan Zweig*. The remark about increasing numbers of refugees changing the perspective on their desirability is cited in Donald Peterson Kent, *The Refugee Intellectual: The Americanization of the Immigrants of 1933–1945* (Columbia University Press, 1953). Zweig complains about the number of people he must attend to in New York in numerous places; my quotations here are drawn from his correspondence with Friderike. My principal source in discussing Zweig's collecting of musical scores in his later years was "Music in Stefan Zweig's Last Years: Some Unpublished Letters," a monograph by Harry Zohn published in *The Juilliard Review* (Spring 1956). Remarks on the looseness of class boundaries in Vienna, Zweig's ability to create a literary atmosphere wherever he traveled, and typically Viennese multiplicity derive from Klaus Mann, "Victims of Fascism: Stefan Zweig," in *Free World* (Apr. 1942). Walter Bauer reports on Zweig's remarks about the life of the spirit in his essay "Stefan Zweig the European" in Arens. Zweig's comments on Salzburg are from the essay "Salzburg: The Framed Town," anthologized in *Stefan Zweig Journeys*, translated by Will Stone (Hesperus Press, 2010). For the mood in New York City I drew heavily on newspaper articles from the era, including Henry N. Dorriss, "Says Spies Infest Forts in City Area," *The New York Times*, June 3, 1941; "Says Bund Mapped Wall St. Hangings," *The New York Times*, October 4, 1940; and "22,000 Nazis Hold Rally in Garden; Police Check Foes," *The New York Times*, February 21, 1939. The observations from Charles Baudouin and correspondence between Zweig and Erich Ebermayer concerning inward change and the desire for counterweights are cited in Prater, who also—perhaps drawing on information supplied by Friderike—reveals that Zweig was receiving anti-aging hormone treatment in New York City. Zuckmayer recounts his exchange with Zweig and writes of his discovery of the American wilderness in his memoir. Remarks on Zuckmayer's head and facility as a raconteur are from Elias Canetti, *The Play of the Eyes*, translated by Ralph Manheim (Farrar, Straus and Giroux, 1986). I was helped in my understanding of the exiles' relation to the American countryside—along with many other aspects of their responses to the New World—by Anthony Heilbut's wonderful *Exiled in Paradise* (Viking Press, 1983). For general information on the period I also relied on Helmut F. Pfanner, *Exile in New York: German and Austrian Writers After 1933* (Wayne State University Press, 1983). The anecdote Thomas Mann recounts of Zweig's charity appears in his essay "Stefan Zweig zum zehnten Todestag 1952," in Arens. Katja Guttman helped me with the translation of this essay, along with Zweig's letter to Paul Zech from June 5, 1941, which is cited in Beck and Berlin, *Stefan Zweig: Briefe 1932–1942*. For the Salzburg Festival of 1933 see, for example, Frederick T. Birchall, "Salzburg Idolizes Bruno Walter, Ousted by Nazis as 'Non-Aryan,'" *The New York Times*, August 4, 1933; and "Austrians Indignant," *The New York Times*, July 31, 1933. Zweig's comparison of the refugees to Odysseus is cited in Robert Van Gelder, "The Future of Writing in a World at War," *The New York Times*, July 28, 1940. The anonymous citation about the Odyssey without the gods appears in "The Exiled Writers," by Benjamin Appel, in *The Saturday Review of Literature*, October 19, 1940. Hannah Arendt's analysis of the "Ulysses-wanderers" comes from her essay "We Refugees," reprinted in Hannah Arendt, *The Jewish Writings*, edited by Jerome Kohn and Ron H. Feldman (Schocken Books, 2007). All citations from Martin Gumpert are from his remarkable memoir *First Papers*, translated by Heinz and Ruth Norden (Duell, Sloan and Pearce, 1941). Zweig's joke about being able to afford exile is cited in Richard Dove's very informative *Journey of No Return: Five German-Speaking Literary Exiles in Britain, 1933–1945* (Libris, 2000), which includes passages from a number of exchanges between Zweig and Rolland that were also important for my book. Brecht pokes fun at the absurdity of the consular office in his drama *Conversations in Exile*. The quotation from Gustav Anders is reproduced in Alan D. DeSantis, "Caught Between Two Worlds: Bakhtin's Dialogism in the Exile Experience," *Journal of Refugee Studies*, vol. 14, no. 1, 2001. Zweig's letter to Jules Romains about the fountain of youth appears in Romains's "Derniers Mois et Dernières Lettres de Stefan Zweig." Hans Natonek's observations about Manhattan being America's alphabet are from his fantastically compelling (and sadly almost impossible to find) memoir, *In Search of Myself* (G. P. Putnam's Sons, 1943). The quotation from Claude Lévi-Strauss—along with other observations by Lévi-Strauss in chapter two—are from his essay "New York in 1941," which is included in the collection *The View from Afar*, translated by Joachim Neugroschel and Phoebe Hoss (The University of Chicago Press, 1985).

Chapter Two

Zweig's comments on the scene at the Metropolitan Opera are cited in Matuschek. Both the accusation against Zweig's epicureanism (by Ludwig Marcuse) and the mockery of Reichner are from correspondence in Hofmann's *Joseph Roth: A Life in Letters.* The fullest account of Zweig's 1935 New York press conference can be found on the Jewish Telegraphic Agency Web site in Henry W. Levy, "Stefan Zweig Tells Plan for Review, Says Folks Don't Trust Intellectuals," January 31, 1935, www.jta .org/1935/01/31/archive/stefan-zweig-tells-plan-for-review-says-folks-dont-trust -intellectuals. Brainin summarizes his own response to Zweig at the conference and in his subsequent hotel room interview with the author in Joseph Brainin, "The Tragedy of Stefan Zweig," *The National Jewish Monthly* (Apr. 1942). Zweig's remark about Jews left inside Germany being hostages appears in a letter he wrote to Joseph Leftwich, which Leftwich cites in his richly layered study "Stefan Zweig and the World of Yesterday," *Year Book III of the Leo Baeck Institute* (East and West Library, 1958). Zweig's incomplete manifesto is reprinted in Berlin's fascinating essay "The Struggle for Survival—From Hitler's Appointment to the Nazi Book-Burnings: Some Unpublished Stefan Zweig Letters, with an Unpublished Manifesto." In recounting the story of the Zweigs' 1938 American tour, I made use of Lotte Zweig's unpublished journal for this period. I'm indebted to Oliver Matuschek for providing me access to this document, along with his research into the correspondence of refugees looking for funds from Zweig, for perspective on the scope of that demand. On the new incarnation of the Cotton Club see, for example, "Night Club Notes," *The New York Times*, September 26, 1936. Additional material about nightclubs of the era, such as my reference to social registerites at the Rainbow Room, was drawn from "Manhattan Night Life," an unattributed article in *Fortune* magazine, vol. 13, no. 3 (Mar. 1936). The Curtiss interview with Zweig is recounted in Thomas Quinn Curtiss, "Stefan Zweig," *Books Abroad*, vol. 13, no. 4 (Autumn 1939). Zweig writes to Hanna and Manfred, as well as to Friderike, about the scene in New Haven. The quotation from Natonek about the panic of refugee experience is from his essay "The Last Day in Europe," reprinted in *Hitler's Exiles: Personal Stories of the Flight from Nazi Germany to America*, edited by Mark M. Anderson (The New Press, 1998). All other quotes from Natonek are taken from his memoir. Zweig's remark about "small fry" is from a letter to Rolland cited in Dove. His comparison of refugees to dogs is quoted in an unpublished lecture by Prater, archived at SUNY Fredonia. The quotation from Feuchtwanger is from his essay "The Grandeur and Misery of Exile," which is reprinted in Anderson. On the spike in crime in New York City see, for example, "Big Rise in Crime Is Reported Here," *The New York Times*, November 12, 1940. The Camus quotations are from his 1947 essay "The Rains of New York," reprinted in Albert Camus, *Lyrical and Critical Essays*, translated by Ellen Conroy Kennedy, edited by Philip Thody (Vintage Books, 1970). The fascinating article by Erich Kahler, "Collectividualists," was published in the special edition of *The Saturday Review of Literature* devoted to exiled writers, published October 19, 1940. Brecht's quip about the exile's real job of hoping is cited in Heilbut. Hilde Spiel's observation about the real America is from her novel *The Darkened Room* (Methuen & Co., 1961).

Chapter Three

Zweig's remark about books being better company than people appears in a letter to Friderike. Victor Klemperer's extraordinary book *The Language of the Third Reich: LTI— Lingua Tertii Imperii*, translated by Martin Brady (Continuum, 2006), was my source for the comments about books belonging to Jews inside Nazi Germany, as well as for a number of other insights that were significant for this book. An English translation by Harry Zohn of Zweig's essay "Thanks to Books" appeared in *Saturday Review* on February 8, 1958. Fleischer records his experience of entering Zweig's bachelor flat in a commemorative essay anthologized in *Stefan Zweig—Spiegelungen einer schöpferischen Persönlichkeit*, edited by Erich Fitzbauer (Bergland Verlag, 1959). The lines from Zweig's 1922 autobiographical sketch are cited in Matuschek, as are the quotations from Zweig's youthful letter to Fleischer, and Fontana's remarks about Zweig as a voyeur. The letter from the sculptor Ambrosi and Zweig's remark about lacking sexual greed are cited in Prater, "Zweig and the Vienna of Yesterday," an essay in Berlin, Johns, and Lawson, *Turn-of-the-Century Vienna and Its Legacy*. Prater's unpublished notes from an interview he conducted with Friderike are also the source of Friderike's remark that Zweig was no "Don Juan," and he reports that Friderike said Zweig's fear of madness was the reason he refused to have children in the essay "Stefan Zweig," collected in *Exile: The Writer's Experience*, edited by John M. Spalek and Robert F. Bell (University of North Carolina Press, 1982). For the rise in suicides in Germany and Austria see, for example, Darcy Buerkle's intriguing essay "Historical Effacements: Facing Charlotte Salomon," anthologized in *Reading Charlotte Salomon*, edited by Michael P. Steinberg and Monica Bohm-Duchen (Cornell University Press, 2006). Hilde Spiel's beautiful study of returning to Vienna after the war, *Return to Vienna: A Journal*, translated by Christine Shuttleworth (Ariadne Press, 2011), was my source for her remarks about being glad her children grew up in England. Geiger's story of Zweig's prowling around the zoo as a flasher appears in his *Memorie di un Veneziano* (Vallecchi Editore, 1958). Romains's observations on Zweig's interrogative style and his confession of violent passions are recorded in his *Stefan Zweig: Great European*. Zweig's observations about Austrian fatalism are cited in the important commemorative essay by Otto Zarek

"Stefan Zweig—A Jewish Tragedy," in Arens. Klaus Mann's comments about Zweig's modest ambitions are taken from his essay for *Free World*. Friderike's remarks on Zweig's scanty allowance for personal pleasure, along with her account of their court-ship and move to Salzburg, come from her memoir of Zweig. Gombrich's observa-tions regarding the palliative effect of music on Viennese anti-Semitism are cited in *Strangers at Home and Abroad: Recollections of Austrian Jews Who Escaped Hitler*, translated by Ewald Osers, edited by Adi Wimmer (McFarland & Company, 2000). The anti-Semitic atmosphere in Vienna around Christian holidays is discussed in Richard S. Geehr, *Karl Lueger: Mayor of Fin de Siècle Vienna* (Wayne State University Press, 1990). Scenes of abuse in the Viennese parliament are recounted in the eye-opening study by George E. Berkley *Vienna and Its Jews: The Tragedy of Success, 1880–1980s* (Madison Books, 1988). The most comprehensive account of Zweig's Jewish lineage is provided by Leo Spitzer in *Lives in Between: Assimilation and Marginality in Austria, Brazil, West Af-rica 1780–1945* (Cambridge University Press, 1989). Leftwich cites the interview with David Ewen in which Zweig reports that he's always been vitally interested in Jewish problems.

Chapter Four

Carl E. Schorske, *Fin-de-Siècle Vienna: Politics and Culture* (Vintage Books, 1981), provides an indispensable introduction to the strange weave of febrile aesthetic production and political disenfranchisement in Vienna that heavily influenced Zweig and his peers. I used the Michael Ford translation of Hitler's *Mein Kampf* (Elite Minds, 2009) throughout. Alfred Zweig's note about their family friends being first-tier Jewish bourgeoisie is cited in Matuschek. Zweig explored the analogy between history and an artichoke in a talk he composed on the topic of "History as an Artist," scheduled for the Stockholm PEN conference of 1939, but canceled at the outbreak of the war. Friderike quotes Zweig's description of the book as "a handful of silence" in her biography of him. Zweig compares the act of writing to opium and hashish in a late letter to Wittkowski, cited by Prater in his essay in Spalek and Bell's *Exile: The Writer's Experience*. Zweig's letters about prizing peace and quiet, along with his important letter to Schickele in 1934, are quoted in Prater. Forster's response to Zweig's *Erasmus* can be found in *The B.B.C. Talks of E. M. Forster 1929–1960*, edited by Mary Lago, Linda K. Hughes, and Elizabeth MacLeod Walls (University of Missouri Press, 2008). On the American response to *Erasmus* see, for example, Percy Hutchison, "Stefan Zweig's Life of Erasmus," *The New York Times*, November 4, 1934. Irving Howe uses the phrase about the "virtues of powerlessness" in relationship to Yiddish literature in the introduction to *A Treasury of Yiddish Stories*, which Howe edited with Eliezer Greenberg (Viking Press, 1954). Gustinus Ambrosi's observations about Zweig as an "eternal pilgrim in the human psyche" are quoted in Harry Zohn, "The Burning Secret of Stephen Branch, or A Cautionary Tale About a Physician Who Could Not Heal Himself," in *Stefan Zweig: The World of Yesterday's Humanist Today, Proceedings of the*

Stefan Zweig Symposium, edited by Marion Sonnenfeld (State University of New York Press, 1983). Werfel reports on the moment when Zweig turned pale at the mention of revenge in his commemorative essay "Stefan Zweig's Death," published in Arens. The citation about *Jungvolk* is from Erika Mann's striking book *School for Barbarians*, translated by Muriel Rukeyser (Modern Age Books, 1938). Mann's account of Hitler's comprehensive transformation of the German education system is essential for understanding how the Nazi phenomenon occurred. My quotations from Zweig's first essay on Herzl, and his exchange of letters with Martin Buber, are drawn from the excellent essay "Autobiography as Farewell I," by Michael Stanislawski, in his collection *Autobiographical Jews: Essays in Jewish Self-Fashioning* (University of Washington Press, 2004). Kraus's remarks on Zionism are quoted in *Karl Kraus* by Harry Zohn (Twayne Publishers, 1971). Zweig's comments on the Jew's sacred mission appear in his study of Romain Rolland in the chapter "The Jews," which is part of Zweig's analysis of Rolland's *Jean Christophe*. The incident at the museum in Munich is reported by Zarek in Arens.

Chapter Five

Zelda Fitzgerald noted the marshmallow odor of the Biltmore in a letter to Scott in the summer of 1930. Among the accounts of the PEN evening I drew on were "1,000 Authors Here Defy Nazi Power," *The New York Times*, May 16, 1941; and a German-language version of Zweig's speech published in the *Aufbau* on May 16, 1941, which Katja Guttman helped me to translate. Klemperer recounts the incident from Tacitus with Scherer's gloss in *The Language of the Third Reich*, which also contains his analysis of the vicissitudes of the term "*fanatisch.*" Comments from Romains about Zweig's sense of Germany's being his intellectual fatherland are from his lecture *Stefan Zweig: Great European.* Scholem's remarks on the lurid illusion to which writers such as Zweig were subject appear in his essay "Walter Benjamin," reprinted in Dannhauser's *On Jews and Judaism in Crisis*. Zweig's statement about the "reasonableness" of the Slavic element in Austrian character was made to Ernst Feder, as reported in Feder's essay "Stefan Zweig's Last Days," in Arens. On Hitler's voice see, for example, Kurt G. Ludecke, *I Knew Hitler* (Charles Scribner's Sons, 1937), and Emil Lengyel, "Hitler at the Top of His Dizzy Path," *The New York Times*, February 5, 1933. Ernst Kris's comments on Hitler's slogans are reported in the article "Expert Analyzes Nazi Propaganda," *The New York Times*, December 8, 1940. Viertel's comment on Zweig's Latin style comes from his essay "Farewell to Stefan Zweig," in Arens. Amelia von Ende's observations on the Viennese race appear in her essay "Literary Vienna," published in *The Bookman*, October 1913. Arendt's interview with Günter Gaus, which took place on October 28, 1964, can be found in Arendt's collection *Essays in Understanding: 1930–1954*, edited by Jerome Kohn (Harcourt, Brace & Co., 1994). Hilde Spiel describes the scene at the Upper West Side party of refugees in *The Darkened Room*. I drew on Dove's poignant account of the plight of refugees in Great Britain for a larger context to Zweig's experience there, and Dove's book was also my source for the letter to Felix Braun in which Zweig speaks of being a Jew without religious faith. The moment when Anna Freud and Miriam Beer-Hoffman Lens stand together admiring Zweig's prose at Freud's funeral is recounted in Elisabeth Young-Bruehl, *Anna Freud: A Biography* (Sheridan Books, 2008). The edition of Stefan Zweig's diary I use throughout is Stefan Zweig, *Tagebücher* (S. Fischer Verlag, 1984). Entries that I quote from Zweig's time in Bath were originally written in English.

Chapter Six

The young refugee's lament about the absence of proper cafés in America can be found in Gerhart Saenger, *Today's Refugees, Tomorrow's Citizens: A Story of Americanization* (Harper & Brothers, 1941). Zweig's observations on the constant motion of New York, so antipathetic to the café spirit, appear in "The Spirit of New York." Comments by Fritz Wittels about the Viennese café are from *Freud and the Child Woman: The Memoirs of Fritz Wittels*, edited by Edward Timms (Yale University Press, 1994). Zarek describes Zweig and Trotsky overlapping at the Café Central. The Ebermayer letter is cited in Prater. Descriptions of the Nazi confetti before the Hotel Regina come from Hilda Doolittle, *Tribute to Freud: Writing on the Wall—Advent* (New Directions, 1974). John Gunther's *Inside Europe* (Harper & Brothers, 1938), from which I took the popular jokes about Austria's diminished stature, offers a compelling eyewitness account of events in Austria in the 1930s. Spiel drew the historical analogy between February 1934 and the Spanish Civil War in *The Dark and the Bright*. The scenes involving Canetti, Broch, and Zweig are drawn from Canetti's *The Play of the Eyes*. The description of John Gunther's efforts to read news about Vienna while in Vienna at the Café Imperial comes from his powerful article "Dateline Vienna," published in *Harper's Magazine*, July 1935. *Interwar Vienna: Culture Between Modernity and Tradition*, edited by Deborah Holmes and Lisa Silverman (Camden House, 2009), was another significant reference point for me in thinking about this period. Karl Kraus's essay "The Demolished Literature," in which his description of the denizens of the Café Griensteidl appears, is included in the invaluable anthology *The Viennese Coffeehouse Wits: 1890–1938*, translated and edited by Harold B. Segal (Purdue University Press, 1995). Kraus's description of Zweig and Ludwig as "elevators of culture" appears in his essay "Pretiosen," from the June 1926 edition of *Die Fackel*. The joke about anti-Semitism gaining currency in Vienna after the Jews take it up is recounted in Berkley. Zweig's wartime propaganda—along with the propaganda work of his Viennese peers—is summarized in Edward Timms, *Karl Kraus: Apocalyptic Satirist, Culture and Catastrophe in Habsburg Vienna* (Yale University Press, 1986). Musil's observations on Kraus are quoted in the exchange of letters between Walter Kaufman and Erich Heller in *The New York Review of Books*, August 9, 1973. Roth's description of the defeated war generation appears in his novel *The Emperor's Tomb*, translated by John Hoare (Overlook Press, 2002). The account of Hitler's return to the Imperial is from Pierre J. Huss, *Heil! and Farewell* (Herbert Jenkins, 1943).

Chapter Seven

My main sources for Zweig's musings on where to base himself were letters to Huebsch and to Lotte's family. Some of the background information on Van Loon's home and experience of refugees comes from the profile story of him by Robert Van Gelder, "Van Loon, the Man Who Can't Say No," published in *The Milwaukee Journal* on May 14, 1941. Van Loon writes of Zweig's visits to him on Long Island Sound and his efforts to find Zweig a home in his correspondence with Ben Huebsch. The introductory chapters of Davie's *Refugees in America: Report of the Committee for the Study of Recent Immigration from Europe* remain one of the best summaries of how rapidly evolving events in countries under Hitler's sway influenced international policies toward refugees. This volume is also my source on the "whispering campaign" mounted against U.S. department stores, and some of the reports on the larger economic anxiety generated by the refugees. The latter subject is also covered in Saenger and Donald Peterson Kent, *The Refugee Intellectual: The Americanization of the Immigrants of 1933–1945* (Columbia University Press, 1953). All three of these books contain many poignant case histories. The story I cite about the draftsman in Pittsburgh is from Kent. For general background on the Jewish movement into exile in relationship to the United States, see also Saul S. Friedman, *No Haven for the Oppressed: United States Policy Toward Jewish Refugees, 1938–1945* (Wayne State University Press, 1971). Klaus and Erika Mann's observations on refugee experience are from their collaborative work *Escape to Life* (Houghton Mifflin, 1939). Desmond Flowers's account of Zweig's response to the fall of France is quoted in Prater's unpublished lecture "Stefan Zweig." Statistics on children as refugees and Holocaust victims are taken from the enlightening study *What Happened to the Children Who Fled Nazi Persecution*, by Gerhard Sonnert and Gerald Holton (Palgrave Macmillan, 2006). Leftwich cites Zweig's speech before a fund-raiser in Brazil for Jewish war victims in which Zweig makes clear his views on the lack of merit in survival. Zweig's escape from England in pursuit of "Latin gaiety" is recounted by Romains in his 1939 lecture. My primary source for the impressions of refugee life in Sanary around Aldous Huxley and Thomas Mann was Sybille Bedford, *Aldous Huxley: A Biography* (Alfred A. Knopf/Harper & Row, 1971). Zweig's misreading of the 1930 electoral results and Mann's response are recounted in Mann's *The Turning Point*. Further details of the Zweigs' trip to Cap d'Antibes, beyond those Friderike describes in her biography, appear in an essay she wrote on Zweig that was anthologized in *Greatness Revisited* (Branden Press, 1971), a collection edited by Harry Zohn. Friderike's typewritten copy of Lotte's love letter to Stefan is archived at Fredonia. I'm indebted to Oliver Matuschek for the insight that Zweig begins to equate Lotte with London in the first phase of their affair. The Alfred Polgar anecdote about the distance of Ecuador is quoted in Erika and Klaus Mann's *Escape to Freedom*.

Chapter Eight

I'm grateful to Norm Macdonald, President of the Ossining Historical Society, for answering a number of my questions about life in Ossining during the period

the Zweigs were there, as well as for general background on the town in the 1930s
and 1940s. I also made use of *Ossining Remembered*, a monograph in the Images of
America series produced by the Ossining Historical Society (Arcadia Publishing, 1999). I drew on details about the sounds and sights in Ossining in 1941 and
1943 from an essay by Sally Walsh, "War Comes to Main Street," published in
The Intelligencer, May 1944. The subject of the refugees' amazement at the abundance of food in the United States crops up in many reports. I drew primarily
on Davie, Kent, and Saenger. Zweig's fascinating essay "The Monotonization of
the World," first published in the *Berliner Börsen-Courier* on February 1, 1925, is
collected in *The Weimar Republic Sourcebook*, edited by Anton Kaes, Martin Jay, and
Edward Dimendberg (University of California Press, 1994). The battle of the
comics and the son who scourges his immigrant father as un-American, as well
as expressions of the difference between Europeans and Americans on subjects
such as art and education, are reported in Kent. Ise Gropius's compelling essay is
reprinted in Davie. Auden's observations on Americans looking like elderly babies
can be found in W. H. Auden, *The Dyer's Hand and Other Essays* (Vintage Books/
Random House, 1990). The description of children as the Trojan Horse in refugee
families appears in Mary Treudley, "Formal Organization and the Americanization Process, with Special Reference to the Greeks of Boston," *American Sociological
Review* (February 1949). Saenger reports the case history involving a father who
wants his Americanized son to become his family's publicists. Henry Pachter's
analysis of the problem with the American education system can be found in
his essay "A Memoir," anthologized in *The Legacy of the German Refugee Intellectuals*,
edited by Robert Boyers (Schocken Books, 1972). Zweig's letter to Rolland about
wanting to become a "moral authority" is cited in Prater. The story of the squatters at the Kapuzinerberg, and the Zweigs' response to their presence, is told in
Friderike's biography of Stefan. Virgilia Sapieha, "The Glass-Enclosed Record of
a Mind," a review of *The World of Yesterday*, appeared in the *New York Herald Tribune*
on April 18, 1943. The anecdote involving Zweig, Roth, and Keun observed by
Hermann Kesten is recounted by Michael Hofmann in *Joseph Roth: A Life in Letters*. Arendt's essential critique "Stefan Zweig: Jews in the World of Yesterday"
is reprinted in Kohn and Feldman's *The Jewish Writings*. Zweig's remarks about
impoverished children and war profiteers are discussed in Lionel B. Steiman's
compelling essay "The Worm in the Rose: Historical Destiny and Individual Action in Stefan Zweig's Vision of History," from Sonnenfeld's *The World of Yesterday's
Humanist Today*. Walter Bauer quotes at length from Zweig's Volta Congress lecture in his essay "Stefan Zweig the European," in Arens. Friderike also cites parts
of the speech in her biography of Stefan. For an introduction to the seminal role
of Wagner's aesthetic theories in shaping Austrian politics, along with Schorske
see William J. McGrath, *Dionysian Art and Populist Politics in Austria* (Yale University Press, 1974). I'm grateful to Dr. Arturo Larcati for responding to my queries about
the Volta Congress with helpful details on the German Nazi and Italian Fascist
domination of the 1932 event.

Chapter Nine

I drew on editions of the *Citizen Register* (Ossining's main daily newspaper at the time) from July and August 1941 for background details on events in the town during the time the Zweigs lived there. The story of Joachim Maass's last encounter with the Zweigs is recounted by Maass in "Die Letzte Begegnung," in Arens's *Der große Europäer*. Eva Tuerbl assisted me with the translation of this essay.

Chapter Ten

René Fülöp-Miller's recollections of conversations with Zweig in Ossining are recorded in his essay "Memorial for Stefan Zweig" in Arens. I'm very grateful to Adrian Christopher Liddell and Nicola Helen Liddell, along with their two engagingly thoughtful daughters, Eloise and Alexandra, for the tour they gave me of the house and garden at Rosemount. The family's dedication to restoring the garden would have been deeply moving to Stefan and Lotte. In addition to helpful insights about Bath society, the Liddells also shared with me a number of documents about the house and Zweig's gardener that were critical for my research. My primary sources for the stories about Zweig, his garden, walks in the Bath countryside, and Edward Miller were Elizabeth Allday, *Stefan Zweig: A Critical Biography* (J. Philip O'Hara, 1972); "Memories of Stefan Zweig," a letter by Robert Draper, published in *Bath Chronicle* (March 3, 1997); and "Rosemount and Stefan Zweig," an essay prepared by the Bath Historical Society in conjunction with an exhibition on the life of Zweig mounted by the society in 1997. All quotations from Zweig's "Gardens in Wartime" are taken from Will Stone's excellent translation of the essay in *Stefan Zweig Journeys*. Werfel quotes Zweig's letter about collapsing together with bombed buildings in his essay "Stefan Zweig's Death," in Arens. Thomas Mann's letter to Friderike can be found in *Letters of Thomas Mann: 1889–1955*, translated and edited by Richard and Clara Winston (University of California Press, 1975). Zweig's letters to Rolland about his frustration with England are quoted in Dove. Romains's report of Zweig's displeasure with the solemnity of English cities is quoted in "Zweig and Wife, Refugees, End Lives in Brazil," an obituary published in the *New York Herald Tribune*, February 24, 1942.

Chapter Eleven

Maria Wolfring's contributions to my understanding of life in Petrópolis, both during the time of the Zweigs' life there and afterward, were enormous and I'm deeply thankful for her generosity in introducing me to the city and her family history. I'm grateful to Kristina Michahelles for having put me in touch with Maria, as well as for answering many questions herself about the Zweigs and Petrópolis. Her assistance in tracking down key photographs for the text was vital. Feder's comments about Zweig's popularity in Brazil appear in his essay in Arens. Zweig's ecstatic pronouncements about having become Marlene Dietrich appear in his correspondence with Friderike.

Chapter Twelve

Zweig's remark about collapsing like Homeric heroes en route to Brazil appears in a letter to Huebsch. Prater writes of the Zweigs' reception in Brazil, drawing on letters and reports from his friends there. Alberto Dines's essay "Death in Paradise" reports on the reviews of Zweig's book on Brazil in *Correio da Manhã*, as well as the response of well-known contemporary Brazilian authors to Zweig's work. The essay contains a wealth of vital information on Zweig's time in Brazil, a fuller account of which can be found in Dines's untranslated book *Morte no paraíso: a tragédia de Stefan Zweig* (Círculo de Leitores, 1981). The introductory essay in Davis and Marshall's *Stefan and Lotte Zweig's South American Letters* provides an excellent overview of the Brazilian political and cultural landscape in the years of Zweig's visits, especially in reference to refugees and the war. For further background information, I relied on *The Brazilian Reader: History, Culture, Politics*, edited by Robert M. Levine and John J. Crocitti (Duke University Press, 1999); Robert M. Levine, *Father of the Poor? Vargas and His Era* (Cambridge University Press, 1998); Jeffrey Lesser, *Welcoming the Undesirables: Brazil and the Jewish Question* (University of California Press, 1995); Daryle Williams, "*Ad perpetuam rei memoriam:* The Vargas Regime and Brazil's National Historical Patrimony, 1930–1945" (*Luso-Brazilian Review*, 2004); and Frank D. McCann, "Vargas and the Destruction of the Brazilian Integralista and Nazi Parties (*The Americas*, July 1969). Zweig's remarks about the "via contemplativa" appear in a letter to Hanna and Manfred. Friedenthal's comments on the Balzac manuscript appear in a postscript to the edition of Zweig's Balzac that he edited, which was translated by William and Dorothy Rose (Viking Press, 1946). Zweig's letter about the "silent cure" of Petrópolis, his rediscovery of Montaigne, and his inability to share in the joy of the Carnival revelers is reproduced in Romains's "Derniers Mois et Dernières Lettres de Stefan Zweig." A typewritten copy of the unpublished letter to Viertel drawn on at several points in this chapter is archived with the Huebsch papers at the Library of Congress. The lines from Zweig about his world being destroyed after Pearl Harbor and the heroism of translating into German are from a letter to Viktor Wittkowski cited in Prater's essay "Stefan Zweig," in Spalek and Bell's *Exile: The Writer's Experience*. Feder reports Zweig's response to the moment his friend the Chilean poet Gabriela Mistral announced her belief that Nazis would invade Brazil, as well as his reaction to the letter from du Gard, in his essay in Arens. I drew also on a more detailed account by Feder of his trip to Carnival with the Zweigs, including Zweig's comments during the drive from Petrópolis to Rio, which was published under the title "My Last Conversations with Stefan Zweig," in *Books Abroad* (Winter 1943).

Epilogue

Zweig's assertion that only the body can truly experience is reported by Geiger. Friedenthal's statement about Zweig's need for personal contact appears in his essay "Stefan Zweig and Humanism," in Arens. Zweig reports sharing Keats's sense of disappearance to Romains in a letter printed in "Derniers Mois et Dernières Lettres de Stefan Zweig." "Fame—*and* Oblivion," the intriguing essay that Zweig wrote about the mysterious force counteracting human productivity and the mysterious disappearance of the physical matter created by writers and artists, was published in the *New York Herald Tribune* on March 11, 1934. In an ironic touch, the paper's byline describes Zweig as the author of *Marie Antoinette: The Story of an Average Woman*, and *The Case of Sergeant Grischa*. The latter book was actually written by Arnold Zweig—no relation to Stefan. Rolland's remarks about Zweig's having become a "Flying Dutchman" out of "a burning desire to to obtain an insight into all phases of life" are quoted in the obituary "Zweig and Wife, Refugees, End Lives in Brazil," published in the *New York Herald Tribune*, February 24, 1942. Zuckmayer describes his response to Zweig's suicide and his authorship of *A Call to Life* in the essay "Did You Know Stefan Zweig?" in Arens. The statements by Frank and Maurois about Zweig's suicide are cited in Prater. The anonymous editorial describing the Nazis as the true exiles is entitled "One of the Dispossessed" and appeared in *The New York Times* on February 25, 1942. My conversations with Barbara Frischmuth took place before and after our joint appearance on a panel as part of the PEN World Voices festival in the spring of 2013. Her insights were critical for my understanding of Zweig's legacy within Austria and the larger spectrum of issues confronting young writers in postwar Austria. I'm very grateful for the time she devoted to addressing my questions. On Zweig's philosophy of potentiality in relation to action, see, in particular, his biography of Erasmus and the collection *Europäisches Erbe* (S. Fischer Verlag, 1960), as well as Steiman's "The Worm in the Rose." A footnote in Steiman's study quotes Zweig's comments about brotherliness, which are from Zweig's essay "Bekenntnis zum Defaitismus," published in *Die Friedens-Warte*, vol. 20 (July/Aug. 1918). Fred T. Marsh characterizes Zweig as "a decadent early Christian" in "Zweig, a Great European Story Teller," a review published in the *New York Herald Tribune*, April 1, 1934. Zweig's remarks about only being interested in writing about the defeated occur in the course of his interview with Curtiss. Zuckmayer's extraordinary account of the scenes in Vienna following the Anschluss appears in his memoir. Zweig describes Vienna as an "accursed city" in a letter to Frans Masereel from 1919, cited in Prater, "Zweig and the Vienna of Yesterday." His statement about Vienna's merriment and the mask having come off in the light of Hitler's arrival in Vienna is from his memoir. The comments about the philosophical correctness of suicide as a response to the Anschluss occur in reference to Egon Friedell in a letter to Felix Braun cited by Dove.

PHOTO CAPTIONS AND CREDITS

Frontispiece: Zweig on bus in New York City, 1941. (Photograph by Kurt Severin, courtesy of David H. Lowenherz)

p. 2: 34 Rua Gonçalves Dias in Petrópolis as it appeared when the Zweigs lived there. (Arquivo Casa Stefan Zweig, courtesy of Alberto Dines)

p. 7: Stefan Zweig in Salzburg, summer 1931. (Theatermuseum, Vienna)

p. 22: Top center: My grandfather and grandmother, framing my uncle George and my father Martin. Top left: My grandmother's favorite cousin, believed to be either Alice Peters or Selma Peterselka. (Same figure on center right of page.) Most other images are of my grandmother. Lower left: My grandfather's parents in a Vienna photo studio. Lower right: My uncle George. (Composite assembled by Tynan Kogane)

p. 28: Medallion on plinth of Schiller statue in Schillerplatz. (Credit: Vladimir Gurewich)

p. 36: Still from film footage shot of Stefan Zweig in Salzburg. (Courtesy of a private collection)

p. 59: Stefan Zweig and Ben Huebsch, probably in the offices of Viking Press. (Arquivo Casa Stefan Zweig, courtesy of Alberto Dines)

p. 84: Stefan Zweig on the steps of the New York Public Library. (Photograph by Kurt Severin, courtesy of David H. Lowenherz)

p. 86: Stefan Zweig and Joseph Roth in Ostend. (Arquivo Casa Stefan Zweig, courtesy of Alberto Dines)

p. 87: Stefan Zweig and Foreign Minister Macedo Soares at a diplomatic function in the Jockey Club, Rio de Janeiro. Left: Alzira Vargas, daughter of President Getúlio Vargas. Right: Jandira Vargas, another daughter of the president. Behind Zweig stands Samuel Malamud, Zweig's lawyer, and the diplomat Jorbe Manoelda Costa. (Arquivo Casa Stefan Zweig, courtesy of Alberto Dines)

p. 116: Stefan Zweig's library. (Courtesy of the heirs of Stefan Zweig and a private collection)

pp. 148–149: Article in *Signal* magazine, the principle Nazi propaganda magazine aimed at occupied Europe, the UK, and the United States. Modeled on *Life* magazine, it was published between 1940 and 1945 in a total of twenty-five languages, with a peak circulation of 2,500,000 copies. (Courtesy of Adam Cvijanovic)

p. 169: Stefan Zweig in a Salzburg café. (Courtesy of the heirs of Stefan Zweig and a private collection)

p. 190: Stefan Zweig at the War Archives in Vienna. (Arquivo Casa Stefan Zweig, courtesy of Alberto Dines)

p. 217: Lotte on the road with Stefan Zweig near the start of their relationship. (Courtesy of the heirs of Stefan Zweig and a private collection)

p. 219: Lotte in Monte Carlo, 1934. (Courtesy of the heirs of Stefan Zweig and a private collection)

p. 269: Right to left: Lotte, Ursula Mayer (Lotte's cousin), and Eva Altmann in the garden at Rosemount. (Courtesy of the heirs of Stefan Zweig and a private collection)

p. 279: Mr. Miller at the time the Zweigs lived at Rosemount. (Courtesy of the heirs of Stefan Zweig and a private collection)

p. 289: King John by William Blake. (Fondation Martin Bodmer, Cologny [Geneva])

p. 295: Path into the forest, Petrópolis. (Author's photo)

p. 302: From the balcony of the Zweigs' home, Petrópolis. (Author's photo)

p. 306: Zweig signing books in Brazil. (Arquivo Casa Stefan Zweig, courtesy of Alberto Dines)

p. 319: The Zweigs' home in Petrópolis. (Arquivo Casa Stefan Zweig, courtesy of Alberto Dines)

p. 332: Stefan Zweig dictating to Lotte in Brazil. (Arquivo Casa Stefan Zweig, courtesy of Alberto Dines)

p. 350: The Zweigs on their deathbed. Stefan and Lotte were repositioned in the course of being photographed. While the fundamental configuration of their bodies remained the same, Stefan's expression appears more starkly harrowing in one photo taken before the shot reproduced here. In that earlier image, Lotte completely enfolds Stefan, while her face buries into him. (Copyright © Wien Museum)

p. 363: Stairs descending from the exhibition gallery in the Vienna Academy of Fine Arts. (Author's photo)

p. 364: Schillerplatz. (Author's photo)

p. 365: Elevator cage in my father's building. (Author's photo)

p. 366: Walking up the stairs in my father's building. (Author's photo)